DAN STUART'S
FISTIC CARNIVAL

DAN STUART'S
FISTIC CARNIVAL

Leo N. Miletich

TEXAS A&M UNIVERSITY PRESS
COLLEGE STATION

The paper used in this book meets the minimum requirements
of the American National Standard for Permanence
of Paper for Printed Library Materials, Z39.48-1984.
Binding materials have been chosen for durability.

LIBRARY OF CONGRESS CATALOGING-IN-PUBLICATION DATA
Miletich, Leo N.
    Dan Stuart's fistic carnival / Leo N. Miletich. — 1st ed.
        p.   cm.
    Includes bibliographical references (p.   ) and index.
    ISBN 0-89096-614-1 (alk. paper). — ISBN 0-89096-615-X (pbk.)
    1. Boxing—Texas—Dallas—History—19th century. I. Title.
GV1125.M55   1994
796.8'3—dc20   94-14957
                                                                CIP

This book is for Ramon Ramirez,
who first triggered the quest for facts
with a single question that rapidly turned
into an obsession.
AND
This book is also for
all the unsung Interlibrary Loan workers everywhere,
without whom most works of research would never
get past the idea stage.

CONTENTS

Acknowledgments   *page* xi

Preface   xiii

PRELIMS   3

ROUND ONE: Dallas, Part One   18

ROUND TWO: Dallas, Part Two   36

ROUND THREE: Hot Springs   60

ROUND FOUR: The Irishman   85

ROUND FIVE: El Paso, Part One   105

ROUND SIX: El Paso, Part Two   127

ROUND SEVEN: Rangers   147

ROUND EIGHT: The Main Event   169

CARSON CITY AND BEYOND   192

Epilogue   209

Notes   213

Bibliography   231

Index   235

ILLUSTRATIONS

"Gentleman Jim" Corbett	*page* 8
Bib Fitzsimmons	12
Dan Stuart	19
Dallas, 1895	30
State Fair program ad	38
Peter Maher	61
Bath House Row, Hot Springs	70
Sheriff Houpt	78
"Gorbett's Ring," Hot Springs	81
Corbett in movie with Pete Courtney	95
Downtown El Paso, 1900	103
El Paso's Myar Opera House	108
Footballers in El Paso	114
Gem Saloon, El Paso	123
El Paso Ministers' Union	133
Texas Rangers	149
Downtown Juarez, Mexico	153
Cartoon of Maher and West Texas sandstorm	162
Cartoon of *bandido*-Ranger hybrid	172
Judge Roy Bean	179
Bridge to Rio Grande sandbar	181
Rangers'-eye view of the fight	183
Cartoon of "The Men in the Ring"	184
Maher and Fitz fight	185
Stuart's prize ring, Carson City	197
Fitz and Corbett clinch for heavyweight championship	200

ACKNOWLEDGMENTS

MY SINCERE THANKS are extended to all who helped dig up multi-tudinous stray facts, quotes, and pictures, particularly: Joan Dobson of the Dallas Public Library; the Reference and Southwest departments of the El Paso Public Library; the ILL staffs of Sue Brown and Carolyn Kahl; Juan A. Sandoval; the Nevada Historical Society; the Library of Congress; and George D. Tselos of the Edison National Historic Site.

I acknowledge the following publishers for permission to use material from these sources: *The Roar of the Crowd* by James J. Corbett, reprinted by permission of The Putnam Publishing Group, copyright © 1925 by James J. Corbett, 1953 Renewed; *A Million and One Nights* by Terry Ramsaye, reprinted by permission of Simon & Schuster, copyright © 1926; *The Fighting Man* by William A. Brady, copyright © 1916, and *George Ade, Warmhearted Satirist* by Fred C. Kelly, copyright © 1947, reprinted by permission of Macmillan Publishing; *The Letters of George Ade,* Terence Tobin, editor, copyright © 1973, reprinted by permission of Purdue University Press.

Thanks and remembrance must also be extended to those hardworking journalists of yesteryear who managed to cover all aspects of the news without benefit of electronic data-gathering equipment, computers, word processors, or motor vehicles, with a special salute to "Colonel" Whit-myer, the elusive "Wun Lung" of the *El Paso Daily Herald,* whose wry comments and unorthodox coverage enrich this account.

And thanks also to Justine and Juliette for making the work so much easier.

PREFACE

GENERAL KNOWLEDGE about Australia and New Zealand in the late 1800s—even among politicians—was so vague that the two countries were often used interchangeably by the press and public alike. To Americans, both were lumped together as "Down Under" and "Australasia" (terms still in use today). Mark Twain noted this geographic and political ignorance in *Following the Equator:* "All people think that New Zealand is close to Australia or Asia, or somewhere, and that you cross to it on a bridge."

Actually, New Zealand is not "close" to anywhere and, at the time of the great fistic carnival, had been a self-governing province for forty-five years (in 1893 it became the first nation to give voting rights to women; Great Britain granted independence in 1931). Still, the interchangeable use of the countries' names in regard to Bob Fitzsimmons—who took on fighters from both—is historically understandable. Both countries had been colonized by Great Britain, and New Zealand had once been considered part of Australia's New South Wales colony.

To preserve the flavor of the contemporary reporting, this book will retain that quaint stylistic linking of the two countries.

DAN STUART'S
FISTIC CARNIVAL

PRELIMS

We stood before each other;
  We had to scrap or die;
I saw his resolution
  As I looked in his flashing eye.

Then he began the fighting
  With all his might and main,
And the crowd behind was crying
  "Bravo! hit him again!"

. . .

The seventieth round was ended,
  He fell with a terrible cry;
I looked him over closely,
  But I couldn't see no eye.

John L. Sullivan,
New Orleans Picayune,
January 30, 1892

IT WAS A SPRAWLING, brawling age, the 1890s, teeming with a roistering and impetuous populace. Captains of industry, moneyed moguls, high hats, starched collars, Prince Albert coats, bloomers, and bicycle races all caught the imagination of an America waking up to its potential, flexing its muscles.

The railroads had pushed into the frontier, expansion, growth, progress and prosperity awaited—if an ambitious man couldn't make his fortune in the grimy, bustling east, then he headed west, west toward the untamed Indians, the gunfighters, the wide open territories. It was understood—a God-given Truth—that able-bodied, stouthearted Americans could do anything they set their minds to!

Except fight each other for prize money.

Now I am determined that these 'knocking-out' contests shall not be revived. There will be no prize fighting in this city. If these men get together and violate the law, it is my duty to arrest them and I will do so. Of course, I cannot and do not desire to prohibit sparring exhibitions, but the law does not permit prize fighting (New York Superintendent of Police Murray, *New Orleans Picayune*, 27 December 1891).

The prize ring, one place where might *is* right and no one believes the meek will inherit anything *but* earth, was in disfavor. In 1895, the year future boxing great William Harrison "Jack" Dempsey was born (and when the original Jack "Nonpareil" Dempsey died), prizefighting was illegal in most of the forty-four United States. In some places it was a felony that could draw a ten-year jail sentence.

There were still fights, to be sure, sponsored by numerous athletic clubs across the country. It was a very popular sport that went by many euphemisms: fistic discussion, fistic argument, physical culture exhibition, the "science" of pugilism, and, of course, the "manly" art of self-defense. The *New Orleans Picayune* dubbed fight fans "followers of Fistiana."

Fighters were idolized by wide-eyed boys, courted by gamblers, besieged by women, and mobbed by cheering fans. They were also roundly condemned from virtually every pulpit in the land. In addition to dime novels, saloons, and smutty paintings hanging in saloons, prizefights gave preachers and moralists a symbol of what they perceived to be society's moral rot.

Reformers were hotly and righteously repelled by the bloody brutality of the bareknuckled era. It was shameless barbarity, they cried, a spectacle for degenerates and bums, an uncivilized outgrowth of drunken barroom and back-alley bruisers. And they drew crowds of thousands, who apparently screamed for blood the way decadent Romans encouraged gladiators and lions alike.

Despite the preachers and the laws, fights were arranged, bets laid, and audiences attracted. People would board trains and travel hundreds or thousands of miles to watch. For them, the attraction was obvious: a fight centered on two well-trained and unaided men competing against each other in tests of courage, endurance, and strength—one would win, one would lose. The raw simplicity of it was stirring at a primitive, elemental level of the brain stem.

In 1895, the *New York World* attempted to analyze the sport's vicarious popularity for fans both rich and poor. It concluded that "the prize fighter touches the popular instinct of admiration for what are regarded as manly if not heroic qualities." This, plus the exhibition of individual combat skills, "moves the common man to the admiration of qualities he would be delighted to possess. It is human to honor and glory in the best man; it is conventional to be horrified at the brutalities of a battle, and human nature dominates in this case with a great part of the people."

Fighters were gypsies in those days, traveling the country by train and as little respected by genteel society as tinhorn gamblers, tramps, actors, and other vagabonds. They picked up money sparring with any local citizen willing to chance getting what was left of his brains beat out. The big purses were for the champs and top contenders, matches generally arranged by athletic clubs as carefully as marriages, complete with large side bets and financial guarantees of performance.

Most prizefights had to be held in private, "out in the woods," in a mill, behind a barn. If prolonged, a fight was almost sure to be found and broken up by police raids well into the twentieth or thirtieth round.

(Many fighters believed it a point of honor that "to the finish," that is, when one combatant could not regain his feet, was the only mix worthy of their participation. In 1893, Andy Bowen and Jack Burk spent seven hours and four minutes in the ring, racking up a record one-hundred and ten rounds.[1] Bowen was killed in a New Orleans match in December, 1894, when his head slammed onto the wooden floor of the ring.)

Deaths in the ring were not uncommon in the early days of prizefighting, mostly resulting from poor training, unpadded rings, and the sharp impact of bare knuckles under what was then termed "London Prize Fight Rules."[2]

Within those rules roared a mighty Bostonian named John Lawrence Sullivan, known also as The Boston Strong Boy, striding the world like a hearty, rough-hewn colossus.

Sullivan—now there was a name to reckon with. He was a large man with a large voice and singularly large appetites, primarily for high living, women, and alcohol. The press covered his varying states of inebriation as closely as it did his fights, and those were some fights: bloody, barefisted brawls that could last for hours. In one four-year period (1881 through 1884) he engaged in twenty-seven fights, lost none, and won eleven by knockouts, twelve by technical knockouts.

He became heavyweight champion of the world when he knocked out Paddy Ryan in Mississippi City, Mississippi, in 1882. It took just nine rounds; Ryan had earned the title in an eighty-seven rounder against Joe Gross in 1880.

The big man was a celebrity for a time, touring the world, meeting crowned heads and presidents while decking local champs.

But even "The Great John L." was harassed at home.

In what is often cited as the "Coney Island Fiasco," Sullivan was to be matched against Frank Herald in September of 1886, but the local authorities ran them out of town. The *New York Times* (which regarded the champion as "a mean and cowardly bully") crowed that Sullivan was lately "disgusted with the failure of his recent attempts to meet ambitious sluggers because of police interference." The paper claimed that "Sullivan is willing to do almost anything in his line to make money, as he is 'dead broke.'"

That fight was moved to Pennsylvania, where the leading ministers of Allegheny City called on the Mayor and Chief of Police, insisting they stop the fight or face a restraining order. The police, standing by, broke up the fight in the second round after Sullivan dropped Herald with one tremendous blow, "his head striking the boards with such force that the sound echoed throughout the building."[3]

The sound of gavels on judicial benches was louder, and Sullivan took to acting on the stage for his livelihood.

The plays he starred and toured in were vehicles crafted just for him, usually containing an excuse for a sparring match. One show, *Honest Hearts and Willing Hands,* included as a prop a real forge at which a barechested Sullivan would fashion horseshoes that he'd later distribute to friends.

An early biographer, Donald Barr Chidsey, noted that the plays always produced a certain amount of "delicious suspense," for one never knew when Sullivan "might happen to be very drunk and bellow straight at the audience remarks which had nothing to do with the show or, for that matter, with decency." The staged fight might even turn real.[4]

To earn money for his prodigious appetites, the world's champion was not above touring the country and offering up to $500 to anyone he couldn't knock out in four rounds.

Sullivan briefly surrendered his title to Jake Kilrain but, bored with an actor's life, decided to get it back and arranged for a fight in Richburg, Mississippi. It was 1889.

It turned out to be the last bareknuckled championship fight, and it lasted a punishing seventy-five rounds before Sullivan knocked Kilrain out cold. But it didn't end there. The fight infuriated Mississippi's Gov. Robert Lowry, and he vowed to make both fighters pay. Warrants were issued for their arrest.

The indictment charged Sullivan with entering a prize ring to "beat, strike, and bruise the said Jake Kilrain, against the peace and dignity of the State of Mississippi." Six of the grand jurymen were at the fight and listed as witnesses.

Sullivan was arrested at the Vanderbilt Hotel on August 1 and spent the night at police headquarters, though not locked up. In fact, according to a reporter from the *New York Times,* the minions of the law uncharacteristically treated the champ with "extreme tenderness." This was looked on as both a reflection of his popularity and the influence of his trainer, Billy Muldoon, an ex-policeman.[5]

Sullivan was removed to Mississippi, stood trial, and was found guilty on August 17. The next day he was sentenced to a year in jail. He posted a $1,500 bond and fled for New York.

At this time there was a brash new American fighter making his name known, a fellow named James J. Corbett. He was a dandy, this Corbett, a San Francisco-reared bank teller and finishing school alumnus with a passion for boxing.[6] The press, never having seen his like before, dubbed him "Handsome Jim" and "Pompadour Jim," while the public settled on "Gentleman Jim."[7]

The small-fisted Corbett was a new breed—not a mauler, a puncher, a stand-toe-to-toe-and-slug-it-out bruiser, but the first "scientific" contender, who used tactics, skill, and fancy footwork to best his adversaries.

His fans were legion, and his detractors scornful. Sullivan called him "that little dude from California."[8] Corbett needed an impressive win and, in 1890, beat the man who went seventy-five rounds with the Great John L., whipping Kilrain in six rounds in New Orleans. In 1891, he chose the British champ, West Indian Peter Jackson, as the next logical step to the title.

Jackson was possibly the best fighter in the world at the time. He had been trying to get a match with Sullivan for years, but John L. "drew the color line." (Some editorialists suggested this was a handy excuse to avoid a hard fight.) Corbett was not so choosey.[9]

The fight was held in San Francisco on May 21, 1891, and it was all Corbett could do to stay even with Jackson. The grueling contest staggered through sixty-one rounds.

Years later Corbett recalled that his hands became numb from clenching them so long: "I would go up and hit Jackson with my hands open and actually didn't know they were open, so dead were they. Towards the latter end of the fight the perspiration brought out all the hair in the gloves, forming a ball, which I used to work around into the palm of my hand; holding this was the only way I could tell my hand was clenched."[10]

The fight ended with a decree of "No Contest," both fighters seemingly on the verge of collapse, though Corbett always maintained he could have won had it not been for the connivance of various gamblers and Jackson's backers.[11]

(Indeed, Corbett could never bring himself to admit defeat, telling

The reigning champion, James J. "Gentleman Jim" Corbett. From Billy Edwards. *The Pugilistic Portrait Gallery* (London and Philadelphia: Pugilistic Publishing Co., 1894).

reporters in 1895, "I am sure I shall never be put out except by a chance blow, which is something that might happen to any man." Fighters were the prima donnas of sport, brandishing huge egos along with their strength. Losing was unthinkable.)

Those sixty-one rounds gained Corbett respect in boxing circles; the following year he got his shot at John L. Sullivan. They had sparred four rounds together in San Francisco a month after the Jackson fight, but this time it would be in New Orleans and for the championship. It would also be fought according to the Marquis of Queensberry rules, with gloves.

With its prefight posturings and international press coverage, the bout quickly—incredibly—became the foremost (and fabled) sporting event of the age. Americans everywhere focused their attention on New Orleans, their emotions, biases, even their patriotism coalesced by the relentless hype of a prizefight. The already mythical status of the invincible and uncouth Sullivan was magnified and then matched by the soaring stardom of Gentleman Jim Corbett.

Before the fight, Corbett wrote to a nervous friend, "I'm in splendid condition." Though the odds were heavily against him, the challenger figured he had youth and clean living on his side: "You know I can go the distance; and no man who has lived the life that Sullivan has lived can beat me in a finish fight." Far from reassured, his friend, Tom Williams, went and laid down $15,000—on Sullivan.[12]

Conditioning won out in the end, Corbett playing the matador to Sullivan the bull, who chased him around the ring, arms flailing, for twenty-one rounds. Then, seeing the champion starting to puff and slow down, Corbett poured it on: "Summoning all the reserve force I had left I let my guns go, right and left, with all the dynamite Nature had given me, and Sullivan stood dazed and rocking. So I set myself for an instant, put just a little more in a right and hit him alongside the jaw. And he fell helpless on the ground, on his stomach, and rolled over on his back!"

Pandemonium ensued—"an uproar like Niagara tumbling over the cliffs, followed by the greatest shower you ever saw, of hats, coats, canes, belts, flowers from buttonholes, everything, falling on me and my seconds and all over the floor of the ring."[13]

Addressing the crowd, Sullivan the fighter gave way to Sullivan the actor: "I fought once too often. But I'm glad it was an American who beat me and that the championship stays in this country. Very truly yours, John L. Sullivan." He was a flabby thirty-four years old; Corbett was a fit twenty-six.[14]

For his part, Corbett modestly acknowledged that for all his stamina and strength, this was not the Sullivan of legend, "but a man who had not been careful of his habits and who had enjoyed too much the good fellowship and popularity the championship brings. I got him when he was slipping."

Bare-knucklers were now yesterday's heroes, the old-timers of the ring. The rules set down in 1867 by John Graham Chambers under the patronage of the Marquis of Queensberry were now the world's standard, unmanly gloves and all (derided by the old-timers as "pillow fights"). The dancing dandy's defeat of slugger Sullivan marked the end of an era and the beginning of another—it was as though the prizefight had been moved from the barroom to the parlor.

Corbett immediately took a fifteen-month vacation from prizefighting, enjoying the laurels of a theatrical career while protecting the crown. He finally defended his title against Charley Mitchell in Jacksonville, Florida, on January 25, 1894, and knocked him out in three rounds. Hardly broke a sweat.

Mark Twain met the champ after a sparring match at Madison Square Garden in 1894 and wrote that "Corbett has a fine face and is modest and diffident, besides being the most perfectly and beautifully constructed human animal in the world."

The humorist offered to have a go at the champ himself. In a bantering mood, the ever-cautious Corbett declined, saying, "You might chance to knock me out by no merit of your own but by a purely accidental blow, and then my reputation would be gone and you would have a double one. You have got fame enough and you ought not to want to take mine away from me."[15]

The Mitchell fight was followed by four widely spaced exhibition bouts against relatively easy opponents—Peter Courtney, Tom Sharkey, and two bouts with Jim McVey. None went past six rounds. It was beginning to look like Pompadour Jim was afraid of mussing his upswept hair.

Corbett and other fighters were still being relentlessly pursued by the forces of moral rectitude who were not put off by the addition of padded gloves. Municipalities where fights were scheduled found themselves bombarded from all directions. When the Corbett-Mitchell title fight was announced, various watchdog groups sprang into action, among them the International Law and Order League. In a letter to the *New York Times* (January 15, 1894), the League's "General Agent," Clarence Greeley, set out a standard battle plan aimed at stopping such encounters.

Greeley saw prizefighting as nothing more than assault and battery and termed Florida's maximum ten-year prison term and $5,000 fine for fighting "tolerably severe," but found enforcement lax: "If there is difficulty in Florida, it will be because of local official sympathy with lawlessness." When Corbett arrived in Jacksonville, Greeley harrumphed that he "was greeted with cheers, and no attempt was made to arrest him or his party."

Greeley called up his own militia after that oversight, mobilizing local members of his League and appealing directly to the governor to send troops—a tactic that had recently worked in Indiana. He urged the "press and pulpit" to back his crusade behind his rallying cry, "On to Florida!"

Such sentiments were spreading and having influence as more and more cities and states closed their doors to fighters. In December of 1894, the Denver police chief said he would jail fighters as vagrants if they didn't leave town. On July 2, 1895, a sheriff's posse broke up a fight in a Muncie, Indiana, mill at 3:45 in the morning—only to be met with a bullet fired through the barricaded door. The lights went out, and in the ensuing tumult all but two of the estimated two hundred spectators got away. The two arrested fans were women.

It was getting to the point where a man couldn't make a decent living punching another man in the face.

Meanwhile, that part of the public that enjoyed physical culture shows was clamoring for Corbett to take on a worthy challenger. Negotiations began for a rematch with Peter Jackson, possibly in England. If the deal fell through, said the *New York Times,* Corbett might be forced to retire "and hereafter confine himself to his task of making the public believe that he is an actor."

Jackson called Corbett a "bluffer" who didn't want to risk losing the title now that he had it. Sullivan's manager Charles "Parson" Davies agreed, saying Corbett would rather pose on the stage for his admiring public.

A challenger closer to home was put forth by a Newark, New Jersey, police captain named Glori, backer and manager of Robert Prometheus Fitzsimmons, the middleweight champion. William A. Scholl of the New Orleans Olympic Club backed Glori's challenge by offering a purse of $25,000, winner take all. Glori offered a $5,000 side bet.

Fitzsimmons had challenged Corbett in 1891, when both were relatively unknown, but had been snubbed. It was now time for the man who bested John L. Sullivan to put up or shut up.

Shutting up was not among Jim Corbett's talents. The *New York Times* reported that "Champion Corbett says that the tall Antipodean is not in his class, and he still adheres to the belief that Fitzsimmons should have a shy at some of the lesser lights. Meantime Peter Jackson, the big colored fighter, is left in the background, and his rights to a battle are being ignored altogether."

The challenger, Bob Fitzsimmons, in 1891. From Billy Edwards, *The Pugilistic Portrait Gallery* (London and Philadelphia: Pugilistic Publishing Co., 1894).

On September 26, Fitzsimmons raised the side bet to $10,000 and offered a charity sparring match to prove his mettle.

In response, Corbett reiterated that Fitzsimmons was not yet in his class and stipulated he must first fight Corbett's sparring partner Steve O'Donnell. This was a favorite ploy of Corbett's, sending his sparring partner out to test pretenders to the throne. (The Community of boxers being small and tightly knit, it came as no surprise that O'Donnell had one been Fitzsimmons' sparring partner as well.)

After Fitzsimmons beat Dan Creedon on September 27 to retain his middleweight title (a second-round knockout), O'Donnell plunked down $1,000 in forfeit money and dutifully challenged the Aussie, but Fitz the upstart was not taking the bait.

He was even contemptuous of Corbett's title fight, claiming Creedon could have whipped Sullivan in two rounds. "Why, there wasn't even a knock-down in that fight; not even the last one. Corbett only hammered him, and the big fellow gradually sat down. He kept getting lower and lower, and when he got down on his haunches, he keeled over, that's all."

John L. Sullivan sobered up long enough to say, "Fitz is the coming man" (and to disclose that he won a hundred dollars and a new suit of clothes on the Creedon fight). Sullivan was convinced Fitz could take Corbett; perhaps Corbett was too.

As Corbett continued to delay, the Olympic Club's board of directors took an astonishing action. On October 3, 1894, they declared Robert Fitzsimmons the heavyweight champion of the world, without a punch being thrown. (As a way to placate preachers, a slugless fight was surely the wave of the future, but fight fans—and Corbett—were not amused.)

They called the new champ the "Antipodean" for his down-under roots, "Lanky Bob" for his ungainly physique (Sullivan said, "He's a fighting machine on stilts"),[16] and "Ruby Rob" for his high coloring and the red hair staging an orderly but spectacular withdrawal from his forehead. His small eyes were said to be a "piercing" blue.

"What a peculiar looking figure he was," wrote Corbett thirty years later, "with his red hair, freckles, and bald front, knock-knees, and shambling gait. But he had a fine chest, neck and shoulders,—from the waist up a splendid looking fighter, but not promising from the waist down."[17]

Peculiar looking, perhaps, but there would come a day when sculptor Gutzon Borglum, the creator of Mount Rushmore, would proclaim Fitzsimmons "the best specimen of muscular development" the ring had produced.

He was born in Helston, Cornwall, England, May 26, 1863. Fitz was sensitive about his age, particularly late in his career—his last fight came at the age of fifty. When pressed by reporters he would open his mouth and laughingly offer his teeth for counting as if gauging the age of a horse.

(There was a considerable amount of gold in them thar molars by then, and not a few diamonds, the latter having been ensconced by a dentist friend who, the story goes, obtained the gems from the donated jewelry of young ladies smitten with the fighter.)

His family moved to New Zealand when he was a boy, and Bob spent many years building his shoulders and arms as a blacksmith in Timaru. He had the same open, guileless, direct approach to life as that of a child, quick to anger, quick to forgive, full of himself and given to simplistic practical jokes: handing a freshly forged, blistering hot horseshoe to an unsuspecting victim was considered a great laugh.[18]

In time he became New Zealand's answer to Longfellow's village smithy: "A mighty man is he,/With large and sinewy hands;/And the muscles of his brawny arms/Are strong as iron bands." And with nary a spreading chestnut tree to be seen.

At age eighteen, despite being awkward and gangly, he knocked out four heavyweights to win a New Zealand amateur boxing tournament staged by former British champion "Jem" Mace. One of his victims was Herbert Slade, a man known as "The Maori Giant." Fitz went on to consistently beat men bigger than himself, and they often outweighed him by as much as thirty pounds or more.

He landed in California in 1890, a quarter-inch short of six feet, with fifteen wins behind him (five by knockout) and three fights later had a shot at the middleweight championship. All he had to do was beat the original Jack Dempsey, "the Nonpareil."

They met on New Orleans' Royal Street, in the Olympic Club's new arena, on January 14, 1891. Fitzsimmons was not a fighter who relied on tactics or the advance scouting of opponents; his only strategy was to absorb everything thrown at him until he saw an opening—his awesome strength did the rest. The *New York Times* would later report that Dempsey "landed enough blows on Fitzsimmons to have won a dozen fights, but was repeatedly knocked down."

The champ hit the deck three times in the tenth, seven times in the twelfth, and six times in the thirteenth. Through the latter portion of the ordeal, Fitzsimmons kept urging Dempsey's seconds to stop the fight and rescue their man from this terrible beating and, in the thirteenth, they threw in the towel. Newcomer Fitzsimmons had a TKO and the middleweight crown.

He lacked the income for the theatrical splash and excesses of a Sul-

livan or Corbett, but he did keep a growing male lion named Nero as a
pet and occasional sparring partner.[19] And he followed the Dempsey fight
with eleven knockouts. He was primed and ready to move into the
limelight of the heavyweight class.

The Olympic Club's gambit was the goading Corbett needed.

The two fighters met in the offices of the *New York Herald* on October
11, 1894. The expected clash between the two did not occur, though
Corbett did some taunting about Fitz having to go on tour to raise his
$10,000 stake money. When Fitz objected, Corbett backed off, saying, "I
want you people to distinctly understand that I would fight Fitzsimmons
if it was only for a five-dollar bill."

Then, his diamond rings sparkling in the light, Corbett produced a
horse-choking roll of bills and nonchalantly peeled off $10,000 in cash.

It was agreed, however, to pay the money in installments of $2,500,
and to accept the $41,000 bid from the Florida Athletic Club to hold the
bout in Jacksonville the following year. They had a drink in a nearby bar
and parted company, Corbett heading for Ohio and Fitz for Philadelphia
(the contract had to be signed outside of New York "so as not to antago-
nize the authorities").[20]

The first sign of difficulty came early in December, when the Jacksonville city council repealed the ordinance that allowed prizefighting. The
New Orleans Picayune called the move "a sop thrown at the high moral
element in Florida." Joe Vendig of the Florida Athletic Club predicted a
new, favorable law would be passed before the fight, with only a higher
licensing fee. He was wrong. In May the state legislature acted accordingly, shutting Florida down to fighters.

Moral fervor was again on the rise.

On December 19, the state of Louisiana joined an injunction suit
against the famed Olympic Club. The state claimed that deliberately
seeking to produce unconsciousness by brain concussion was "unlawful as
being contrary to the law prohibiting assault and battery," and "liable to
result in homicide."

Even with possible sites dwindling, Corbett was satisfied not only that
the fight would take place, but that it would be his grand finale. Speaking
in Memphis, Corbett declared, "After I whip the Australian, I will retire
from the ring, never to don the gloves again. It is my only ambition now
to become an actor."

He then proceeded to give himself a good review (possibly because the
critics were not so inclined).

"I do not think I flatter myself when I believe I will make an actor. I never expect to be a Booth or a Salvini, but I think I can do light parts very creditably. When my fight with Fitzsimmons is over, I intend to secure a play better suited to my ability than I think 'Gentleman Jack' to be. Something in light comedy." Something like that, he'd take to Europe. He added, "While I do not take any pride in my profession, I take pride in the thought that I have elevated the ring. I believe I have."[21]

The Olympic Club won its court battle and offered $25,000 for the fight, but Corbett, still smarting from the Club's effort to dethrone him in a bloodless coup, refused to fight there.

The ever-waiting Fitzsimmons remarked that the site didn't matter: "I'll fight Corbett anywhere on the globe," he said, mentioning a bullring in Mexico City as a possible alternative, or a finish fight in private for a $10,000 side bet. A Denver promoter named Reddy Gallagher, ignoring official police animosity, said he had a couple of Colorado bankers willing to put up forty grand for the fight. Laredo, Mexico, matched Denver's forty grand two days later. The Australian was getting restless over delays and gossip. "Corbett says I'm easy meat, but he wants three months to train. I'll fight him in three weeks or to-morrow night. One thing I want to deny, and that is that I said I would pull Corbett's nose. If I had said it I would have done it."[22]

The verbal sparring that was to become a staple of this drawn-out encounter was starting to heat up.

By May of 1895, the Olympic Club was again in trouble and glove contests were banned, replaced by wrestling and billiards. It was beginning to look like a lockout for the two fighters. Indignant, Corbett declared, "I don't propose to be chased over the country without a show of meeting him," and lamented, "I don't see one chance in a thousand of the Fitzsimmons fight coming off."

And then from out of the West came the cavalry to the rescue. Fitzsimmons, staying in New York's Hoffman House, produced a telegram from Dallas, Texas, dated May 21, 1895. Corbett's manager, William A. Brady, also received one. It read:

"Corbett and Fitzsimmons, New York: Will be in New York before June 1, ready to talk business."[23]

It was sent by a man named Dan Albert Stuart, and nothing would ever be the same again. The world of prizefighting was about to witness a stunning and bizarre chain of events, all triggered by that simple telegram.

Because of Dan Stuart, new state and federal laws were passed, international relations were strained, three militias were called out, governors were outraged, troops mustered, ministers formed protest unions, bad poetry was inspired, John L. Sullivan fought a goat and fell off a train, thousands of people descended on a quiet frontier town, cowboys and Indians squared off in a frontier football game, a trainload of revelers made a three-hundred-mile odyssey across the Texas wilderness, Bat Masterson had a showdown with a Texas Ranger, a bear was wrestled, there were chases, arrests, insults, threats, low comedy—and a lion got hit in the snoot with a punching bag.

Oh, it was some spectacle, that Dan Stuart's fistic carnival.

ROUND ONE: Dallas, Part One

Am almost certain everything will be closed our way by to-morrow night. Am trying to make terms that will leave the Yankee money in Texas.

—telegram from Dan Stuart

DAN STUART WAS A GAMBLING MAN, what was once commonly termed a "sport." A gambler dealt almost exclusively in games of skill and played to win. A true sport was as freewheeling, spontaneous and financially swashbuckling as any Wall Street speculator, cheerfully covering wagers of outlandish amounts on everything from a horse race or poker hand to where a fly might land next or how long it would take ice to melt and a puddle to dry. Wherever there was money and action on which to risk it, a sport could be seen reaching for his wallet and figuring the odds. The contest was the attraction; winning was simply a bonus. All sports were gamblers, but not all gamblers were sports. Dan Stuart was both.

His base was the Coney Island Jockey Saloon and Restaurant (later the Coney Island Turf Exchange) at 216 Main Street in the Western metropolis of Dallas, Texas. He lived just up the street.[1]

A native of Vermont (said to be descended from the Stuarts of Scotland), Dan Albert Stuart came to Texas in 1872 at the age of twenty-six.[2] He was a portly, genial, prosperous-looking man with a fashionable full mustache and dark hair parted straight down the middle. He could easily be mistaken for a banker or merchant, and his integrity was such that Dallas bankers were ready to advance him as much as $10,000 on his word alone. The *New Orleans Picayune* called him "the wealthiest sports man in Texas."

"His is a very modest and retiring sort of a man," reported the *Picayune*, "averse to being talked about or flattered." As various state governors and lawmen would soon discover, Dan Stuart was also irrepressible.

Dan Stuart, the Dallas sport who only wanted to stage a prizefight and ended up challenging lawmen, governors, and presidents. *New York World,* February 22, 1896.

In one bold move, Stuart's prizefight plans brought new life to a city still struggling to escape the effects of the Panic of 1893, a financial depression that momentarily slowed the city's growth. More than the politicians in either Dallas or Austin, the quiet gambling man was about to fill the city with an estimated twenty thousand to thirty thousand freespending sports and just in time for the tenth annual Texas State Fair and Dallas Exposition.

A visionary, Dan Stuart thought big and planned ahead. To make it easy for visitors to reach Dallas he arranged for special excursion rates with the railroads and the laying of new sidings so tourists could live in the hundreds of passenger cars that brought them, a veritable Pullman City.[3]

And could the championship of the world be held in just any old arena? No—Texas was going to show the world it had style in a grand way. Even before the articles of agreement were signed, Dan Stuart was making plans for a monument to sport, a 52,500-seat Dallas Coliseum. The roofless amphitheater would have an elevated ring, a press area large enough for three hundred reporters, and two hundred dollar luxury boxes.

Considering all the obstacles still in his way—including a sudden offer of $25,000 to stage the fight in Canada (contingent, said The *Chicago Tribune,* on the buying out of "some municipal government of some small town near Montreal"),[4] an uncertain governor, and personal problems badgering the pugilists, Stuart's outward show of confidence was as infectious as it was baseless.

The *Chicago Tribune* noted "something in the demeanor of those Dallas people that inspires the followers of rough sports with confidence" and predicted that the staging of the fight was "a certainty." Indeed, such was Stuart's reputation that sportsmen across the country began making travel plans for October, destination Dallas. All he had to do was pull it off. At the time, nothing seemed simpler.

Before Stuart ever reached New York, the fighters were wrangling. Corbett, Fitzsimmons, Joe Vendig from Jacksonville, Corbett's manager William Brady, and Fitz's legal adviser Emanuel Friend, all got together on May 27, 1895, to discuss the business side of the fight.

According to the *New Orleans Picayune* of May 28, the talk quickly degenerated to desk pounding (by Corbett) and a colloquy reminiscent of boys on schoolyards.

Corbett: "You said I was afraid of you."

Fitzsimmons: "I did, and I'll tell you how I came to say it."

Corbett: "I don't want to hear your explanations, I want to prove to you that I am not afraid of you or any other man."

Fitzsimmons: "I never saw a man that I was afraid of yet either."

Corbett: "Will you tell me that I am afraid of you to my face?"

Fitzsimmons: "I say I am not afraid of you."

Corbett: "Shall I prove to you right here that I am not afraid of you?"

Fitzsimmons: "As you like."

And so on, with Corbett "livid with rage" and Fitzsimmons grinning the while. The only things missing were chips to knock off each other's shoulders. The main thing decided was that they should settle matters in the ring and not in the lawyer's highly breakable office.

As promised, Stuart arrived the first week of June. He had put together a syndicate of businessmen back in Dallas, raised the capital, and brought with him a certified check for $41,000. Canada and everyone else was suddenly out of the running.

"There is no doubt about the bringing off of the fight," Stuart told an Associated Press reporter on June 3. "There is no Texas statute which will be violated by such an exhibition, and I can assure you that the gentlemen who are anxious to have the fight take place there would not have anything to do with it if there was anything illegal about the transaction."

More of Dan Stuart's grand design was revealed over the course of his visit. In addition to the title fight as the main event there would be a number of other bouts with the best fighters available—in keeping with the state fair hoopla, he was going to put on a fistic carnival the likes of which had never been seen before.[5]

The fair was to run from October 15 to the end of the month. The fight would climax the festivities and be held in the new amphitheater (he brought the plans with him to New York as a selling point). The agreed-upon prices would be $10, general admission; $25 for reserved seats; and $200 for private boxes.

The unusual time of ten in the morning was set for the opening bell. Stuart assured everyone that while this was innovative, it was also for the best: "It will all be over, including the applause, by dinner time, and hence will not interfere in any manner with other events."[6]

Corbett's backers pronounced themselves satisfied, and Fitzsimmons said Stuart seemed to be on the level. As for himself, "Give me a fair, trustworthy referee and I have no doubt that I shall prove myself the better man." Regarding the champ, Fitz assured fans that "when he meets me he will tackle a better man than he has ever met before."

That said, and some more problems with the stake money ironed out (and placed in the capable hands of New York racing tout Phil Dwyer), Dan Stuart again issued a positive, upbeat opinion: "The people whom I represent are solid businessmen and there will be no possible chance of a slip-up occurring."

Indeed, things seemed to be going smoothly—it was learned on June 7 that the Dallas fight would have as honored spectators the Prince of Wales and the Marquis of Queensberry himself.[7] And for saving its forfeit money, the Florida Athletic Club voted Dan Stuart in as its president and treasurer.

The *Picayune* fairly rejoiced as it called Dan Stuart "a sporting man with plenty of money and grit." Corbett would train in Asbury Park, and Fitzsimmons was talking of a camp in Galveston. What could possibly go awry?

For starters, the Dallas Pastors' Association was having none of it. The moral shepherds of the city gathered at the Dallas YMCA hall on the morning of Monday, June 10, 1895, and proceeded to issue a ringing condemnation of the proposed fight, the language of which was so strong that two offended pastors refused to sign it. Led by Methodist E. L. Spraggins, the clergy set forth their objections in no uncertain terms:

> Whereas, we learn with shame and sorrow that it is proposed to hold in our midst a contest between two noted pugilists; and whereas such contests are brutalizing in an unspeakable degree; and whereas such a contest will concentrate in our midst a horde of gamblers, thieves, pickpockets, thugs

and harlots, whose presence even scattered throughout the country is a
perpetual menace to the welfare of the community, and where concen-
trated here would debauch our city and state in an unlimited degree; and
whereas, while we have the fullest confidence in the integrity, ability and
courage of our chief executive, Governor Culberson, but whereas there is
some doubt as to the adequacy of our statutes to enable the state authorities
to effectually interfere to prevent the besmirching of the fair names of our
city and state in the eyes of the civilized world in this matter; therefore, be it

Resolved, that we express our most emphatic disapproval and abhor-
rence of the proposed outrageous, abomination.

Other "indignation meetings" began popping up like prairie brush-
fires,[8] but yet to be heard from was the young governor of Texas, forty-
four-year-old Charles A. Culberson. Would he try and stop the fight as
the governors of Florida, Mississippi, and Indiana had stopped such
encounters? He was publicly mum.

The *Chicago Tribune* thought Culberson would resist the tide of moral
outrage; it editorialized that "everybody—that is, every member of the
'dead game' fraternity—expects to find the Governor with 'a front seat
and a tab' when the mill comes off." The paper noted that in withstanding "the billow of indignation that will roll upon him on the eve of the
fight and the broadside of resolutions that will be fired at him he will
show a gameness that is worthy of a State where so many people have died
without first removing their cowhides."

Publicly, the governor remained silent, even when Dan Stuart was
given a hero's welcome on his return from New York, the fight (and its
influx of tourist money) signed, sealed, and soon to be delivered. "Dallas
Starts Going Wild," the *Picayune* headlined.[9]

In less than a week, Stuart and his syndicate of backers established a
fund of $50,000 for construction of the stadium and let out a contract of
$18,000 for lumber. Stuart the optimist would not even comment on the
personal peccadilloes of his star performers, though back in New York
they were hot items—Corbett was trying to answer adultery allegations in
his messy (and oh, so juicy) divorce proceedings, and Fitzsimmons was
about to go on trial for first degree manslaughter.

It was tough for both men to concentrate on training routines in June
and July.

One of the few official items of fight business conducted that nervous
summer was the traditional measuring and weighing. Corbett was heavier
and, at 6' 1½", nearly two inches taller; Fitz had a bigger chest and a good
edge in reach (with ten-inch fists at the end of his long arms).

Both men also showed up at Madison Square Garden on June 8 for a benefit to help the ailing Jack Dempsey, and thousands of fans came—Fitzsimmons and Corbett, however, sparred with others. The benefit raised $6,000.[10]

What New York really cared about anyway was the gossip, and Gotham got it.

Ollie and Jim Corbett's marriage had been shaky for some time. After the Charley Mitchell fight Corbett purchased a house at 146 W. 88th Street in New York for his wife while he remained at their Jerome Avenue residence (the Sullivan fight paid for that one). He gave Ollie an allowance of $100 a week and put the new house in her name.

Athletes attracted women, and there had always been talk of Jim's womanizing. Ollie had tried to ignore it. Then it became a little too public for comfort—they nearly separated after an affair with a woman named Hattie Clark (which ended when a bookmaker beau threatened to shoot the champ on sight).

More affairs were brought to light during the divorce as Ollie charged her husband with "improper conduct" in Zanesville, Indianapolis, Charleston, West Virginia, and other romantic hideaways. The juiciest testimony came on July 15, when an actress in Corbett's touring theatrical company took the stand.

Marie King told of a woman named Vera who accompanied Corbett in Pittsburgh, Parkersburg, Cincinnati, and Indianapolis. "She used to come to the theatre with Jim and leave it with him, and was his companion at all times." In late April, she saw them enter a stateroom on a train and lock the door. They were, said Miss King, "very affectionate," and the other actors always called Vera "Mrs. Corbett."

By the time it was revealed that the two had registered as "J. J. Corbett and wife" at a hotel in Corning, Ohio, the heavyweight champ was ready to throw in the towel and change his wife's allowance money to alimony.[11]

The trouble facing Fighting Robert Fitzsimmons was far more serious than who was bedding whom. On June 30, 1895, testimony began in Syracuse, New York, in the boxer's manslaughter trial. He was accused of causing the death of Cornelius Riordan, his sparring partner, on November 16, 1894.

Con Riordan was no stranger to boxing. The Melbourne native was thirty-one when he died and had been a fighter since he turned twenty. He had been a sparring partner for Peter Jackson, fought against Jim Corbett in San Francisco, and held the record for the shortest fight in history, having knocked out Billy Cole in Melbourne in just eight seconds. As part of Fitzsimmons' vaudeville act at the Jacobs' Theatre in

Syracuse, Riordan would nightly come out on stage and, with "Yank" Sullivan as referee, spar with his lanky boss.

At 10:30 on the night of the sixteenth, there was the usual mixing it up, and suddenly Riordan was down, apparently having been struck on the chin by one of Fitz's feared uppercuts. The audience, thinking it was part of the act, applauded and then watched a local fighter, James Dunfee, spar with Fitz.

Riordan was still unconscious when the curtain came down and was moved to the Hotel Candee, where doctors applied electricity in hope of reviving him. He was pronounced dead early the next morning. Shortly after midnight, Fitzsimmons was arrested.

When told of Riordan's death, Fitzsimmons exclaimed, "My God! You don't mean to tell me Connie is dead. I can't believe it. I did not hit him hard enough to injure a child." Fitz told the press: "Do you suppose I would strike my sparring partner with any force? I knew he had been drinking hard, but did not know he was in such a condition. Invariably when I sparred with him he turned blue around the mouth, and it was a sign for me to let up." And that is what he did: "The blow that caused the trouble was light as I could make it, merely slapping him with the back of my hand. He fell down and then staggered around. I put my arm around him to assist him off the stage. When he fell I thought he was faking."

He was soon free on $10,000 bond—referee Sullivan and an ex-sheriff named Thomas O'Neill put up the money. It wasn't much longer before the telegraph wires were humming with opinions.

Light-heavyweight Joe Choynski dismissed the "light" blow theory right away, saying (from personal experience), "Bob hits too hard in play, and without intending to hurt people. He is too awkward and too powerful to gauge a blow and reduce its force, but he is not naturally brutal. He is earnest and fierce enough when boxing, but is a kindly, well-meaning fellow."

Fighter Jim Hall, noting Riordan's was not the first ring death by far, said there should be medical supervision of boxing matches: "The man was not only drunk, but half dead from disease, and any doctor would have kept him off the stage."

The harshest criticism from his peers came from Jim Corbett, who wasn't overly kind to Riordan either. "I knew Riordan well," commented the champ. "As an amateur he was clever, but he was no sparring partner for Bob, and I blame Fitzsimmons for using such a wreck for a punch bag. Riordan will be found to be diseased and a man who should never have been in a position to take punishment." His retroactive prognosis on

Riordan was, "He was at any time liable to drop dead after an exertion such as running a foot race or a lively boxing match."

After the autopsy, Dr. D. M. Totman concluded that the victim had been dealt a powerful blow to the chin and this produced a blood clot in his brain. Riordan was said to have been in perfect health.

Fitzsimmons hired a lawyer.

Four days after the fight, the Syracuse Common Council passed a resolution prohibiting boxing.

A day before the inquest, Fitzsimmons sought to tell his side of things to the public. The *New York World* printed a long letter from the distressed fighter that attempted to give a blow-by-blow description of the fatal round, again emphasizing Riordan's drinking habits and the possibility he was clowning around (some spectators, he said, yelled "Fake!" when Riordan sat on the stage and "fell over backwards"). He disavowed all blame: "I knew I had not hit him hard enough to hurt a flea."[12]

The verdict at the inquest was "Not guilty," but the district attorney, S. J. Shove, took the case to the grand jury just the same.

The trial began nearly eight months later.

Judge Ross's courtroom was packed each day. Police Captain Quigley, an eyewitness, testified that Riordan did not throw his head back as if punched, and Dr. U. H. Brown said he clearly heard Riordan's head strike the stage floor. But the most decisive recitation came from New York doctor F. A. Lyon. By the time Dr. Lyon was through contradicting the "perfect health" autopsy report, one had to wonder how Riordan ever lived through the opening bell. The *Austin Daily Statesman* reported the testimony this way:

"From the description given of Riordan's heart, [Dr. Lyon] would judge that he was affected with hiperthrophy [*sic*], which gives the heart a spasmodic action. He thought that the kidneys were affected with Bright's disease; also from the description of Riordan's condition he would judge he had enlargement of the liver and an affection [*sic*] of the left lung."

Dr. Lyon had examined Riordan a year before his death and at that time also diagnosed a case of dropsy. He had warned the Australian to stop drinking and avoid violent exercise.

The jury was out less than four hours and the announcement of "Not guilty" was greeted with cheers from the crowd.[13]

Fitz gave an exhibition that same night and reported he would soon go into training for the Dallas fight. He and his new manager, brother-in-law Martin Julian, would be at Coney Island until time to leave for Texas.[14]

If there was to be a fight at all. One day before the trial ended, Nat

Finley, the Texas State Comptroller, pronounced prizefighting to be illegal.

The simmering Texas summer had just hit the boiling point.

In 1889, the Texas legislature had passed a law allowing prizefights, bullfights, and other dangerous contests, the only provision being that the organizers pay the state a $500 "occupation tax." Despite this, Gov. Lawrence Sullivan Ross had stopped a fight by calling out the militia.

Ross was succeeded in 1891 by Gov. James Stephen Hogg, a man who went down in Texas history chiefly for naming his daughter Ima. In the first year of his administration, prizefighting became a penal offense.

Depending on which side of the issue one stood, the 1891 law completely superseded the law of 1889, or they coexisted and canceled each other out. Taking the latter road, Dan Stuart applied for a license and cheerfully offered the $500 fee to the Dallas County tax collector.

That woke up the state's bureaucracy and set the judicial wheels rolling.

The matter was duly passed upward to the state comptroller's office, and on July 2, Nat Finley wrote back to Dallas, laying down the law as he saw it:

"This department will not attempt to legalize the proposed pugilistic encounter in this state by the issuance of a license therefore, or by authorizing you, as tax collector of Dallas county, to receive any tax for such performance when the same is manifestly unlawful and has been so expressly declared by the people of Texas through their legislature."

In Finley's corner was the author of the 1889 law, State Representative Mills, who noted that not only was the law repealed entirely in 1891, but the maximum sentence for violations was a $1,000 fine and a year in the pokey.

Into the fray jumped two of the state's best lawyers, George Clark and Bill Crawford. They would argue that a conflict existed in the law—it made fighting a felony but with a misdemeanor punishment. Plus, the law as written was so vague it could not be understood let alone enforced.

The two attorneys met with Martin M. Crane, the state's attorney general (and one-time lieutenant governor under Hogg), on Tuesday, July 9, and forcefully presented their case.

While calling the opposition's arguments "most elaborate and ingenious," Crane found himself unable to agree with them. He said, in essence, that no matter how poorly written or how dense the language, if the original intention of the legislature was to prohibit prizefighting, nothing else was relevant. Lapses in the wording were no excuse or shield or reason for overturning a law. Accordingly, the sheriff was duty-bound not just to stop the fight but also to arrest all spectators for "unlawful assembly" and for encouraging the lawbreaking. "He has the power to call to his assistance any number of men he may choose," warned Crane. "Should he deem it necessary he can call on the governor for the militia."

What went unspecified was how the sheriff and his deputies could successfully arrest 20,000 or more people.

In any case, the statement appeared solid, irrefutable, and worse, was hailed from pulpits near and far. The *El Paso Daily Times* noted, "The authorities are strongly backed by the moral sentiment of the state."

First to weigh in as God's heavyweight was the Reverend George W. Cravens who was reported in the Austin press as ready "to run the principals, promoters, and the whole crowd into the sea."

At a meeting on July 16, a large group of Austin ministers got together and drafted an address to the citizens of Texas. The *Daily Statesman* observed that the address "will bristle in many respects." That was an understatement.

The address termed all participants in the fight "ministers of brutal transaction" and "law-breakers," labeled the fight itself "a wicked exhibition" that, if held, would be an "outrage" and an "insolent defiance of the right mind." The Austin clergy declared, "These prize fights constitute violent threats to all the interests of order and virtue as well as of Christianity."

They enumerated their objections under four categories:

First—They involve an enormous and useless waste of the time and wealth of the people.

Second—They attract to the unfortunate place selected for the criminal exhibition a vast throng of those disorderly and dissolute persons who find their enjoyment in these savage scenes, whose presence is a perilous threat to the community. It must expect to be cursed by an enormous impulse in its very midst to the sins of profanity, intoxication, lewdness, betting, gambling, prodigality, breaches of the peace and even homicides.

Third—An example is displayed with the greatest publicity, which applies a seductive but poisonous temptation to the natural feelings of inexperienced youth.

Last—The proceeding is brutal, cruel, dangerous to the participants, always involving causeless wounds and bloodshed, and sometimes the crime of actual murder, inflaming and debauching the souls of the spectators and even of the most distant readers.

The ministers decided that even bullfights were more humane because the bulls were headed for the butcher's block anyway.

"We see not how these prize fights can be judged less barbarous than the gladitorial murders of the ancient arena which made a pastime for the pagan rabble of Rome. We know not how the civilization of any people and the honor of the commonwealth can be more deeply disgraced than by the toleration of such crime." That such an event might come off even after being declared illegal was particularly galling, "a darker evil" to be boldly fought lest it make Texas seem "hospitable to barbarism and infamy."

Where that could lead was, to the ministers, obvious: "From time to time one and then another of our towns will be invaded by the prize fighters of the whole continent with their debauched hoards of followers. Our excitable and inexperienced youth will be seduced into imitation: their ambition will be fired to seek the brutal honors of the ring instead of [the] sober pleasures and credit of scholarship, industry and domestic virtue. Our other wholesome laws for restraining vice will be trodden in the mire. Our State will sink beneath Mexico in disrepute, poverty and decadence."

The address, signed by chairman A. J. Rose, urged the writing of letters and telegrams in support of the governor and attorney general, and promised to publish them for all to see.

In Dallas, over four hundred of the city's leading businessmen gathered at the Commercial Club on July 19. Their purpose was to find ways around Crane's decision and bring off the fight as scheduled, stating it would be good for the state, good for the city, and, incidentally, highly profitable to themselves.

They were also feeling threatened by a bid for the fight from Galveston where it could legally be pulled off out in the waters of the bay rather than on the sacred soil of Texas. The businessmen resolved to get a lawyer and, sports that they were, started betting two to one against Galveston getting the fight.

Moral support for Crane came all the way from Baltimore in the form of the fifth international convention of the Baptist Young People's Union of America. Amid resolutions calling for strict observance of Sunday closing laws in all states and the abolishing of Sunday newspapers, amusements, and excursions, was this: "We extend our earnest sympathy to the noble people of Texas, who are now using all their powers to prevent the occurrence of the proposed Corbett-Fitzsimmons fight in the Lone Star State, under the conviction that such a fight would tend to demoralize not only Texas but the whole civilized world."

Dan Stuart, the Great Demoralizer, did not appear worried. A news wire report reprinted in Austin, right under Governor Culberson's nose during breakfast, was almost defiant in tone:

"There is nothing about the movements of the men who are getting up the big glove championship contest to indicate that they are worried in the slightest degree over the manifesto of the attorney general of Texas, or the alleged uprising of the moral element of the Lone Star State against the project." Tickets for the "monster amphitheater," it said, were already out, and offices would open nationwide within a week. "Madison Square Garden is a pretty big place," observed the article, "but the Dan Stewart [sic] building will seat ten times as many persons. Dan does not expect to crowd the house. It would take 52,518 customers to bring this about. He believes, however, in being fully prepared for a rush."

A rush? When completed, the stadium would hold seven thousand more people than lived in Dallas at the time. In terms of seating capacity, it would be history's second largest building![15] The stadium would be located in "the widow Browder's cotton patch" a quarter mile northeast of the fairgrounds.[16]

Tickets went on sale in Dallas on August 8 and went fast. At the cotton patch, three miles from the Dallas courthouse, twelve acres had been cleared by August 15, four of them set aside for refreshment stands and the parking of "carriages and hacks by the thousands." A hundred workmen were standing by, and ten flatcar loads of lumber were arriving daily. The New Orleans Picayune predicted the battle would draw "the largest assemblage of people ever gotten together on the western continent."

Whether the battle they had in mind was the fistic one, or the legal one, or the moral one, was not yet clear.

Betting pools were springing up across the country from New Orleans to San Francisco, from Denver to Chicago, from Cleveland to Memphis, from Pittsburg to Indianapolis. And the bets were not just on who would win the big fight (opening odds were five to four against Fitzsimmons, and fourteen to four against Corbett), but also who would prevail in the political ring—it was three to one in favor of Stuart.

The governor could no longer stand above the fracas. His office was being deluged with letters and telegrams denouncing the fight. The Evangelical Pastors Association of Marshall, for one, claimed the fight violated the laws of God.[17] The Austin Ministerial Association called for a public mass meeting to protest the event (and took the occasion to also denounce free Sunday entertainments as a desecration of the Sabbath and an occasion of youthful corruption).

The next condemnation came from a convention of retired Civil War soldiers who decried the fight and the "thugs" it would bring to Texas, their resolution to the governor stating: "We, the surviving members of

The rapidly growing modern city of Dallas, as seen from the Oriental Hotel in 1895. It wasn't New York, but Dan Stuart was about to teach the Gothamites about Texas determination. Courtesy Dallas Historical Society.

the Eleventh Texas Cavalry of the late C.S.A., in reunion at Clarksville, Tex., respectfully tender to you our hearty support and service in your efforts to uphold the supremacy of the law to the prevention of said fight or contest taking place within the borders of our State."

Mightily pressed by the forces of good, Governor Culberson did the bureaucratic thing. He issued a proclamation. It was a beaut.

Branding anyone involved with a prizefight a contemptuous felon, Culberson derided "any supposed temporary pecuniary benefit" as insufficient cause to "disregard the will of the people." Texas, he said, "with her hospitable and intelligent population and limitless resources, needs not the incentive of violated law to induce immigration or investment." Therefore, the governor urged the state's peace officers "to prevent the commission of such offense and cause offenders to be punished and all persons contemplating future infractions of said law are warned to desist therefrom and are put upon notice that to the limit of executive authority I shall take care that the law is faithfully executed to the end that such offenses may be prevented and offenders punished."

The governor may not have realized the scope of what he was trying to suppress when he wrote of the "supposed temporary pecuniary benefit" of the fight. If all the seats were sold, the net amount of the gate receipts alone would be $1,225,244.94. In addition to the revenues for local businesses and the city's coffers. No wonder that among the fight's most ardent supporters was Col. Frank P. Holland, Mayor of Dallas.

Holland said it was not a fight at all, but, rather, "an athletic exhibition, the greatest physical culture exhibition, the most scientific boxing contest in the world." It might very well be "the premiere event in the domain of sport."[18]

And then a scheme came forth from out of the capital, a scheme so outrageous, so lunatic, so tongue-in-cheek, that had it been implemented, it just might have worked.

It was reasoned by certain unnamed Austin promoters that the main objection to the fight was not its legality but simply its location. If it came off in Dallas or Galveston, no one in the state government would be able to attend without spending a lot of time and money. So the solution must be to hold it in Austin.

The plan, set forth in the *Austin Daily Statesman,* called for tiers of seats on either side of the Colorado River around Mount Bonnell. The ring would be in the middle of the river on a floating platform, the whole lit "as light as day" by electric lights. Supplementing the bleachers would be steamboats anchored close to the ring. Those fans most concerned with how this might look to the voters (the governor, sheriff, and others) could be seated "where the shadows fall the heaviest" so they might enjoy the fight in anonymity.

As for the "the religious and moral world," Dan Stuart could arrange and heavily advertise *false fights* in both Dallas and Galveston as decoys, luring the heavenly heat away from Austin.

It sounds nearly foolproof, but no one paid much attention to it at the time. Except Stuart, who filed it away for future consideration.

Meanwhile, the *Dallas Morning News* reported that over four hundred people would be coming to the fight from San Francisco; Omaha was sending two hundred; large parties from Kansas City, Denver, Colorado Springs, and even Salt Lake City had booked themselves onto the Union Pacific, Denver and Gulf Railroad.

And Dan Stuart started hedging his bets by sending a representative to see the governor of Chihuahua, in the event the fight had to be held in Mexico. The *El Paso Daily Times* openly hoped for such a twist, saying it could mean twenty-thousand visitors to the border city who would spend upwards of $800,000 during the week of the fight.

In the present atmosphere, almost anything could happen.

And it did: Jim Corbett and Bob Fitzsimmons got into a hell of a fight. Not in a ring, but in a hotel lobby.

There had been a lot of boasting and swaggering in the newspapers by each of the two men, as was becoming a customary prelude to title matches. On August 10, 1895, both fighters were on the road with their respective entertainment troupes when their schedules brought them by chance to Philadelphia at the same time.

Jim Corbett and his entourage were relaxing in the bar of Green's Hotel near midnight when Bob Fitzsimmons stepped up to the registration desk, alone.

Corbett's younger brother Joe spotted the challenger and exclaimed, "What do you make of that?"

What they made of it was that Fitz, in coming to Corbett's hotel, was being openly disrespectful and "looking for trouble." What happened next depends on whose account one chooses to believe. All agree that Corbett started it.

In his autobiography, Corbett wrote that he deliberately became "the aggressor," going over to the front desk and offering an impertinent insult. Fitz blew up, words were exchanged ("though I cannot recall the exact dialogue, it had pepper enough") and Corbett, responding to gossip in the papers about Fitz threatening to yank his nose, beat him to it: "I grabbed hold of his nose and twisted it so it hurt."

The next day's *Austin Daily Stateman* had it that the champ "gave Fitzsimmons' nasal organ a smart tweak."

To no one's great surprise, Fitzsimmons took offense.

Corbett claimed his "thoughtful" friends grabbed him and held him back, but "not a soul thought of doing the same for the other man." The newspapers reported, however, that the two immediately clinched and were separated simultaneously. Joe Corbett was in the thick of it, gripping Fitzsimmons from behind and pinning his arms. One account has him trying to butt the Australian, and taunting, "You can't whip me, to say nothing of my brother."

Corbett wrote that while he was helplessly sat on by at least ten of his good friends, Joe and Fitz "wrestled all over the lobby" until finally breaking apart. Enraged, Fitzsimmons picked up a decanter and threw it at Joe but missed.

"Then what must Fitz do," recalled Corbett, "but step in the dining room, seize a castor from the table, and hurl it, pepper, salt, vinegar, oil and cayenne and tabasco, as red as his hair, at Joe—Joe who had simply held him, when it was I who had twisted his nose. Joe ducked and the salad dressing splattered the wall."[19]

According to the papers, Fitz was stopped by a security guard *before* he could let loose of the castor.

As things settled down, Jim Corbett walked up to Fitzsimmons and spat in his face.

Later, Martin Julian told a *Houston Post* reporter, "That was a bum proceeding. Corbett and his heelers found Fitz alone and they took advantage of it. Never a word would have been said had the members of the company been present. The insult was offered by Corbett and Fitzsimmons was held, with his hands at his back, by two or three while Corbett attempted to spit in his face. And then that half brother who was with him, caught Fitz about the neck, giving him the 'strong arm.' It did Corbett no good. His title of Gentleman Jim was proved to be 'unearned.'"

Boys will be boys. But the way things were shaping up in Dallas, that could be the only fight fans were going to get.

Oh, sure, Mayor Frank Holland was still sounding optimistic—passing through St. Louis, drumming up business for the fair, he predicted the fight was "a sure thing." The law, he said, was about to be history. Dan Stuart, he assured skeptical Missourians, "is a good, practical businessman, and is not taking any chances. We expect to have an enormous inpouring of the best people of the country in October, and that is the main reason that the businessmen of the state, and particularly of Dallas, are supporting Mr. Stuart."[20]

In a similarly optimistic vein, Fitz continued to train at Coney Island while, on August 22, Messrs Supton and Innes, representatives of the Arkansas Pass Railroad, began scouting Corpus Christi for a suitable Texas headquarters for the challenger. (The railroad was planning on running two paid excursions a week to the training site.) A group of local businessmen had leased a home for him north of the city, right on the beach. Stuart, meanwhile, was consolidating his support by arranging to advertise a tie-in between the fight and the upcoming boat races set for Austin.

If Dan Stuart, his star challenger, and the mayor were not paying heed to the newspapers, that changed very quickly the next day when the *Austin Daily Statesman* published letters passed between Governor Culberson and Dallas Sheriff Ben Cabell on how to stop the fight, the gist of which made it to a terse headline three days later: "SHOOT THEM DOWN."

The letters, released by the governor's office, began simply enough with

Culberson reiterating his intention to stop the fight and adding, "From my long acquaintance with you I have no doubt you intend to perform your duty fully under the law as you understand it." He did, however, ask for reassurance on how much effort the sheriff would expend "to prevent this offense."

The two were indeed well acquainted, Culberson hailing from Dallas. But if the governor expected a rousing cry of solidarity from the sheriff, he was mistaken. Ben Cabell was no fool. His father, William L. Cabell, had been a Confederate general *and* a four-term mayor of Dallas; Ben had not only been taught how to obey orders but also how to protect himself from vague ones. Political savvy ran in the family.[21]

He wrote back asking for very specific guidelines.

In addition to asking for writs and other backing, the sheriff pointedly wrote: "I would therefore, respectfully ask you as the chief executive of the State . . . whether I would be justified in using such force as may be necessary to prevent it, even if it required the shooting down of citizens, and would you advise me to use such force?"

On August 17, the governor responded, and he too tried to cover himself. He felt that the sheriff first needed to state unequivocally whether or not he actually intended to stop the fight, whatever amount of force was called for.

On August 20 came the sheriff's return volley: "I endeavored to be plain and frank in my former letter." He then asked again, "to what extent will I be justified in using force to the extent indicated by my former question?"

It took two days for the exasperated governor to reply that it was mandatory that all public officers—such as sheriffs, and particularly the sheriff of Dallas County—"give notice at once of the firm purpose to enforce the law that none may be deceived." Otherwise, "non-residents unable to do so at home shall ply their prohibited avocation here." The governor closed by saying all necessary and expedient force "will be used to prevent this proposed infraction of the law of the State." He referred further details to Attorney General Martin Crane.[22]

Crane had no trouble fielding the tossed hot potato. On August 27 he told a stunned state that a prizefight would be covered under the anti-riot laws, and "Homicide is justifiable when necessary to suppress riot." In such a case, Sheriff Cabell would be empowered—with or without a warrant—to call in the state militia. "If the riot can be suppressed in no other way except by taking life, it is his duty to suppress the riot, and let the consequences take care of themselves."[23]

In other words, to prevent the possible injury or death of one of the fighters in the ring, the sheriff should be prepared to kill them both and the spectators as well.

Crane had just thrown a very wet blanket over Dan Stuart's party.

Amid renewed rumors of the fight going to Juarez, Mexico, for a guarantee up front of twenty thousand pesos, reporters cornered a chastened Dan Stuart. As lumber continued to pile up in Mrs. Browder's cotton field and hundreds of workmen went on hammering and sawing, the fight's savior and chief promoter was asked about the triple play between Cabell, Culberson, and Crane.

And the suddenly somber Stuart, perhaps sensing crosshairs on his chest, said, "I am closed tighter than a clam."

Round one belonged to the governor.

ROUND TWO: Dallas, Part Two

I intend to stop this fight if it takes the entire
police force of the State to stop it.

—Gov. Charles Culberson

DALLAS WAS PROUD OF ITSELF. Returning from his short trip up north, Mayor Frank Holland reported that Dallas was seen as a "coming" city with good credit, which was fortunate because he needed to borrow $40,000 during the trip to meet the city's payroll (one moneyless payday had already passed).

From its frontier origins near the three forks of the Trinity River in 1841 (incorporated in 1871), Dallas had grown to be one of the state's most prosperous and expanding cities. The Commercial Club was planning on sending a railway car of Texas products and resources to the Atlanta Exposition, a kind of "Texas on Wheels" to tout the commonwealth.

A Commercial Club report on the city's most exploitable virtues was presented to the public on September 10. Calling theirs "the wealthiest and most populous county of Texas," and putting the current population at roughly forty-nine thousand (if Oak Cliff was included), the businessmen hailed Dallas as the number one city in the state, and thirty-first in the nation.

The real value of taxed property was set at $33,000,000. There were over thirty miles of sewers, two-hundred and fifty public arc lights illuminating the Texas nights, fifty schools and colleges, forty-eight churches, one synagogue, sixty-four miles of streetcar tracks (mostly electric), and five banks.

In addition, "Dallas [excelled] any city in the state in the number and character of newspapers and periodicals published," boasted of a fire department—with an electric alarm system—that was "the pride of the state," had the best hotels in the southwest, and had never suffered an epidemic or drought; sunstrokes were "of most rare occurrence."

Five railroad trunk lines entered the city, with more on the way, and the last state fair had bigger receipts in sixteen days than the great St. Louis Exposition had garnered in forty-eight.

The city also had a two-million-dollar debt, not mentioned in that glowing report. But things were looking up—after all, the new cotton crop, an area staple, was selling at a brisk six-and-a-half cents a pound, and it was almost time again for the state fair, surely a harbinger of an economic boom.

The plans for exhibits and displays were nothing short of grandiose, ranging from agricultural to mechanical, with amusements from bike and horse races each day to a fiery reenactment (eight nights running) of "The Last Days of Pompeii" (reserved seats seventy-five cents). There would be a simulated naval battle, a bombardment of Fort Sumner, and "The Falls of Niagara" represented in "living fire."

For the adventurous armchair traveler, the fair would feature a recreation of the streets of Cairo, complete with "Egyptian snake charmers, Bohemian glass blowers, mystic mazes, bewildering illusions and all that is new, striking, novel and grotesque in this country and the old." Music lovers were going to be treated to the "grandest carnival of music in the history of the south" at the fair's music hall, starting with The Royal Hawaiian Band and Glee Club and ending patriotically with the military band of John Phillip Sousa playing "Songs and Dances of the Sunny South" along with other perennial favorites (the Daughters of the Confederacy would be soliciting funds for a memorial to the defeated men in gray).

To keep visitors coming back for more, events were programmed around special days: October 25 would be "Republican Day," and October 26 would be "Educational Day and Drummers' Day"; this would be followed by "Colored People's Day," "Comic Opera Day," "Populist Day," "Free Silver Day" (featuring the oratory of William Jennings Bryan), "Chrysanthemum and Woman's Council Day," and, to really drum up tourist business, "National Passenger and Ticket Agents' Day."

A thousand dollars worth of fireworks would be set off nightly.

The only event still up in the air, still "to be announced" for the last day's big finale, was the heavyweight championship fight. And that, two months beforehand, was making a lot of people uneasy, the governor included.

Dallas was proud of its governor, the first chief executive who called

YOU GUESS . . . .

WHO WILL BE THE WINNER
IN THE COMING

CORBETT-FITZSIMMONS

Glove Contest.

. . . . .

From now until October 31st, 1895, we will make to order and present, free of charge, choice of any suit in our house to the person guessing closest to the "time"—HOURS, MINUTES AND SECONDS—it will take for

CORBETT and FITZSIMMONS,

to decide in their great contest who will be the **Champion of the World.**

COME IN AND GUESS.

HULSIZER & HUNTER,

ROYAL TAILORS,

322 Main St., DALLAS, TEXAS.

Local businesses delighted in fight tie-ins, as this ad from the State Fair program shows. Courtesy Dallas Historical Society.

the city home.[1] And right now, the eyes of Texas (and the nation) were upon him.

Charles Allen Culberson was born June 19, 1855, in Dadeville, Alabama. The family moved to Texas a year later. His father, David Browning Culberson, set the pace for his son as a lawyer, judge, lieutenant colonel in the 18th Texas Infantry during the Civil War (though he had opposed secession), adjutant general of Texas, and U.S. Congressman since 1875. Dave Culberson was a popular man in Texas.

Charles studied law at the University of Virginia, and settled in Dallas with his wife Sally in 1887.[2] He was elected the state's attorney general in 1890 and won his first term as the twenty-second governor since annexation in 1894.[3]

An astute politician (who was rapidly becoming known as "the veto governor"),[4] the clean-shaven Culberson stood a broad and burly 5'9" and was such a stickler for observing the letter of the law while still getting his own way that one political crony said he "could give a bulldog cards and spades for clean grit."

That same politico, a Dallas county official who declined to be identified beyond the name "Jim," told a *Chicago Tribune* reporter all about his pal the governor.

Jim spoke of the governor as "good people" and "one of the boys" who was also "about as swift a politician as Texas has afforded since the days of Sam Houston." Jim claimed to have been among the Dallas officials (along with Sheriff Cabell) who delivered the necessary money and votes to get him elected against "a rather strait-laced and religious party [who] had what you would call the religious element behind his game." Which was why Culberson was not now playing fair:

"I want to say right here that we, the very people who nominated Culberson, are the very ones who are now trying to pull off this Corbett-Fitzsimmons match," Jim declared, "and when Culberson gets in the way he touches us where we live. His attitude toward the fight is going to bother him hereafter—the more so as it is nothing but a political play on his part."

As if to emphasize that the governor was not exactly a saint himself, Jim got a little personal. "While he seems to be siding with the pulpits," noted the gossipy official, "Culberson himself couldn't be called the pulpit sort. While he doesn't drink too much, Culberson stands ready without the slightest hesitation to sample most any kind of invigorator that ever lived back of a bar in a bottle. When he is irritated he can swear like a teamster, and he doesn't hesitate to garnish the ordinary conversation with a reasonable degree of profanity."

Jim predicted the fight would come off after the requisite amount of "fuss and feathers beforehand." Texas wanted the fight, he said, "and when the Texas public takes a yearning for anything it generally gets it."

That remained to be seen.

Round two opened up with Dan Stuart striding into the ring and throwing a sharp jab: "The championship contest will be pulled off according to original agreement. If not in Dallas, then not far away. This is official and positive."

The man would not stay down for the count.

On the first day of September, the law granting a boxing license upon payment of a $500 tax would automatically come into conflict with the statute outlawing such fights. It was time for a test case.

On August 30 "flaming hand-bills" began appearing on poles, fences and walls all over the city of Dallas. They read: "Grand physical culture exhibition between Tommy Cavanaugh and Jim Bates, six rounds; Spider Kelly and Gene Mitchell, ten rounds."

Sprouting almost overnight on a Main Street vacant lot just east of the post office was a mini-amphitheater of twelve thousand seats with a ring in the center.

The fights promptly took place the next night as a lead-in to an exhibition of rat killing by a dog named Bulger. Cavanaugh and Bates, Kelly and Mitchell duly presented six rounds each of "scientific sparring" and were applauded. Bulger killed a dozen rats in fifteen seconds. No one, man or animal, was arrested.[5]

The next day Dan Stuart triumphantly telegraphed the following message to Joe Vendig, manager of the Florida Athletic Club: "Pay no attention to absurd rumors from Austin, Tex. I reiterate 1000 times stronger than before that parties coming here to see the Corbett-Fitzsimmons or other fistic contests on Oct. 31, will not be disappointed. Lumber all delivered on grounds ready for building."

His was, of course, a biased opinion, but there were plenty of supporters to cheer him on.

A Dallasite named W. J. Connor returned from a Colorado vacation and told reporters that "it looks out there as if the whole of Colorado is coming, and that the name of Dallas is on every tongue"; a Kansas City businessman named N. R. Bagby said much the same of his city, "and those who will attend will be representative men." The *News Orleans Picayune* said, "There is not a prominent lawyer in Dallas who does not believe Crane is wrong. At all events there seems no doubt in the city that the fight will take place at the time appointed."

The city auditor, C. G. Morgan, returned from his vacation in Mississippi to say that "On the cars, in the hotels and on the plantations they all talk of Dallas and Corbett and Fitzsimmons. It strikes me that it is a big thing for Dallas and for Texas."

The editor of the *Waco Telephone* noted the efforts of "those who are possessed of conscientious scruples against prize fights" to stop it, and predicted the fight would come off and be "the greatest drawing card that Dallas ever had." W. G. Crush of the Missouri, Kansas and Texas Railroad, sent out twenty thousand arena diagrams all over the country from his St. Louis terminal.

On the other side stood the various state officials sworn to follow the lead of the governor and attorney general. The county attorney for Dallas, John P. Gillespie, admitted the question involved "many complex and intricate questions of statutory construction" and that the answer was shrouded in "doubt and uncertainty." But would he stop the fight? "I should consider it my official duty to prosecute the offender."

With the battlelines thus drawn, and two seemingly contradictory laws now in force, representatives of the Dallas Athletic Club stepped into the office of Tax Collector Louis Jacoby on September 2 and laid down five hundred dollars for a fight license, the opponents to be welterweight Tom Cavanaugh of Buffalo, New York, and Jess Clark from San Francisco, said fight to be held that night in the same amphitheater where Bulger the terrier had so ably acquitted himself.

The money was offered by F. T. Hubbell and fighter Jim Bates, referee and president of the Dallas Athletic Club. The conversation went like this:

> Bates: "Mr. Jacoby, I wish to get a license for a glove contest tonight."
>
> Jacoby: "I refer you to Mr. Finley at Austin."
>
> Hubbell: "We have the money here and would like to get a license today. Can't you issue one?"
>
> Jacoby: "I have no blanks and I have never been furnished with any. I have to use the blank described by law, or I would lay myself liable."
>
> Hubbell: "How much is the tax?"
>
> Jacoby: "Five hundred dollars for the state and $250 for the county."
>
> Hubbell: "Well, if it is $500 we will pay it, and if it is $750 we will pay it."
>
> Jacoby: "I couldn't take your money. I wrote to the comptroller for blanks to issue a license to Mr. Dan Stuart. He said in one letter to collect the tax and in another he instructed me not to and did not send any blanks."
>
> Hubbell: "Well, if you haven't those blanks here I will hand you the money now and you can send me the license as soon as you can get the blank."

Jacoby: "I couldn't take your money."
Hubbell: "Then you understand I tendered it."
Jacoby: "Yes, I think we understand each other."

Sheriff Ben Cabell was in the crowd outside the office. He informed Hubbell and Bates that should the fight now be pulled off without a license, everyone connected with it would be arrested.[6]

Elsewhere in town, Judge Clint of the criminal court impaneled the grand jury and instructed them on the prizefight particulars, asking the members to be "conservative and prudent."

And as luck would have it, the Dallas Pastors' Association reconvened that day after a summer holiday. According to the Dallas Morning News, only eight ministers attended, but between the Reverends C. L. Seasholes, Baptist, W. G. Templeton, Presbyterian, and W. Irving Carroll, Congregationalist, there was ample brimstone for Dan Stuart's fire.

Reverend Carroll was all for calling a halt to the wrangle—not the one in the ring, but the one in the pulpits: "I think it is a prostitution of our holy functions to assemble here every Monday morning and declaim against evils that may come on the community. Our influence should be directed to the salvation of souls by the word of God, and not by calling upon sheriffs and attorneys to administer human laws."

Being compared to the same ladies of the evening he was used to condemning apparently didn't set well with the Reverend Templeton. Not for one minute did he believe he was prostituting anything. "Brother Carroll looks at it from one standpoint and he is sincere, but I think he has prayed in bad company," Templeton admonished. Claiming Dan Stuart had never entered a church, the Presbyterian noted, "There are some unpleasant things the preacher has to do, and one of them is to denounce sin and call the attention of the people to where it is."

Sin no doubt appreciated the free advertising.

Brother Seasholes chimed in with a call to arms: "If Governor Charlie Culberson would call on me Sunday morning when I was preaching the gospel of Jesus Christ I would get down from my pulpit, shoulder a Winchester and defend the laws of Texas."

That reaped a chorus of amens, and he added, "I love sinners but I hate evil. When Jesus Christ saw the temple being desecrated he whipped them out, and that is what Dallas has to do—whip them out."

After that, Reverend Carroll could only repeat that the Association was "not a city vigilance society or a municipal league," and compare their efforts to "a preacher with his little perfume bottle trying to purify the filthy sewerage of political corruption!" (Not exactly what Dan Stuart would call a ringing endorsement.) He then offered to resign.

The meeting ended with a prayer for harmony.

The day was filled with talk and tension. By 9:00 there was a crowd on Main Street waiting to see what would happen. "The full-fledged sport was in the majority, and the curiosity seekers and the irrepressible small boy brought up the rear," reported the *Dallas Morning News,* while "the windows of the federal building overlooking the ring had a good representation of the fair sex."

The fight started at 9:55. During the twenty-third round, Sheriff Cabell and two deputies stepped into the ring and placed both fighters, their seconds, and the referee under arrest.

In response, the *Morning News* began referring to the "war-like presence" of Governor Culberson, and to "Knife-to-the-Hilt" Crane, while denouncing the possibility of militia interference as "ridiculous."

A few days later, with the test case hearing set for the sixteenth and the testees still behind bars, ticket business actually picked up, including a good many requests from newspaper editors who had been condemning the fight.

The *Detroit Journal*'s Washington correspondent reported that in the nation's capital the fight was big news. "All events of that character awaken a lively curiosity and provoke much discussion," went the report, backed up with a bit of recent history: "During the progress of the short fight between Corbett and Mitchell neither house of congress had a quorum on the floor. But both houses could boast of more than a quorum around the telegraph offices in the lobby."

As for this fight, the lawmakers favored Corbett. "Such at least is the opinion of every cabinet officer at present in town although all declare they take but very little interest in the matter. Several in private add, however, that whichever man whips, the fight will be well worth seeing." The public agreed, and a fare war was already developing among the railroads serving Texas.

The *Washington* [D.C.] *Post* noted the public's fascination with the fight: "Corbett and Fitzsimmons are becoming as household words. They are putting children to bed [in Texas] by threatening not to let them see the Corbett-Fitzsimmons fight unless they are good and go to sleep."

The paper interviewed a prominent Texan, Col. William Greene Sterrett, who candidly assessed the situation two days before the hearing.

On Dan Stuart and his committee's resolve, Colonel Sterrett said the fight's backers were "ardent, romantic souls, who in addition to a great fund of sentiment, have great wads of wealth and limitless nerve." He saw these as all the necessary attributes. "They have money, enterprise and know-how, and they're going to pull off the fight or send somebody home on a shutter."

Colonel Sterrett was not worried about interference, arguing that if Sheriff Cabell were in charge it would be a "fangless" operation. His certainty that the fight would occur rested on his knowledge of his fellow citizens: "the great common heart of Texas throbs for this fight, and ever since the days of Sam Houston when the heart of Texas takes to throbbing for anything it gets it. And such being the case, it'll get the fight."

While it was still uncertain whether Sheriff Cabell would be with or without fangs on the scheduled day of the fight (after all, he *had* waited twenty-three rounds before breaking up the Cavanaugh-Clark fight), his leanings might have been construed when his father, General Cabell, left for Honduras carrying a dozen fight posters with him.

The officer freely explained, "I shall hang these diagrams in the large offices at Puerto Cortez and advertise Dallas and the championship glove contest. They will attract great attention in that country."

Just in case "Dan Stuart has slipped a trolley in his legal advice," all was not lost. The *Austin Daily Statesman* again helpfully came up with an alternative plan. Mexico, the paper reported, was now out of bounds. President Diaz had issued "a hostile proclamation" against the fight, and that country had "a quaint but emphathic way of enforcing such decrees."

But there were a series of sandbars along the lower Rio Grande called "bancos" that dotted the river along its last hundred miles before reaching the gulf. Such a banco, an isolated two hundred acres of ambiguous nationality surrounded by water, existed near Rio Grande City. Peace officers on both sides considered it a neutral no-man's-land of "Amerexican" soil. "A man could organize a Trilby club or sing 'After the Ball' thereon with perfect safety of life and limb."[7]

Corbett would train in San Antonio and Fitzsimmons in Corpus, and both sites were closer to the banco than Dallas. (Dallas, however, was easier to reach. To get to Rio Grande City one had to make train connections to Hebbronville, and then ride a bumpy eighty-five miles by stagecoach.)

Still, it was a plan worth considering. It was filed next to the idea about decoys.

All the free advice was not deterring Dan Stuart, whose optimism was based on the judge's reputation. Selected to preside over the hearing was the Honorable James M. Hurt, Chief Justice of the Court of Criminal

Appeals, a man "known to be a liberal, broadminded man," said the *Picayune,* "who would have been thrown overboard had he been a passenger on the Mayflower, and would have been a liberal stockholder in the bears baited in Salem."

Jim Bates, Tommy Cavanaugh, and Jess Clark spent two comfortable weeks in jail, refusing to put up the thousand-dollar bond. They were not even disturbed by a mock trial conducted by fellow inmates who found them all guilty (each was fined two dollars).

Clark was called before Judge Hurt at 10:10 on the morning of September 16. The courtroom was packed with spectators, including some fifty lawyers, a number of prominent businessmen, and a passel of preachers. Six lawyers were representing Jess Clark; opposing them was Knife-to-the-Hilt Crane, law books piled high around him.

After a day of arguing, court adjourned at 5:00.

Court reconvened at 9:00 on September 17. The final arguments were heard, and Judge Hurt rendered his long-awaited decision. He began by reminding listeners he personally thought prizefighting should be a felony, as he considered it "the most brutal of acts." This discouraging prologue was followed by:

"But my private opinion has nothing to do with the law. I am not responsible for the condition of the laws of your state; I am not responsible for this confusion in regards to the statutes; I am not responsible for the fact that it requires the highest intellect and the most searching examination, such as the present, to determine whether we have a law against prizefighting or not. I do not believe that under the provisions of our statutes," Judge Hurt decreed, "that this man has violated a law." Having gotten everyone's undivided attention, he added, "And I shall discharge him."

Applause briefly broke out, and was just as quickly silenced by Judge Hurt's gavel and a threat to jail everybody.

The enthusiasm engendered by the verdict could not be long restrained—the *Picayune* proclaimed, "Dallas is a happy city to-night. Everybody is glad and heartily congratulating each other." Stuart fired off a telegram to the Inter-Ocean news wire in Chicago: "The highest criminal court in the state of Texas has decided there is no law against prize fighting. There is nothing to prevent the greatest contest in the history of the prize ring from taking place as advertised."

Tight-as-a-Clam Dan Stuart, now freed of judicial pressure and uncertainty, at last opened up to reporters. It was undoubtedly difficult not to sound smug.

"I naturally feel elated," he said. "Governor Culberson probably could not have done less than he did do, both by the proclamation and otherwise." After giving his worthy opponent his due, Stuart took the high moral ground: "I wish to reiterate emphatically that there never was an intention on my part to violate any law of Texas."

With a million feet of lumber standing by in the cotton field, Stuart gave the go-ahead: "The force of workmen on the building will be doubled at once and the contractors, the Grigsby Brothers, say that the amphitheater will be ready for occupancy by October 20th at the outside. I have asserted and do now assert that there is nothing brutal or offensive in glove contests of this character."

There was no cheering in the governor's house. It was bad enough that during the trial the newspapers had dug up a decision he had allegedly made in 1894 as attorney general that declared prizefights legal in Texas subject to a "manly art exhibition fee" of ten dollars.[8] But to lose the test case after so much posturing had to have been humiliating.

The final ignominy came when the governor opened his morning paper on September 18. Front page stories heralded the coming fight with the glaring headline, "DAN STUART TRIUMPHANT."

He must have fumed. He must have wadded up the paper and hurled it away. It must have made him crazy, for in his mind—as would soon become evident—he may have been on the ropes, but the round was not yet over. Not by a long shot.

As the fistic stand-ins were making a party of their jail time and test case, Bob Fitzsimmons, just back from Canada, began his first days of serious training for the big fight.

A reporter for the *New York World* tracked him to a small, green cottage "just outside the hurly-burly of Coney Island. Ducks, chickens and a lion live in friendship together in the front yard. Sometimes the lion chases the duck, a sight interesting to those who know a little about Coney Island slang. But the lion does not hurt the duck, because the duck gets away."

Just your typical house by the sea.

The reporter followed Fitz through a training day, an unusual one in that the challenger trained himself, setting his own schedule and routine. This ranged from an early morning salt bath and run along the sand, to playing with his lion, sparring with his six-year-old son Charles, and punching a bag with great art (at last "knocking it free of its moorings with one swing of his right"), and practicing his lightning footwork. At day's end he rode a bike to Brooklyn and back. Sometimes his roadwork would entail hitching a fast trotting horse to a light wagon and holding on to the backboard as it took off.

All of which so impressed the *World* reporter that he observed, "A great deal will be written about Mr. Fitzsimmons as a fighting wonder in the next few weeks."

Most impressive was the wonder's "very blue and very piercing eyes. They are wonderfully blue." And when he made a rare miss punching the bag, the eyes held "a glitter to which Mr. Corbett is entirely welcome."

But it all kept coming back to physique. "His body is a very attractive catapult. It has a collection of muscles piled up along the spinal column, such as can be seen on no other man," gushed the reporter. "From these muscles and some others he gets the power to hit a terrible blow without drawing back his hand." The years of pounding a blacksmith's anvil clearly had a good effect: "His shoulders are so well trained that he can lift either up almost above the top of his ear, making an absolute protection on that side of his head."

Aside from a beer at meals, Fitz "has no alcohol to get out of his stomach, and no stomach to work off." Indeed, "according to his friends, Fitzsimmons is the happy possessor of no bad habits."

For an expert opinion, the *World* sent along Mike Donovan, boxing instructor at the New York Athletic Club, a one-time teacher of Jim Corbett. After a sparring match, Donovan wrote, "No man in the ring can hit a harder blow than Mr. Fitzsimmons can, and no man—I don't care who he is—can hit as hard a straight blow."9

Another Donovan, Joseph, was sent out after Corbett by the *Dallas Morning News*. The champion began training a couple of weeks after Fitzsimmons, on the first day of the hearing before Judge Hurt. All during training, Corbett kept up his end-of-career litany.

"This is positively my last fight. It may look like a good thing to be champion, but when this is over I'm done with the fighting business. To be sure I've made money at it—a great deal of money—but I've had to spend heaps of it, and I'm not worth as much as is popularly supposed. I've made some good investments, however, and hereafter I will attend fights as a spectator." No one is on record as having believed this.

Joe Donovan filed this comparison report back to Dallas:

"Fitzsimmons is a wonder in the way of knock-out hitting, yet, if he and Corbett were to measure their striking strength by test, on a registering machine, it is very probable that Corbett would equal or out-hit him." The difference was in style. "Fitzsimmons, in the ring, lets fly his powerful batteries at every opening, holding nothing in reserve; Corbett keeps half the force of his blow home, to take care of himself. The first goes in head and heels; the second goes in only as far as he can get back safely. Fitz deals in one-punch knock-outs; Corbett never, unless his man has been jabbed till he is too weak to throw a quick and dangerous counter."

While the old-timers of the ring would have scoffed at the admission, "The big Californian is a student of safe fighting; it has been his study for many years." Gentleman Jim, in other words, "believes in seeing his way, and he will not leave his fortifications till he does."

Joe Donovan quoted Corbett the ring master on the importance of strategy: "I have spent many hours in mental planning for every contest I ever had with the result that when I get in front of my man my itinerary of routes is spread in big letters. Let my man start any way he chooses. I like him to do the starting, always—and he is going to fall into one of the paths already chalked out for him."

(Fitz belittled the idea of a battle plan as "ridiculous," asking, "How can I tell what I'm going to do when I don't know what he is going to do? I'm going to be ready for anything.")

Over the coming weeks, the paper reported that Corbett's training was more traditional and arduous than that of the "attenuated" Australian. The Asbury Park headquarters consisted of "a barn as hot as purgatory and a hand-ball alley as sultry as the jungles of India." Corbett walked for miles, rowed on Loch Arbor, used weights, pulleys, bags, and sparring partners, romped with his dogs and generally put in a day that would, assured the weary journalists covering him, collapse a dray horse. Indeed, "the labor of the exiles in the lead mines of Siberia is child's play compared to it."

If the fight went more than ten rounds, Corbett was seen as the easy winner.

Once the question of the law was seemingly settled by a judicial referee, the matter of a fight referee became big news. Many a prize had been lost because heavyweight gamblers had bribed a ref and the choice was not always an easy or unanimous one. Charles "Parson" Davies, John L. Sullivan's stage manager, suggested the ex-champ as the logical choice as well as being a man "as honest as man can be." Corbett thought there might be a small lingering conflict of interest working against him and rejected his old opponent.

It was said at one time that both fighters found Jere Dunn acceptable for the task. Dunn was a notorious gambler with a reputation for decisively violent action—he had killed his wife's lover right on Broadway, and later killed a prizefighter named Elliot after a battle in a Chicago restaurant. If nothing else, Dunn's decisions in the ring were sure to be taken seriously. But that choice fell by the wayside, as did Jake Kilrain and newspaper editor Lou Houseman, both rejected by the champ's handlers.

As Corbett and William Brady continued to find fault with suggested men (there was still no referee by late October), Martin Julian snapped, "Fitzsimmons will fight your man at any time and at any place." He assured them, "No referee will win this fight for you." The debate wore on.

Meanwhile, the task of filling out the fight card was advancing rapidly. Tommy Ryan and "Mysterious" Billy Smith would fight in the welterweight division, and both were said to be "as game as Georgia chickens." The heavyweight fight set for November 1 would pit Corbett's sparring partner Steve O'Donnell against the champion of Ireland, Peter Maher, then in England chasing down a bout with Peter Jackson.[10]

While Culberson and Crane were regrouping, the amphitheater began to rise out of the cotton patch. Calling it "the colloseum [sic] of modern times," the *Dallas Morning News* was certain "its dimensions will be chronicled in histories and encyclopedias when the effete civilization of the present is forgotten, and the great monuments of to-day are moldering ruins."

Architect Silven was equally proud of his immense creation: "There will be used in the building 1,120,000 feet of lumber of the best class of Texas pine." Cut into planks and placed end-to-end, the lumber would stretch for 192 miles. The wood weighed 7,840,000 pounds, was hauled to Dallas on 117 railroad cars, and would be held together with over 26,000 pounds of nails.

The octagonal structure would be four hundred feet across, or two hundred feet from the ring to an outside wall.

As work progressed, the stadium became the city's biggest attraction, hundreds—and sometimes thousands—of curious citizens coming by each day to listen to the sawing and hammering and watch the framework grow. One visitor, Louis Wortham, told the *Morning News,* "Every kodak [sic] fiend in the country has visited the grounds and taken snapshots of the arena."

And whether by design or luck, the state's reporters were hard pressed to find any citizens who did not applaud Judge Hurt's decision.

Capt. John Crotty, manager of the Austin regatta, was "happy as a song bird" about the whole affair: "It is simply fine. It will be the finest kind of thing for our regatta, don't you know, as all the sports will come right from Dallas down here. I am going to Dallas tonight to shake hands with Stuart."

Austin Alderman Charles E. Anderson: "I know hundreds of gentlemen in the North who will attend and I think this talk of toughs only being present is being over done. I never saw a prizefight in my life, but I think I will attend this one."

Ex-lieutenant governor Barnett Gibbs was astonished at all the fuss: "For the Lord's sake, when are we to quit hearing all this agitation about the glove contest?" He complained it was taking up far too much news-paper space and snorted, "It is ridiculous to dignify it to the importance of either a moral or political issue. There is not enough immorality in it to make a smart man see devils and not enough politics to carry a county, and in ten days after it is over it will be forgotten."

After some more quibbling about agitators making a play "for quasi-moral and political points," Gibbs concluded, "Public opinion is funnier than a circus."[11]

Albert Armstrong, a resident of Ardmore, acknowledged that "Extraor-dinary interest is manifested in the coming glove carnival throughout the Indian Territory. In all the little towns the leading men are getting ready to attend." He added, "We had a glove contest at Ardmore last night which was largely attended."

Jerome Kearby, the leading Populist candidate for governor, suggested Culberson be impeached, and the Reverend Dr. W. C. Young of Dallas remarked, "There are twenty worse things going on in the town about which we have been making no fuss."

From Galveston to Waco, Sherman to Plano, El Paso to Fort Worth, Ennis to Kaufman, McKinney to Austin, public sentiment rallied behind Stuart and urged the state's officials to accept the situation as it stood. Orders for tickets increased, and the *Dallas Morning News* published an unsigned poem titled, "Crane and Guv Bird." Odds are it didn't go down well in the capitol.

> The crane and guv bird set out for a race,
> And sparred for points with an airy grace;
> "Now come," said the guv bird, "I'll set you a pace."
> "Go long," quoth the crane, "or I'll punch your face."
>
> Then the guv bird screamed,
>   And the crane guffawed,
> And the blue bird beamed,
>   And the black crow 'cawed,'
> And the whole menagerie
>   Hummed and hawed.
>
> Said the Crane to himself: "The saucy thing,"
> And he flitted his tail and flirted his wing
> As brutal prize fighters do in a ring,
> And he came up to Dallas to smash the thing.
>
> Then the guv bird screeched,
>   And the cranie scowled,
> And the old crow preached,
>   And the coyote growled,

And the whole menagerie
　　Hooted and howled.

"Great scott!" shrieked the guv bird, "what'll I do?
My main vote play's gone up the flue;
Now how, Mr. Crane, can I keep up with you?
I'll call out the rangers and the whole to do."

Then the guv bird limped,
　　And the crane it soared,
And the blue bird whimped,
　　And the coyote roared,
And the whole menagerie
　　Got on board.

Then the crane came on to Dallas town,
Not for once heeding the guv bird's frown,
His soul elated instead of cast down,
But he came across a judicial frown.

And then the crane swore,
　　And the guv bird chewed,
And the coyote tore,
　　And the blue bird stewed,
And the whole menagerie
　　Boo-hoo-hooed.

The guv bird got hot and hissed through his bill,
"I'll do it in spite of judges, I will.
By jinks, 'twill not be said I'm ticked until
I'm down to my last goldarned quill."

Then the guv bird humped,
　　And the judge he laughed,
And the old crow jumped
　　On the blue jay's gaff,
And the whole menagerie
　　Went clean daft.

Well, the fight is on for a month or so,
And politics is in it and religion also,
But the guv bird's soul is full of woe,
For he knows no one can give a knock-out blow.

And the crane is flitting
　　To the guv bird's tune,
And the blue jay's knitting
　　A cap for a coon,
And the whole menagerie
　　Is up in a balloon.[12]

The guv bird and Crane were not being idle. If it was no longer a legal matter, it had developed into an obsessive and vindictive power struggle, one in which the governor was determined to assert his will and have it prevail. No matter what the cost.

One day after the hearing, Crane and Culberson conferred for over an hour. Neither man was prepared to yield to Judge Hurt, and in the evening the governor issued a statement. "The opinion of a single judge," wrote the man sworn to uphold the laws of the state, "settles nothing but the particular case decided." Precedent only counted when it was on his side. He wanted the full court's ruling, and until he got one, "the proposed prize fight at Dallas shall not take place if enough men can be found to execute the law, of which I have no doubt."

Within days there were ominous rumors circulating around Dallas and Austin, rumors of a possible and extraordinary special session of the state legislature. If there was not a viable law against fighting, it was said, the governor would write one and get it passed before the brawl could be pulled off.

Reaction to this news came fast. Barnett Gibbs snorted, "One-half of the people of Texas are opposed to glove contests, the other half don't care a cuss about them; but nine-tenths of all of them are opposed to extra sessions and militia." He was adament against wasting any more time or money on this issue. "Whatever a man's opinion on prizefighting may be, he should not expect a governor to override an opinion of a chief justice. Ants are very troublesome, but the mayor can't order out the fire department to kill them off."

The possible cost of a special session was estimated to run anywhere from $15,000 to $50,000 depending on how long it took. And time was a major consideration. State Sen. Oliver P. Bowser of Dallas told the *New Orleans Picayune* that the idea was just not practical, predicting weeks wasted on getting quorums, appointing committees, debating, amending, and filibustering, all with the fight just forty-one days away. The situation was not helped by the legislature being at odds with Culberson at adjournment.

The idea of a special session, said the *Picayune,* "is ridiculed by everybody."

Judge George Clark of Waco said, "The threats of the governor are more conducive to lawlessness than a hundred prizefights." As an observer of Texas politics, it had been a long while since Clark was impressed by any chief executive. "We had opera bouffe under [Governor] Hogg, ad nauseam, and this has been succeeded by the object lessons of the kindergarten under Culberson. Hogg was sublime in his spectacular displays of basso profundo ignorance, while Culberson receives our sympathy in his tottering efforts to learn the rudiments of statesmanship."

Even the governor's father, Congressman Dave Culberson, thought Charlie was going too far. He told reporters in Rockport, Texas, that his son would have to back down as the duties of the governor were executive in nature and not judicial. Judge Hurt's opinion, said the elder Culberson, would stand until the legislature wrote a new law.

As if that wasn't enough familial disloyalty, the governor's own wife came out against him.

Speaking to reporters in Chicago, Sally Culberson stated, "If Texas wants the prizefight, let them have it, I say." She favored majority rule. "At least nine men out of every ten in Texas want the prizefight, and after all he was elected to carry out the will of the people, and the people want the fight." There were also the economy and individual rights to think about. "Then think of the money it would cost to convene the legislature. I do not see, anyway, why one man should have the power to decide what the rest should do," scolded Mrs. Culberson, "the governor is trying to stop something popular sentiment is in favor of having. It's all foolishness, and I've told him so."[13]

The court was against him; lawyers, judges and businessmen were against him; sports fans and the nation's press were against him; even his own family told him to back down. Where could Governor Culberson turn to find support?

The religious community.

An editorial in the *Texas Christian Advocate* restarted the holy war. While admitting Judge Hurt was probably sincere and legally correct, the paper would not accept that opinion as final. "This is what we call a first-class fiasco all around. There is absolutely no remedy unless the governor calls a special session of the legislature," declared the editorial. "Better that the exchequer of the state were emptied a hundred times than this foul indignity and outrage should be perpetrated."

Two days later the Reverend W. K. Homan, editor of the *Christian Courier,* rendered onto the Dallas Y.M.C.A. members a pulpit-pounding diatribe condemning "the works of the flesh" (among which were witchcraft, fornication, heresies, revelings "and such like"), and, of course, prizefighting.

"I am an optimist," he told his rapt audience, "but the world is surely rotten; rotten at least in spots, and Dallas is one of the spots just now."

Getting down to the main subject, the Reverend Homan denounced the profit motive as evil: "The argument that such a disgraceful affair would bring money to Dallas and Texas is an old one, for Judas Iscariot laid aside his moral convictions when he sold his Lord for thirty pieces of silver. Whenever wicked men want to establish an evil in a community the very best way to do it is to introduce it under the guise of 'business.'"

The Good Samaritan lesson in his *Bible* notwithstanding, the Reverend Homan was unambiguous about what kind of unacceptable freeloaders were attracted to fights. "They say it will bring distinguished people here. There is one of them here now in our city hospital. He is a tramp from Chicago. He was asked what he came here for and he said because of the fight. He was asked if he knew of others coming, to which he said yes, every tramp in his knowledge would be here if he could get here."

The Ministers' Association of Austin met on September 21 and passed some resolutions against the fight and took the side of "our noble governor" in his efforts to stop it by any means. Believing themselves to "represent the finer feelings and higher moral instincts of our whole people regarding this question," the ministers offered not just moral support but, "if need be, the personal presence of the brave, heroic and law-abiding men from every part of this great State."

At the First Methodist Church in Dallas, Elder Alderson referred to "the Christ-given civilization which we enjoy," and said news of the fight sent "a thrill of horror" through "the lovers of law, peace and purity from one end of the state to the other." Condemning "this incarnation of all brutality," he called on Texans to boycott the state fair—not just the upcoming one, but all future ones should the fight take place, lest Texas be the birthplace of "the universe of thugdom."

Elder Alderson brought up Fitzsimmons' manslaughter case in Syracuse and argued that all who leave a fight "feel as if they had just emerged from a protracted debauch," and labeled prizefighting "the prolific mother of all crime" and a kind of "hellish 'black death'" that would sweep across the state. The person of the governor, preached Alderson, "ought to be sacred in the eyes of every Texan, as providentially girded of God with the sword of executive authority."[14]

The Dallas Pastors' Association met again on September 23 to announce to an eagerly waiting world that "the number of fallen women is increasing" in the city (they carefully counted over eight hundred). They also thanked the mayor for his "untiring energy" in bringing business to Dallas—with the notable exception of the prizefight, for which he was chastized. And a new statistic was added to the argument, namely that during a fight in New Orleans that city suffered "from fifty to seventy-five holdups per night."

And so it went, in pulpits and prayer meetings all across Texas. But, like it or not, the fighters were on their way.

Peter Maher arrived in New York aboard the steamer Circassia on September 23 from Glasgow. He headed right for Texas.[15]

Fitzsimmons left for Texas just a few hours ahead of Maher on a special three-car train, along with his entourage that included Emile Roeber, a German wrestler; his lion, Nero; his pregnant wife, Rose; her brother and Fitz's manager, Martin Julian; trainer Charlie White; and Fitz's mother-in-law. Baggage included four crates of live chickens—for Fitz, not Nero, to prevent anyone from tampering with his food.

Fitzsimmons was confident he would win the fight in four rounds. This was not based so much on training as on superstition. He told reporters that he had had prophetic dreams before some of his biggest contests. Recently Corbett appeared in a dream, and hit the floor in four. The challenger therefore considered the match a sure thing. (Just to be safe, however, he would as usual take his lucky talisman into the ring— the tip of a kangaroo's ear tucked inside his shorts.)[16]

Corbett's training facility at the San Antonio Jockey Club was standing by for his arrival early in October.

Ever since Judge Hurt's decision, the attorney general's office had been swamped with so many requests for boxing licenses that Attorney General Crane, unamused by these actions, fired off another strong opinion:

Judge Hurt's decision, he wrote to Comptroller Finley, "is not supported by any logical reason." He suggested that the legislators who passed the license tax statute must have been "chartered libertines," as the wording "does not even seem to give you the privilege of saying whether the fight shall be with bare knuckles, with gloves, with knives or with pistols."

With three hundred workmen banging away at the stadium and 600,000 feet of lumber already nailed in place, the governor came off the ropes, and he came out swinging. What happened next was so swift that it stands alone and unique in the history of Texas politics.

At 11:00 o'clock on the evening of September 26, Culberson issued a stunning proclamation. After a brief rehash of the situation, he wrote, "an extraordinary occasion has arisen requiring the legislature to be convened in special session." He set the special session for high noon on Tuesday, the first of October. He had given the representatives less than five days to assemble. Chief purpose of the move—which "should require a session of only a few days at a small cost"—was:

"To denounce prize fighting and kindred practices in clear and unambiguous terms, and prohibit the same by appropriate pains and penalties, putting the law into immediate operation and making necessary provisions for its enforcement" in order to avert an "affront to the moral sense and enlightened progress of Texas." This being "the undoubted will of the people."

If it wasn't exactly the will of all Texans, it did reflect a national fervor—just the day before two fighters in Kansas were sentenced to a year in the pen for following their trade. However, when the *Picayune* asked an attorney for the Florida Athletic Club how the proclamation would affect "the great digital diversion," the lawyer said the club's legal department was "serene."

Asked about the proclamation, Dan Stuart replied, "Hanged if I know anything about it, but I think the grammar and spelling are all right."

Stopping over in New Orleans, Fitzsimmons was asked for his reaction. "I don't think it will amount to anything. It's the businessmen of Dallas who are back of the fight; and they will pull it off, despite the governor and his legislature and militia, and so I'm not worrying about it. But, then, I'm not going to let them pull down that $5,000 forfeit which they have put up. I am not the least bit afraid that the fight won't come off."[17]

That attitude did not last long.

As legislators hurriedly packed to head for Austin, the state was buzzing with talk of the session. Representative John F. Reiger remarked, "It will cost the state $60,000 to indulge this whim of the governor's."

"TEXAS STIRRED UP" was the headline on page one of the *Dallas Morning News*, followed by two pages of opinions.

Collin County Rep. J. R. Gough: "Pugilism, like bull fights, does not belong to our age or country, but is a relic of the dark ages, and is unworthy an enlightened Christian country like ours."

Rep. R. B. Allen: "A special session called for the purpose of passing a law to prevent such contests as have been of almost daily occurrence in the state for many months past is unwise and unfortunate, to say the least."

McLennan County Rep. Cullen T. Thomas: "Texas is no pauper and her reputation should not be bartered for a few thousand dollars. It is a good opportunity to teach the northern and eastern states that Texas stands for law and order and civilization."

In Gainesville, Texas, there was a town meeting with a brass band to show support for the governor.

The mayor of Longview, W. T. Whitlock, succinctly said, "Don't think it necessary. Too big gun for small game."

Ex-governor Frank Lubbock pronounced himself "delighted," saying, "What is right is right, and we can not let a wrong be perpetrated because it costs a little to prevent it."[18]

Ex-Senator Rutabaga Johnson called the session idea "extremely foolish," though he too was opposed to "immoral acts inconsistent with a high civilization," and especially "immoral exhibitions which are solely conducted for money."

In Georgetown, handbills announced a town meeting at the courthouse for "Every law abiding Texan who is opposed to plug-uglies disgracing the name of your state."

So many telegrams of support and approval flooded into the governor's office that you'd have thought Stuart had suggested tearing down the Alamo.

In the nation's capital, at least one newspaper suggested that "Corbett does not want to fight and will count the governor as his best friend from this time on."

As the weekend quickly passed, there were rumors of Dan Stuart moving up the date of the fight, of having it in Indian Territory, of sending lobbyists to Austin, but none of it could be confirmed.

The Fitzsimmons express rolled into Texas to cheering crowds on the morning of September 28, stopping first in Houston. He was presented with a St. Bernard mascot for his stay by James Lawlor, proprietor of the Lawlor Hotel, on condition Nero didn't make a snack of him.

Martin Julian said Fitz would be ready to fight as scheduled at the end of October, "whether Mr. Bloody Corbett is there or not. If Corbett crawls, Fitzsimmons is open to fight any man in the world for the heavyweight championship."[19]

In response to the rumor of the fight being taken to Indian Territory, the secretary of the interior promptly informed the War Department about the possibility of a trespass, and that department immediately put the troops at Fort Sill on alert. "It is understood," said the *Picayune*, "that the whole machinery of the government may be called upon to prevent the fight in the territory."

Things were getting rapidly out of hand—Dan Stuart's hand, at any rate.

A committee of businessmen was formed in Dallas to protest the session—twenty showed up. Their resolution astonishingly called for a law against prizefighting, but only after October.

A group representing the workers engaged to build the arena sent its own, stronger, resolution to Austin. Calling the session a "scheme for self-aggrandizement [that was] in no way calculated to control the morals of the community," the laborers protested that the only ones hurt would be their families: "God knows whom it will benefit, but we do know at whose door it will fall with a heavy thud." They then thanked Dan Stuart for his providing their children "with temporary relief from the pangs of thirst and hunger."

The fighters appeared unperturbed. On Sunday night, September 19, Fitzsimmons gave a sparring exhibition at San Antonio's Grand Opera House and then headed for Corpus;[20] in New York's Madison Square Garden the next day, Corbett gave a similar exhibition before seven thousand fans. He was on the train when the special session was called to order.

Both the House and Senate were convened on time and, to the surprise of many, each had a quorum. The governor sent both groups a message that left no doubt as to what he desired from them. He called prizefighting a "commanding insult to public decency," an event that would bring "ignominy and shame" on the state. Culberson said swift passage would stop "one of the most disgraceful orgies that ever promised to discredit and dishonor Texas."[21]

The lawmakers agreed and the *Dallas Morning News* headlined it on October 3:

THE AGONY ENDED
Anti-Prize Fight Bill
Passed with a Whoop.
FEW OPPOSING VOTES.

There were five votes against Culberson in the House, only one—John M. Dean's of El Paso—in the Senate.[22]

Total elapsed time from presentation of the bill to passage by both houses was 180 minutes, the fastest such work then on record. Governor Culberson signed the bill making prizefighting a felony on October 3 at 4:50 P.M.[23]

In Dallas, construction stopped on the historic amphitheater now turned white elephant, railroads began frantically rescheduling their special trains to the fair, and a disappointed—and far less wealthy—Dan Stuart looked around at his busted dream and appeared to throw in the towel.

"I have nothing to say in criticism of the governor," Stuart told reporters. "He has done, I take it, what he thought was his duty." He continued to try and stay above it all. "I will still proceed under the law as it is and hunt other fields. You see I am now, and have been, strictly law-abiding." As for the fight, he answered, "Yes, sir, the contest will not come off in Texas."

The citizens of McKinney, Texas, had a local harness-maker fashion a special belt for the governor and sent along a note praising the "firm and manly stand" taken by their "fearless executive" on behalf of "all citizens who believe in public decency." The belt was inscribed, "Champion of Texas."

Supporters in Jacksonville (Cherokee County), Texas, also sent a belt—leather, studded with silver plates—and a buckle engraved with: "Jacksonville Championship Belt, Charles A. Culberson, our governor, 1895."

Round two, and perhaps the title, belonged to the man now being hailed (and blasted) as "the young Christian governor," Charles A. Culberson, heavyweight political champion of Texas.

ROUND THREE: Hot Springs

Catch Fitzsimmons or stop him, regardless of cost or consequences. Don't fail.

—Arkansas Gov. James P. Clarke to
Deputy Sheriff Jesse Hurd

TEXAS LAY EXHAUSTED. The great communal outpouring of rhetoric and energy was over and everyone could relax and heave a mighty, Texas-sized sigh. Right or wrong, moral or immoral, sport or brutality, there was now an ironclad law against prizefighting.

Some cheered, of course. The governor was heartily thanked from pulpits and papers across the state and the nation for protecting civilization as it was then known. The irony was that immediately following the passage of this law upholding "the will of the people," the fighters began arriving—and were greeted enthusiastically by adoring crowds wherever they appeared.

When Peter Maher hit Dallas just hours after the law was passed, the *Morning News* reported a large crowd of well-wishers and could not resist adding, "It is doubtful if his excellency, Gov. Culberson, would have found so many and such warm friends."

After registering at the Grand Windsor, the handsome, mustached champion of Ireland expressed dismay at what Culberson had wrought. "I was astonished," he said, adding that in Irish or British bouts "the clergy will not back out from seeing an exhibition with gloves, and it does not make them less charitable or religious. This thing is put on."

When Corbett's party rolled through Beaumont on the Southern Pacific, the champ's manager said, "We will go to Dallas, ready to do anything Dan Stuart wants, and we will fight Fitz anywhere, even in a balloon. We are here to fight," William Brady insisted. "If Dan Stuart can't raise $41,000, we will fight for anything." They settled in at the Jockey Club in San Antonio, two miles from the Alamo.

Peter Maher, Champion of Ireland, about 1891. From Billy Edwards, *The Pugilistic Portrait Gallery* (London and Philadelphia: Pugilistic Publishing Co., 1894).

A later biographer of the governor's wrote that "the disgraceful and degrading practice of 'prize-fighting' was permanently, no doubt, banished from the boundaries of this great commonwealth of ours," and offered this assessment: "It is doubtful if any other one act of his entire four years' administration ever brought to him such universal approval as did this one."[1]

Perhaps approval wasn't *that* universal. Far from defending the good name of the state from dishonor, some people thought Culberson had made it a laughing stock.

The *Philadelphia Times* suggested, "The only chance for a prize fight in Texas hereafter will be in holding it on a dark night in a back county where sheriffs are unknown and the court is on a perpetual vacation."

The *New York World* chided the legislators for overlooking other common acts of far greater violence. "This is the Texas idea of the evils of fighting. To strike out from the shoulder is brutal and low. To put a bullet through a man's heart or rip him open with a bowie is a gentlemanly way of settling a difficulty."

The editorial noted, "There has rarely been seen in any American state such a ridiculous instance of disproportion between the thing to be done and the instruments and agencies brought into action to accomplish it. It is, besides, a bit of hypocrisy and humbug. With its murders, lynchings and other frequent deeds of actual and criminal lawlessness, Texas is made to seem absurd by the hysterical activity of the governor."

The following poem appeared in the *New York Sun,* the *Augusta Chronicle,* and other papers across the country:

Texas Talks

I am the state of Texas,
The great and only Lone Star,
The biggest in the
Firmament of the union.
Once I was
The Bully Boy of the Brazos,
The Rip Snorting Rooster
Of the Rio Grande,
And I could lick my weight in wildcats,
And chew up a steer
And use his horns for toothpicks;
I could hang a horse thief
In four minutes by the watch,
And shoot a town full of holes
On seventeen drinks of whiskey;

But I am not that kind any more;
I am a changed being;
My ways are ways of pleasantness
And all my paths are peace.
I am a sucking dove.
And if anybody wants to kick
My tail feathers off,
I offer myself as a willing
Sacrifice.
I have forsaken the wild and woolly,
And shall go to Boston
For art culture
And the study of the intellectuals
And beans.
The cowboy shall know me no more
Forever.
And the maverick
Shall no longer claim me as a brother;
That is the kind of a Texas
I am.
And if those prize fighters
Try to pull off a fight
In my midst,
By gravy,
Something's going to happen!
I won't have it under no circumstances,
For I've turned over a new leaf,
And they don't want to forget it.
That's me!
But if they want to lynch a hoss thief,
Well—
In some particulars
I am still the same old Texas!

"The new law," lamented Dan Stuart, "does away with my investments." Those investments were considerable—about $20,000 to date—and the only way to recoup was to have a fight.

Things were glum at 216 Main Street. People were no longer crowding into the Florida Athletic Club's Dallas headquarters to buy fight tickets. As if fate wanted to rub his nose in it, Dan Stuart could step outside and glance four doors down the street and watch entertainment-hungry crowds heading into Kirby's Drug Store at 213 Main, eager to buy tickets—for the circus.

The Barnum and Bailey Circus would stop in Dallas on October 11 for two shows. And, as the ads said, the circus—unlike the prizefight—was known the world over for "its HIGH moral character" and the "morality of its 1000 employees." It was also "the only show indorsed [sic] by the clergy," and "the only reputable show never exhibiting on the Sabbath day." Plus having twenty-four "ponderous performing elephants," two droves of camels, fifty aerialists, a hundred equestrian acts, a three-eyed steer and a gorilla named Johanna. Admission fifty cents; kids half price. What outlawed prizefight could compete with "2000 tons of pure, moral amusement"?[2]

Dan Stuart may have been bruised, battered, and legally thrown out of the state by the Texas legislature, but he was by no means an orphan of the political storm.

Over the next few days the president of the Florida Athletic Club and his right-hand man and chief organizer, W. K. Wheelock, were besieged with site offers as cities all over America and across its borders vied for the fight. Various newspapers gleefully carried the details headed with:

"California's Chances," "May Fight in Canada," "Will Fight Near Paris [Texas]," "Melbourne Bids for the Fight," "New Brunswick the Field," "May Fight at Ardmore," "Considering Mexican Points," "Texarkana as an Applicant," "Guthrie Still Wants It," "St. Joseph Will Make a Bid," "Oshkosh Wants It Too," "Want It In California," "Ardmore Anxious," "Can Fight at Henry," "Juarez the Only Place," "London Wants the Fight."

The fight's not over until somebody counts "Ten!" Early speculation centered first on the Nueva Laredo bullring, or on a quick crossing into Indian Territory, the refuge set aside in Oklahoma, Kansas, and Nebraska for "the five civilized tribes" (Choctaw, Chickasaw, Cherokee, Creek, Seminole).[3]

The Territory was certainly a tempting idea. The lands of the Choctaws and Chickasaws were within easy reach of Dallas—especially as Bryan Snyder, assistant general freight agent for the Gulf, Colorado and Santa Fe Railroad, offered to move every stick of lumber of the dismantled amphitheater from Dallas to Ardmore free of charge.

In addition, by treaty the land was governed by a council of Indians. The United States government was responsible for keeping out undesirable non-Indians but had little other authority. A public mass meeting held in Ardmore on October 4 was heavily favorable to the fight; the Chickasaw legislature, however, was said to be in opposition.

It was generally conceded that the United States could not block entry by the fighters unless so requested by the Indians. But that was in theory; other treaty provisions were often overlooked when they proved inconvenient to government authorities. An attorney named Caswell Bennett suggested that "if the scrappers can procure themselves to be adopted as Chickasaw citizens there is no authority that can interfere. Nothing could be done any way except to arrest them for a misdemeanor after the fight."

"The Indian," said the *Dallas Morning News*, "is naturally a lover of sport and gaming devices, and the coming contest appeals strongly to his natural instincts." The paper endorsed Bennett's idea to have the fighters skirt the law by becoming honorary Indians.

Unofficial word came on October 4 that the Choctaws were willing to adopt the fighters. Fitzsimmons was skeptical but willing. Corbett's response was to say he'd accept the honor and would gladly paint himself red, wear eagle feathers, and do whatever else was necessary in order to fight Fitzsimmons.

That warpath was blocked three days later when Commissioner Browning of the Indian Office wrote a letter to Agent Wisdom at Muskogee, Indian Territory (I.T.). Browning labeled the fight "a great detriment to the peace and welfare of the Indians." He told Wisdom that he could call on the U.S. Marshal for help and, if necessary, "troops will be furnished to prevent the fight."

No one connected with the fight wanted to tangle with the U.S. Cavalry, and Ardmore lost its moment in boxing history.

Dan Stuart, Joe Vendig, William Brady, and Martin Julian had a four-hour conference about the matter in Texas on October 8, the very day they were all served with subpoenas issued in the name of the Travis County grand jury. Corbett's brother Joe and other trainers were arrested that afternoon in San Antonio. All were ordered to appear in Austin the next day.

The charge came from article 960 of the Texas penal code, conspiracy to commit a felony—a prizefight—within the state.

It was a political move on the part of Austin District Attorney Albert Burleson. He had issued the writs himself without the grand jury's knowledge. The trainers and managers were asked a few rudimentary questions regarding the existence of any fight contracts and allowed to leave. The tough questions were saved for the district attorney.

According to the *El Paso Daily Times,* the DA's arbitrary action displeased the jury and he not only received a dressing down for it, "the investigation [was] very likely to be a fizzle."

But if the main purpose was to run the fighters out of Texas, the fizzle had a lot of sizzle. Forced to make a quick decision, the Florida Athletic Club went over all the promising options again, met with those committees already present in Dallas—and then made the worst possible choice: headquarters was moved to Hot Springs, Arkansas.

Five days prior to the grand jury incident, Gov. James P. Clarke of Arkansas had told an interviewer in Little Rock, "I commend most heartily Governor Culberson and the Texas legislature for their prompt and decisive action." His position was in complete accord with theirs, Clarke voicing a blanket condemnation of boxing "as being wrong from a moral standpoint and brutal when taken in the light of an exhibition."

Prizefights were once a felony in Arkansas, but that was changed to a misdemeanor in 1891 (Clarke was then one of the legislators holding out for felony). The minimum fine was $1,000; maximum was $2,500—for principals and spectators alike. As governor, Clarke unequivocally gave notice that if anyone sought to stage a fight in his domain, "I will enlarge the walls of the state penitentiary if needs be, to accommodate the crowd."

Clarke's opinion was not shared by the Hot Springs committee formed to lure the big fight to Arkansas. Hot Springs had no city ordinance against boxing, and Mayor W. W. Waters was part of the fight committee then in Dallas. A local attorney named H. H. Martin proffered the opinion that, "under the law the governor of the state has no power or authority to interfere, except upon certain contingencies that cannot possibly arise in this case."

As for the populace of Hot Springs, the deal "caused general rejoicing." The *Austin Daily Statesman* estimated that "nineteen-twentieths of the people here evince satisfaction that Hot Springs has been selected." Surely the meeting of the Methodist pastors and their immediate resolutions against the fight was nothing to be concerned about. Why, "bonfires, brass bands and red paint" were ready to greet the mayor when he returned in triumph.

On the day before Barnum and Bailey's morally pure circus rolled into Dallas, Dan Stuart's carnival was rolling out.

As the fighters broke camp, William Brady fired a parting shot: "The wave of ostensible righteousness that the announcement of this contest has set rolling over the land had its origin in an itching desire on the part of politicians and preachers to seize onto anything of sufficient magnitude to give them notoriety." As for their labeling Corbett a beast, brute "and other choice epithets," Brady snapped, "I consider Corbett more of a man than any of these gentlemen, and any man who calls him a beast should be prosecuted for libel."[4]

The *Dallas Morning News* had to agree, saying that during the champ's brief stay he had been visited by nearly every prominent man in town, was generous with his admirers (no admission was charged to watch him train), and impressed everyone "as a big-hearted, modest, overgrown school boy."

The hasty move to Hot Springs was not seen as expedient by Fitz's brother-in-law. On the contrary, scrappy Martin Julian was saying that it was all the champion's doing: "Nothing anybody can say can convince us that Corbett and Brady are not trying every scheme to get out of meeting Bob."[5]

(Julian was also upset that a New York judge had attached their stake money over the non-payment of a bill owed to the Metropolitan Job Printing Company in the amount of $3,078.34. In addition, attorney Emanuel Friend attempted to withdraw $5,000 of that money, saying the original investor had changed his mind. Julian cried "Foul!" at that, and Fitz severed relations with the lawyer by saying, "he charged me double money on two or three occasions and is sore because he can't work his game further.")

The fighters, as usual, were doing far more yapping than fighting. The *Chicago Record* complained that "Corbett's mouth seems to be wound up for an indefinite period of unrestrained activity. Even Corbett and Fitzsimmons have their limitations. There are only 120,000 words in the English language."

The *El Paso Daily Herald* posed a riddle for its readers: "In what way will the Corbett-Fitzsimmons mill differ from the usual pugilistic show? They will punch two bags of wind instead of one."

Corbett's latest version of the scuffle in Philadelphia, for example, asserted that it happened in the office and not the bar, and laid it all squarely on Fitz. "Fitzsimmons was a little the worse for liquor or the squabble would never have occurred."

In Corpus Christi, Fitz responded. "He is going around the country telling people that I am a big fake and a drunkard. Do you see any sign of dissipation on me? Jim simply lies when he says I was drunk when that altercation occurred." His own version of the event made it appear as a deliberate mugging. "I was at the hotel counter registering my name when he came in with a big gang of toughs for the purpose of doing me up so I would never be in a condition to fight him." Corbett, he maintained, "shan't escape me. I am going to get at him if I have to chase him into some corner and hammer the big barroom dude."

Which is pretty much what was said by Corbett: "He is a faker of the worst kind. He is trying his mightiest to get out of this fight, but I will fight him if I have to chase him into a corner so that there could be no escape. I am ready to fight within an hour." A safe enough stance, given the miles separating them. "Fitzsimmons is a sly one. He worked things very smooth after that little affair in Green's Hotel," Corbett slyly confided to reporters. "Why, do you know Fitzsimmons was beastly drunk that day?"

Fitzsimmons: "Corbett doesn't know how to infight, and he won't until I teach him something."

Corbett: "I am going to make this foreigner take his medicine or crawl."[6]

If Governor Clarke had his way, both men would be crawling—to some other state.

Clarke was not a man to trifle with. Six months earlier, on April Fools' Day, Clarke had ordered the sheriff of Little Rock to stop a prizefight. Then eight days later, the governor himself got into a fight—not unlike Corbett and Fitz—in a hotel lobby.

On the afternoon of April 9, State Representative Yancy of Phillips County stood in the House of Representatives and said he had been offered a bribe to vote against a railroad commission bill. Representative Jones of Marion County rose and declared the governor to be behind it and called the chief executive a demagogue and a back-stabber.

This did not sit well with the pugnacious governor. That evening Jones was in the lobby of Gleason's Hotel in Little Rock having an after-dinner cigar, when the governor entered. After exchanging some unpleasantries, the governor spat in Jones's face.

Said Jones: "I returned the insult by spitting in his face. When I did this he turned loose of my arm and made for his pistol. I then saw that my only chance was to knock him down and I struck with all my might at his face with my left hand, but he quickly sprang back towards the door and my blow failed to reach him. He was going for his pistol. I sprang and grappled with him."

Two other state representatives, Roberts and Pope, joined the discussion and all four men seemed to have at least one hand on the governor's gun as they wrestled around the lobby, Clarke yelling, "Turn that pistol loose," and finally, "I promise you positively that I will not kill him."

Under the circumstances it was difficult to put much credence in the governor's troth. He was held in check while Jones made haste up the stairs.

Clarke was arrested by a constable that evening and released on his own recognizance. He vigorously refuted Jones's version but did not deny the essentials. In fact, the governor's account had him yanking Jones out of a chair by his hair, prompting some offensive profanity, at which point Clarke admitted spitting in the lawmaker's face.

"He was furious already, and this only added to it," Clarke reported. "Jones is a stalwart fellow, and I found it necessary to my defense to resort to a weapon." As for those legislators who felt compelled to restrain him, "I was at once disarmed by an overpowering force." Not unlike a small boy, Clarke denied that Jones had been able to land any return saliva.[7]

Since it wasn't for money or a title and no tickets were sold or bets laid, the governor's fight did not count as a prizefight. Besides, pulling a gun was definitely against the Marquis of Queensberry rules. But it was plain that Clarke was not as easygoing or even-tempered as Culberson.

Consequently, it should not have come as much of a surprise when Clarke, on October 11, declared the 1891 misdemeanor law invalid and the felony statute pertaining to unlawful assemblies and riots still in effect.

Responding to a letter from Hot Springs Judge A. M. Duffie, an old classmate, Clarke wrote, "You shall have my prompt and cheerful cooperation in any effort you may make to suppress the proposed fight." The glove contest, he argued, "has aroused and will continue to arouse the indignation of the people" and would spark "an invasion of the State by a class of persons and for a purpose that will not be tolerated elsewhere."

To Sheriff Robert Houpt the governor was equally firm, branding the fight "an affront to the people of the State." Clarke urged Houpt to "employ all diligence" in stopping the match.

The governor next sent a telegram to Dan Stuart. "Such an act will be a palpable violation of our law and will be resented as an insult to our State pride," Clarke advised the Texas sport. "It is not only my duty but my pleasure to place [at the sheriff's] disposal all necessary means of enforcing his orders. Your contemplated fight will, therefore, not take place and it will best promote the satisfaction of all if you will abandon at once your efforts to bring it about."

At least he refrained from threatening to spit in his face.

Clarke the battler also sent telegrams to Corbett and Fitzsimmons, saying: "I am well enough satisfied of the nature and extent of the power and authority with which you will find yourself confronted to say that it will prove entirely sufficient to deter you from engaging in a prize fight in Arkansas. This is enough for you to know." He assured each man that the matter was not open to discussion, fistic or otherwise.

This was not looked on as a good omen in Hot Springs, a city that needed all the monetary help it could get. From over forty springs bubbled water reaching an average of a 143°F, and at that moment the owners of the seven hundred hotels in the area were even hotter.

Bath House Row in Hot Springs, Arkansas—just some of the many facilities tapping into over forty natural hot water sources in town, all eager for new customers. The carnival would mean a much-needed economic boom, if the governor did not interfere. Courtesy Garland County Historical Society.

The city was in an economic depression caused mainly by a smallpox epidemic the previous spring that had, understandably, greatly reduced business at the health spa. Not only was October the start of "the fashionable season" at the springs when enormous crowds would gather at the resort for their health, but the fight had promised to fill every vacant room, and plans were underway to draft private homes for the lucrative overflow.[8] Extra train tracks were already being laid and the amphitheater site cleared at Whittington Park.

Eighteen thousand tickets were sold to date, and a town meeting called by the mayor to raise the $5,000 guarantee produced the sum inside of thirty minutes. Two hundred workmen were prepared to labor night and day to rebuild the arena (though a hitch had developed in Texas where the Hope Lumber Company had tied up the material with a $4,000 lien).

Even Sheriff Robert Houpt was against premature ejection of the stars: "That crowd would have dumped $500,000 in Hot Springs and the law would not have been violated." He had five hundred men on alert to stop it. He favored attracting a crowd, but not a fight. "If 50,000 people came to Hot Springs to see a fight they would have been disappointed. I intended to use my authority on the day of the fight, and I would have succeeded."9

To make sure everyone understood the situation, Governor Clarke rolled up his sleeves and dramatically stated, "There may be a fight at Hot Springs, but it won't be a prizefight." He insisted he would "regret to be compelled to adopt harsh methods, but the law gives me the authority and supplies the means." And he was just the person to make use of both. "It is just as impossible for those people to conduct that fight at Hot Springs as it would be for them to make the rain cease falling."

At one point, Clarke pledged, "If there is no law to stop the fight any other way except by the use of military force, I shall use it."

The *El Paso Daily Herald* reported that Clarke would resign before allowing a prizefight and commented, "As only few governors die and none resign it is surmised that the governor has a well loaded club laid up in the corner of his office."

Over two thousand people attending the Columbia Baptist Association meeting in New Lewisville, Arkansas, congratulated the governor on his stand and passed a resolution calling prizefighting "a relic of barbarism and inseparable from gambling and kindred deviltries."

On the same day, October 14, the ministers of Hot Springs called a mass meeting in the Central Methodist Church to denounce the fight—and who should appear to speak in its defense but William Brady. The *El Paso Daily Herald,* calling Brady "the oily-tongued shrewd sporting man," said he offered to put up $10,000 forfeit money that the fight would not be brutal.

The champ's manager "captured the house," observed the *Dallas Morning News,* "and when he finished such an acclamation of cheers and handclapping went up as was never before seen or heard in that sacred edifice, and which showed the drift of sentiment. The church people were completely nonplused, and in a few minutes more the house was practically empty."

With high hopes, Jim Corbett, Steve O'Donnell, and Peter Maher entered Arkansas at 8:00 the next evening and got off the train at Corbett's camp at Spring Lake. Little did they know they were preceded into the area by Brig. Gen. George P. Taylor some two-and-a-half hours earlier.

General Taylor was commander of the state's troops. After an hour's meeting with the governor that morning, the general was sent to Hot Springs to reconnoiter, and to warn the citizens of their danger. He said the state guardsmen were in good condition and he could have 850 "well drilled and fully equipped men in Hot Springs" very quickly. Taylor was accompanied by George Neeley, captain of the Neeley Rifles.[10]

They were talking martial law.

Having declared the boxing law void, Clarke was now acting under an 1838 law passed to fight outlaws and border terrorism. According to General Taylor, this gave any Arkansas governor extensive rights "perhaps never before conferred on the civil head of any state."

While Fitzsimmons was wisely staying in Texas and giving a wrestling exhibition in Corpus Christi, Corbett was wandering about the Arlington Hotel in Hot Springs trying to get himself arrested in order to force a test case into court. This seemed to amuse General Taylor, who said that as long as the two men were safely apart in two different states, no one would be jailed.[11]

Every company of militia had now received orders to be ready to move to Hot Springs on short notice. This was confirmed by Colonel Hollenberg of the Arkansas Guards' First Regiment, who added, "We do not propose to have any tricks played upon us."

On October 16, Governor Clarke himself arrived in Hot Springs on the noon train. He was met by the mayor, sheriff, and a citizens committee which gave him a reception at the Arlington. They all held a meeting afterwards, arguing for three hours about the nature of glove contests; nothing was resolved.[12]

The next afternoon a warrant was issued against Jim Corbett charging him with conspiracy to commit an unlawful assault on the person of one Bob Fitzsimmons. The sheriff hauled him into court and bond was set at $10,000 by Judge W. A. Kirk.

The champion refused to put up bail and his lawyers took the next step by applying for a writ of habeas corpus on the grounds that the arrest was illegal, there being no valid law against prizefighting. Corbett was allowed to leave for a theatrical engagement in Little Rock while the matter was being thrashed out. A deputy went with him.

Corbett's comments on the affair prompted the *Chicago Tribune* to describe him as "a cyclone almost entirely surrounded by mouth." But this time he felt he had a right to complain.

"I am disgusted with Fitzsimmons," railed the champ. "While my time, that ought be put in training, is being taken up in this way, Fitzsimmons is loafing around Corpus Christi playing cards and congratulating himself. I am getting the worst of it," carped Corbett. "He wires he won't be here until the day before the fight and it begins to look as if he does not intend to come at all."

Even the usually implacable Dan Stuart was getting riled. On October 18, he wired Fitz that if he was not in Arkansas in three days, the fight would be called off.[13]

In New York, John L. Sullivan expressed the concern of all fighters. "I wish in my heart to see it come off as the future of boxing depends upon its final outcome. They are 'knocking' the game all over the country, but it will rise again as sure as you live." Of the two contenders, "Fitzsimmons and Corbett are both good fellows, and they should be allowed to box."

On October 19, Judge Leatherman set Corbett free. The judge's decision said that "a contest with gloves under the evidence in the case is not dangerous to human life and the parties are not liable to inflict serious injury upon each other." Judging that it appeared to be less physically hazardous to health than baseball, football, or horse racing, Leatherman held the contest to be legal and granted the writ.[14]

There was jubilation in Hot Springs amid every indication that the governor's hands were now tied. The fight was on at last.

In the statehouse, the governor was not admitting defeat. He termed the habeas corpus release "a ruse," and declared, "I was never more determined than at present to prevent the fight and I am sure beyond peradventure that I will do so."

One avenue was the possibility of the state's supreme court reversing Judge Leatherman's decision. There was also more talk of the militia invading Hot Springs, and that angered the sheriff.

Sheriff Houpt fired off his own letter to the governor: "I beg to assure you of my ability to cope successfully with any situation that is likely to confront our people." Along with feeling personally insulted, Houpt did not relish the prospect of military occupation, telling the governor that "bringing the militia into this county for such a purpose is entirely unnecessary and will be extremely humiliating to our people."

Meanwhile, it was announced in Hot Springs that the lumber in Dallas had been freed and would arrive on October 19. The *Austin Daily Statesman* that day reported that construction would be rapid: "Whittington Park is situated at the end of the valley and is surrounded on three sides by a steep mountain slope, forming a natural support for the seats. All that will be required will be the placing of the seats on the mountainside in stair step fashion. An immense canopy will cover the park."

As sports around the nation held their breath in anticipation, a minister named John R. Lowery, "the celebrated Arkansas evangelist," was expelling his. On Sunday morning, October 20, Lowery told his flock:

"There are some as good people in Hot Springs as ever walked the face of the earth, but that city stands in the same position before God Almighty today that Sodom and Gomorrah occupied at the time the earth opened and swallowed them up. The place is in danger of hellfire, and the fact that a few gamblers of that city raising a purse of $50,000 and offering it to a crowd of drunken rowdies to come to Arkansas and disgrace the state in the eyes of the whole world is no reflection on the good people of that town."

The evangelist seemed equally concerned with profit sharing. Referring directly to the stakeholders, Lowery exclaimed that "these people, who are now so anxious to disgrace us all, have never raised anything for the spreading of the gospel of Jesus Christ."

A small group of like-thinkers in Conway passed a resolution affirming that a prizefight "would cast a stigma on the whole state which could not be removed in a generation." Mayor Waters and others in favor of the fight were said to represent only "the toughs, gamblers and scum."

The athletes were no doubt getting used to this sort of thing. As matters stood there were just two people now standing in the way of the fight—Bob Fitzsimmons, who was declining to sign the "pillow fight" agreement or move his training quarters to Hot Springs, and Governor Clarke who, it was rumored, still had a bombshell to fire.

The first to move, to everyone's shock, was the Florida Athletic Club. At half past noon on October 21, the club called off the fight, citing Fitzsimmons' refusal to change the date of the fight to November 11 for advertising purposes, refusal to sign the new agreement, and refusal to train in Hot Springs. Dan Stuart announced that Corbett's new opponent would be Peter Maher.

Gentleman Jim was irate and vowed that unless Fitz met him in Hot Springs, he'd personally "send him to a hospital" whenever they might meet on the street.

Martin Julian was even more upset, if not outright paranoid: "We think there is something else behind that has not come to the surface yet," charged the combative manager. "We don't propose to be led into any trap they may set for us." He vowed there would be a fight to the finish, "until either Corbett or Fitzsimmons is carried out of the ring."

Julian also said he would claim the $2,500 forfeit if there was no fight as scheduled. That, in turn, caused Joe Vendig to hold a press conference at which he vowed never to give up the forfeit money if Fitz didn't follow orders.

Dan Stuart reluctantly withdrew his support after Julian charged collusion with the Corbett camp. Angry and insulted, Stuart retorted, "There is only one way on earth to make money, and that is on the level." With a certain amount of sadness, Stuart said, "I dismiss the whole subject with the well known and much used American vulgarism—'rats.'"

The next day, the habeas corpus case made its way into the Arkansas supreme court.

While tempers erupted in court, there were vilifications enough to go around outside as well. "Brady has been earnestly haranguing and wildly gesticulating," the *Dallas Morning News* reported, particularly about not yet seeing the color of Fitzsimmons' money. (Phil Dwyer had been ordered to use part of Fitz's attached stake to pay off his debt.) Julian was pressing his case just as passionately in the press.

On October 22, Corbett called Fitz a cur and abruptly announced his retirement from the ring. This came after a particularly loud meeting with Julian, Stuart, and Vendig. A half hour later he changed his mind and said he'd stay in Hot Springs until the end of the month.

Julian guaranteed he could raise the stake money again from an Eastern backer and went off to get it. The governor was hinting at a special session of the legislature. Everyone was on edge.

On October 22, responding to stories that he had backed out of the fight, Fitzsimmons telegraphed a statement to Arthur Brisbane at the *New York World:* "Say for me that I now challenge the world for a $10,000 a side bet and will let the gate receipts be given to some charitable institution in New York city. Am now convinced Corbett does not want to meet me and is looking for easier game." He did not mention his depleted funds.

The next day the state supreme court unanimously ruled that the 1891 prizefight law was valid after all and fighting was still a misdemeanor. Jim Corbett was rearrested.

Joe Vendig was disgusted. "It is all over with us. The Florida Athletic Club has shut up shop and temporarily gone out of business. It has cost us some $80,000 to find out that we were on a dead one." Even a noted plunger had his limits.

In the aftermath of the court decision and Corbett claiming his title by forfeit, Fitzsimmons angrily lashed out. "Corbett has acted a coward and a sneak in the whole business, and if I ever meet him I'll tell him so to his face."

On October 26, Corbett again changed his mind. "I have decided to remain in training until Nov. 1. Mr. Fitzsimmons will have a fight if he comes here and any grandstand play he may have contemplated will be blocked."

Julian and Fitz said they'd be in Hot Springs in a few days with the necessary stake and would either have a fight or collect their forfeit money. Made aware of this, Governor Clarke promised, "The men shall not fight on Arkansas soil."

But if that was the case, why had the Hot Springs Athletic Club rented a circus tent? "They have not by any means abandoned hope that it can be done," reported the *Dallas Morning News*, "provided Fitzsimmons succeeds in running the gauntlet from Corpus Christi across the Arkansas state line to Hot Springs," said gauntlet bristling by then with armed peace officers.

With that, the quarry was off and running.

Based on information from an undercover detective named South who was planted in Hot Springs by the governor, Arkansas Att. Gen. E. B. Kinsworthy immediately issued arrest warrants for Fitzsimmons and Julian. Deputy Sheriff Jesse Hurd set out for Texarkana to intercept their train. As his authority he had the governor's message: "Catch Fitzsimmons or stop him, regardless of cost or consequences."

On the opposite side, Western Union sent nine extra operators to Hot Springs, and the Iron Mountain Railway started laying side tracks for the expected crowds.

"Every south bound train," reported the *El Paso Daily Times,* "is loaded with sporting men." Fitzsimmons and Julian passed through San Antonio at 8:00 P.M. on October 29; in Hot Springs, Joe Vendig and W. K. Wheelock of the Florida Athletic Club were arrested. More warrants were issued for Corbett and Brady even though they were already under arrest.

In Detroit, John L. Sullivan was preparing to accompany Paddy Ryan and "Parson" Davies to Arkansas. The ex-champ was asked for his opinion. "Will they fight? Well, I guess they will, or leave the country. They have been bamboozling the public long enough with windy war, and have to get to business now or get out of the game."

That's just what Governor Clarke had in mind. Authorities in every railroad town were put on the alert to search all incoming trains. Tickets for the fight were going on sale just as every peace officer was combing the state for the elusive boxer.

The hunt for Fitz had an air of hysteria. Deputies began boarding trains and searching every car as immense crowds gathered at depots to watch. Wild rumors sprang up of switching trains in the night and eluding pursuers on horseback.

The search went desperately on, journalists hot on the heels of the deputies clomping through train cars. It was a merry chase, with the sheriff of Hot Springs on the one hand and emissaries of the governor on the other, each group frantically following up rumors and leads, trying to be the first to spot the fugitive.

Sheriff Guinnette of Magnolia had a posse armed with Winchesters waiting for him to appear. Governor Clarke had called out the first regiment companies of militia at Pine Bluff, Helena, Cabot, and Jacksonville. The McCarthy Light Guards, Fletcher Rifles and Eagle Light Battery of Little Rock were told to be ready to move at a moment's notice. The Helena commander said he had forty-eight men and a thousand rounds of ammo if needed; thirty-eight men were ready to march at Forest City.

It was beginning to look like a war.

Most of his baggage and the circus tent arrived safe in Hot Springs on the evening of October 30—but where was Fitz?

"Governor Clarke continued with renewed energy his efforts to bar the gates against Fitzsimmons," the *Dallas Morning News* told eager readers, adding that it was plain Houpt was now "on the side of the sporting element." The possibility of a fight between competing lawmen over custody of the coveted pugilist was termed "extremely ludicrous."

Sheriff Houpt, a warrant now out for his own arrest, was more than a little involved at this point. Joe Vendig had arranged for a switch of trains at the Cotton Belt crossing, and Houpt was to see that Fitz and Julian made that connection. The sheriff's only problem was to convince Ruby Rob he was on the level, and the fighter was no longer in a mood to trust anyone.

Houpt crossed into Texas and intercepted Fitzsimmons and Julian in Marshall. He and a deputy named Cooper revealed Vendig's plan to get him to the springs by way of a clear track to Malvern and then overland to the fight site, but they encountered stubborn resistance.

Fitzsimmons the naturalized American took umbrage and stood four-square on his Constitutional rights, saying that as a citizen he was free to travel through Arkansas without fear of police molestation. Apparently he hadn't been reading the papers.

Martin Julian had his own reasons for being leery, not trusting Joe Vendig and being convinced the Corbett camp was in league with the Florida Athletic Club to somehow deprive Fitz of a fight or the title. Back on September 30—before the special session—Fitzsimmons had gone on record with the *New Orleans Picayune* as saying, "I think Stuart is an upright man, but I don't like Vendig, and you can put that down."

This animosity towards Vendig—who was characterized even by the *Chicago Tribune* as "Circular Joe"—was so strong that the *Trib's* sports reporter George Siler wrote that just bringing up his name at such a

Sheriff Houpt (*seated*) was ordered to stop Fitzsimmons even if he had to shoot the fighter, but Houpt was playing a tricky game with both sides, his loyalty shifting from the governor to his town of Hot Springs as armed troops began hunting the man from Down Under. Courtesy Garland County Historical Society.

crucial moment "was a remarkably idiotic piece of blundering, if nothing worse."

When the train crossed the Red River and moved on through the border-straddling city of Texarkana, it was boarded by Miller County Sheriff Dillard and a Little Rock officer. They found Fitz and his wife seated with Sheriff Houpt, and a jurisdictional tug-of-war ensued with Julian deciding, disastrously, to go with the Little Rock contingent.

The scheduled fight date of October 31 passed without a punch being thrown, and with both fighters in custody.

As if one couldn't have a carnival without a clown, John L. Sullivan and party arrived in Hot Springs at noon on October 31. With no fight to observe, Sullivan "imbibed freely during the afternoon" and offered his services as second behind Maher who, he said, "will lick that duck O'Donnell." Maher's backer, John J. Quinn, said he'd think about it. Sullivan was persistent, buttonholing Quinn and saying, "I wanter git inter the ring agin; not as a fighter, but as a second, and I wanter get in right."

The ex-champ was also contemptuous of the authorities, telling the *El Paso Daily Times,* "I know very well if they are dead on fighting they can do it, governor or no governor. It strikes me, though, Corbett don't care about fighting and Fitzsimmons don't want to."

Sullivan then launched himself on a trip down memory lane. "When I fought Kilrain we had a worse time than this. We were chased into the woods; had no special trains and no deputy sheriffs to help us, and more than that there was $1,000 as a price over our heads and prison wall before us. In spite of all that Jake and I found a ring and had our little trouble out. Now if we did it under such circumstances these fellows can do it too, and nobody need tell me they can't, particularly if they want to get at each other."

The good ol' days notwithstanding, this time the law won.

Fitz and Julian were put up at the Capitol Hotel in Little Rock with two deputies. When it was charged by William Brady that they had deliberately gone with Dillard to avoid the fight, Julian erupted.

"That statement is a lie, pure and simple," sputtered the former acrobat. "We knew nothing about any arrangements that had been made to get us safely to Hot Springs, if any such arrangements were made. We were left completely in the dark to feel our way out if we could. Neither Fitzsimmons nor myself is a mind-reader, and we could not be expected to pick out friends from enemies simply by looking at them."

Julian termed the whole incident "a put-up job on the part of Brady, Vendig, and the whole gang to keep the fight from coming off." With his flair for truculence, Julian was fast becoming a liability to Fitzsimmons' quest for the title.

Not far from the hotel, the governor was in a jolly mood. "He is enjoying the satisfaction of holding a prize fighter captive within a stone's throw of the Capitol," reported the *New York Times,* "and is reluctant to relinquish the pleasing sensation." Clarke was busy telling the press that he had "fresh ammunition for any possible phase of the situation."

Certain of the citizenry also enjoyed having the celebrities close at hand: the hotel's rotunda and the street in front were jammed with curious bystanders—what the *Austin Daily Statesman* termed "a surging, jabbering mass of humanity."

All the prisoners met with Governor Clarke who received them in a manner befitting a gracious victor, shaking hands warmly. Behind the graciousness was a will of iron. Deputy Hurd leaked it to the press that if Corbett and Fitzsimmons attacked one another in Little Rock, he had orders direct from the governor to kill them.

(Twenty-one years later, Brady confirmed it. Clarke, he wrote, took note of a rivalry that existed between Hurd and Houpt—having killed seventeen and eighteen men respectively. Clarke then told his captives, "Now, I instruct both of these officers that if you, Corbett and Fitzsimmons, as much as bat an eye at each other in this state while I am governor of it, you will go back home in a box.")[15]

Then Clarke turned amiable. "Happily, things now assume a more peaceful aspect, for which we are duly thankful."

There was no chorus of "Thank you" from Hot Springs. The mood in the city was one of dashed hopes and shattered dreams. According to the *New York Times,* "the town has fallen into a state of chronic expectancy after three weeks of ups and downs with almost hourly fluctuation. The proverbial brand of deferred hope, which is believed to make the heart sick, is generally known to the citizens of Arkansas."

Brady was not in a great frame of mind either and to an offer to hold the fight in El Paso for $20,000 said, "If I go down there I will have the same trouble with the courts as I have been having here, and I will be bullied in this way no longer." An offer from Louisiana was similarly dismissed.

When Governor Clarke offered an olive branch—leave the state and all charges would be dropped—everyone readily agreed. It was an offer easy to accept. And what Sullivan had so aptly termed a "windy war" was over. Well, almost.

The *Chicago Record* could not let the pugilists go their separate ways having exchanged only heated words. As a public service, the paper concocted a match of its own so sports fans would not feel cheated. It was a masterpiece of satire. The semi-imaginary fighters were named Gorbett and Fitzgibbons, and the fictive bout went like this:

> This is how it was finally pulled off.
> Gorbett slept soundly until about 8 o'clock, when he arose and talked three friendly rounds with his manager, Grady. . . .
> When seen by a reporter he said: "I never felt better in my life. I believe I could talk all night . . . I've gone through the dictionary twice, and besides I've got some new words furnished to me by the professor at Harvard, and if I don't make that Australian look sick I miss my guess. . . ."
> The champion . . . excused himself and returned to his quarters, where he did some light work with a book of synonyms.

After the *Chicago Record's* make-believe bout between "Gorbett" and "Fitz-gibbons," the people of Hot Springs gleefully erected a sign over Jim Corbett's training camp at Whittington Park proclaiming the site as "Gorbett's Ring." While that proved to be the full extent of the fistic carnival's impact on the town, the ring kept attracting tourists for years (this picture was taken three years later), proving that there was enormous public interest even in a ring where no fight occurred. Courtesy Garland County Historical Society.

In the meantime all was activity at the Fitzgibbons quarters. The Australian's manager engaged the auctioneer of Covington, Ky., to have a trial bout with his man the first thing this morning. After six rounds the auctioneer had to feel his way back to his corner. . . .

There was much betting, Gorbett being the favorite. This was due to a report that Fitzgibbons had seriously strained a submaxillary muscle while practicing on the word "pusillanimous." Manager Joolen denied the report with great indignation. . . .

It was learned today that Fitzgibbons had been taking points on invective from the boss canvasman of a circus. This fact did not apparently disturb Manager Grady, who said that his man was prepared for any emergency. . . .

Gorbett left his training quarters and started to the scene of battle. That he was in excellent condition was shown by the fact that just before leaving the house he blew 935 pounds on the lung tester. It is claimed that Fitzgibbons has never succeeded in blowing more than 875.

Gorbett was the first to enter the arena, and was received with loud cheering. Fitzgibbons came in a few moments later attended by his seconds. The muscles of his jaw stood out like whipcords, and it could be seen at a glance that all rumors as to his lack of condition had been false.

When the men had taken their corners and the excitement had subsided, Prof. Homer Jackson, the referee, explained the terms of the contest. Neither man would be allowed to use any foreign or obsolete words, but there would be no restrictions as to grammar or pronounciation. . . . If either contestant ceased talking until 10 could be counted by the referee, the adversary would be declared the victor. . . .

The gong sounded.

Round 1—The men began talking at the same instant, Gorbett using 180 words a minute and Fitzgibbons surprising his most ardent admirers by doing 185. Toward the end of the round he called Gorbett a "pompadour stiff," but Gorbett cross-countered and called him a "nut-headed kangaroo," thereby seeming to have the best of the argument when the round ended.

Round 2—Both men came briskly to the mark, but Gorbett was on the offensive. He called Fitz "coward, hound and freak" no less than 42 times, and each time with a new combination of adjectives. Fitz was worried, but he managed to retaliate with cries of "fakir!" "fakir!" and also called his opponent a "dude." Both men were slightly winded at the end of the round.

Round 3—Fitzgibbons began this time, leading off with a scurrilous denunciation of Gorbett's record. Gorbett kept his head, and on three different occasions branded Fitz as a "cheap guy," and told him he had been chased out of Australia.

Rounds 4 to 20—Both men showed remarkable versatility and endurance, and although the talking was incessant and each man delivered strong epithets, there was hardly a perceptible advantage until the 18th round, when Gorbett, changing his tactics suddenly, assailed Fitzgibbons with long words, calling him a "hydrocephalous monstrosity, a nebulous icthyosaurus and a downtrodden idiosyncrasy." Fitzgibbons was taken by surprise and seemed unable to reply. The referee counted six and then the Australian recovered sufficiently to say "rats!" thus saving himself. In the next two rounds he talked gamely, but it was evident he had not entirely recovered from the "icthyosaururs."

Round 21—Fitzgibbons assumed the offensive, calling Gorbett a "swell-headed sissy," but the latter proved his wonderful condition by resuming at the rate of 180 words a minute, designating the Australian as a "lunk-head, chump, sucker, bloke, gazaboo, tramp, bum, beggar and wind bag."

Fitzgibbons stood him off with great difficulty, and when he returned to his corner he was tired and puzzled.

Round 22—Gorbett . . . followed the Australian around the ring, denouncing him as a "long-legged, pin-headed, knock-kneed, double-jointed, lantern-jawed, freak of nature." Then as a climax he thundered: "You're nothing but an incomprehensible mass of imbecility, a homogeneous conglomeration of maniacal eccentricities." With a low moan Fitzgibbons fell to his knees and rolled over on his back. His lips moved but no sound came forth. . . .

The house was in an uproar of excitement. As the champion was being escorted in triumph to his dressing-room he said: "I had over 3000 words that I didn't have to use at all."[16]

Well, a dream fight was better than no fight at all.

One reason being offered for the easy compliance with the authorities was that Julian, protestations not withstanding, had failed to raise the missing portion of the stake money.

The *Chicago Tribune* said flatly, "he failed utterly." The paper also accused Julian of knowing months in advance that the money would not be forthcoming and "hoping some complication would arise which would help him to hide the fact." The paper charged that Fitz "was handicapped by his lack of money and by a manager who had not the business shrewdness of Svengali Brady."

So, the story went, they let themselves be arrested, journeyed to Little Rock and gave in to the governor.

Whatever the truth, on November 1 one or the other fighter should have been the undisputed heavyweight champion basking in the acclaim of Dallas multitudes. Instead, the only star in Dallas that day was William Jennings Bryan pontificating on free silver to twenty thousand listeners. The two fighters were in a Little Rock hotel dining room, none the worse for wear.

As Corbett passed Fitzsimmons' table, the champ did some quick and fancy footwork, smiled, and blew a kiss to his rival. Fitzsimmons grinned. Corbett raised a hand beside his mouth and, in a stage whisper, called out, "Boo!" Fitz went on smiling. Corbett blew him another kiss and left the room.

They would not see each other again for fourteen months.

That day Robert Fitzsimmons announced, "There will be no fight in Arkansas. I am done with the Florida Athletic Club and have no use for the citizens of Hot Springs. I am a law abiding citizen. I don't want to go to prison if I know myself."

Not to be outdone in this contest of press releases and provocative quotes, the champ had a news flash of his own shortly thereafter—Gentleman Jim Corbett, "disgusted with Fitzsimmons' dunderheadedness . . . and angry at being chased around the country from state to state," hung up his gloves.[17]

Dan Stuart, game to the end, was in El Paso on November 12 scouting yet another possible location when he received a telegram from William Brady:

"Corbett surrenders the championship and belt to Maher and will back Maher for $10,000 against Fitzsimmons."

Round three, and perhaps the bout, was over, and Dan Stuart was left standing alone in center ring, without a fighter to call his own.

ROUND FOUR: The Irishman

If I've heard it one time,
  I've heard it one thousand and two.
I've heard it from the Chinamen
  The Gentile and the Hebrew.

I hear it in early morning,
  I hear it last at night,
It's ringing, jingling in my ears—
      What's
      the
      latest
      about
      the
      fight?

  —*El Paso Daily Herald,*
      October 22, 1895

THE ON-AGAIN, OFF-AGAIN PRIZEFIGHT took up a lot of column inches in papers from coast to coast. At times it looked as if everyone from New York to Chicago to San Francisco had an opinion and thought about nothing else. One might conclude from all this rapt attention that there was little of interest going on in the world. But sport was entertainment, and entertainment was diversion; Americans in 1895 needed diversion.

Grover Cleveland was president, the ex-governor of New York heading into the final year of his tempestuous second, nonconsecutive term while rapidly losing control of the Democratic party to William Jennings Bryan, the free-silver advocate presently stumping the hinterlands like a financial revivalist. The president faced fierce economic problems at home and a wide range of uprisings, massacres, and wars abroad.

These were violent times.

In Asia, the war between Japan and China ground to an end with Japan being seded Formosa; the Queen of Korea was assassinated with Japanese help as troops from many nations (including U.S. Marines) landed on that country's shores.

The Ottoman despot of Turkey, Sultan Abd al-Hamid II, was well into his plan to eradicate Armenians. The ghastly death toll from his organized butchery was hardly credible to Western minds—fifty thousand massacred in Constantinople alone. Soon the body count in this attempted genocide would reach hundreds of thousands.

This was so unnerving that Elder W. P. Ebert of Frankon, Indiana, declared, "We Seventh Day Adventists believe the present Turkish rising foreshadows the end of the world, the destruction of its kingdoms, and the second coming of Jesus Christ." He saw the conflict as being foretold in the Bible: "The nations are now moving towards that battlefield and all their terrible implements of modern warfare will be there when the seventh vial is poured, when the battle of Armageddon, which is described in symbols in Revelations 16, chapters 7 to 21, will result."

After a four-year exile in the United States, activist José Martí formed the Cuban Revolutionary party and set out in 1895 to liberate his island home from the brutal grasp of Spain. He died in May at the Battle of Dos Rios, but the revolution went on.

Italy and Ethiopia opened hostilities that year as well.

In mid-December both George M. Pullman, the railroad car tycoon, and meatpacker P. D. Armour—targets of labor unrest and radical unionizers for exploiting workers—were sent bombs through the mail. The devices were intercepted en route.

The pages of newspapers were often filled with robberies, murders, rapes, vicious strikes, renegade Indians, mob violence, and lynchings—suspected criminals awaiting trial pulled from jail and strung up, shot, tortured, and sometimes dismembered.

On December 29 in Kentucky, William Dever, living with the widow of Tom West, whom Dever had been accused of murdering (the case was dismissed as self-defense), was shot down by a mob of some seventy-five men. They also set fire to the house and burned Mrs. West to death. Dever's ten-year-old daughter barely escaped alive from this vigilante madness.

That same day, in Texas, a black man accused of murdering a white woman was taken from police custody by a mob of two hundred men. Henry Hilliard was burned alive while tied to a stake in the Tyler public square in front of some seven thousand spectators. It took fifty minutes for him to die.

The *Chicago Tribune* reported in November that "it is getting to be almost as unsafe to live in New York as in some remote region where law is unknown. People are held up daily, and crime was never before so flagrant here." Preaching in Brooklyn, the Rev. Thomas Dixon concurred, calling New York "the most Godless city on the American continent," while its 500,000 inhabitants were heathens "in heart and spirit."

Once newspaper readers got past the fight news and grisly details of contemporary life, they ran across items such as these: Rhodesia was founded; the posthumous volume three of *Das Kapital* by Karl Marx was at last published; Louis Pasteur died, as did the man known as "Darwin's Bulldog," Thomas Huxley.

It was the year Marie and Pierre Curie got married; ace reporter Nellie Bly (Elizabeth Cochrane) married Robert Seaman. King Camp Gillete invented the double-edged safety razor. Couches would never be looked at in the same way after 1895 for that was the year Sigmund Freud laid the foundations of psychoanalysis with the publication of *Studien uber Hysterie.*

In France, after long and arduous struggle, Impressionists like Monet, Renoir, Degas, Toulouse-Lautrec, Manet, and Cezanne were finally gaining recognition and revolutionizing art (Van Gogh had already been dead five years). Rontgen detected X-rays; Marconi developed the wireless; Thomas Hardy published *Jude the Obscure;* H. G. Wells wrote his first novel, *The Time Machine;* Wilde's *The Importance of Being Ernest* premiered in February; George Bernard Shaw had two new plays produced, *Candida* and *Arms and the Man.* Kipling gave youngsters of the world his *Jungle Book.*

Gustav Mahler composed his *2nd Symphony,* while the first complete performance of Tchaikovsky's *Swan Lake* was applauded in St. Petersburg. Heartthrob pianist Ignace Paderewski was touring the states and charming women (he had to skip El Paso, the city feeling that the $2,500 performance fee and $5 tickets were unjustified; one columnist thought that "Paddy" was "holding himself entirely too high for common mortals").

London saw its first motorcar exhibition in 1895, and in America Henry Ford was gearing up to start his own automobile factory. Auguste and Louis Lumière perfected a motion-picture camera, as did Thomas Edison and a number of others (Chicago's Olympic Theatre screened an Eidoloscope movie for the public during the week of August 26, while in Paris the first public movie was shown in December at the Hotel Scribe).

The Women's Christian Temperance Union held its national convention in Baltimore in mid-October. One speaker decried the tragedy of drunken railroad workers: "Thirty thousand railroad men are killed or maimed every year, about three go under the wheels every hour."

According to the *New York World*, the coming thing for 1896 would be a return to higher heels on women's shoes—up to five-and-a-half inches. Admitting that wearing such a shoe would be a feat "of no small pain, labor and difficulty," the paper noted (perhaps sarcastically) a higher motivation: "It makes the wearer look very much taller and it makes her feet look very much smaller. Here, indeed, are ends worthy of such suffering to attain."

There were growing numbers of women, however, not solely interested in passing fashions. Diverse efforts aimed at securing women's rights had become united in 1890 as the National American Woman Suffrage Association working for the right to vote, going about it one state at a time. The "New Woman" crusade often brought about unusual encounters. On November 7, 1895, twenty-five "fair co-eds" shocked the campus of Northwestern University by wearing bloomers to class. The *Chicago Tribune* gave it front page coverage.

In San Francisco, there was an ordinance against wearing the garb of the opposite gender, and, sure enough, a woman was arrested while riding a bike in knickerbockers, a ridiculous garment seen as exclusively male (and why men didn't care to share the ludicrous attire is anyone's guess).

There were times when the "old" male could not fathom the "new" woman and bridled uncomprehendingly at incidents of role reversal. On November 16, a young man named Cosias Drescler was brazenly accosted by four young women on New York's Allen Street; two attempted to kiss him. Cosias ran, crying out for help, and a constable arrested two of the ruffians.

In court, the officer explained to the magistrate, "They're what are called 'new women,' your Honor. They stand on the corner and insult respectable men. We've had many complaints from mothers." The judge fined Maggie Keegan, twenty-two, and Annie Lynch, twenty-four, two dollars each.

Preachers, of course, knew better how to deal with brazen hussies. The Rev. Dr. Joseph Pullman, in trying to determine the root cause of crime in Bridgeport, Connecticut, zeroed in on newspapers and the theater as the main culprits. With that in mind, he put himself deliberately into the path of sin on November 24 by attending a pantomine show armed only with a notebook, in which he furiously jotted "copious notes."

The following Sunday his sermon not only denounced theatrics but referred to the show's star, Miss Jane May, as a "swell Parisian courtesan." The Reverend Pullman was immediately sued for slander and arrested during a prayer meeting. Jane May hired the noted attorney, fearsome agnostic, and eloquent writer and speaker, Col. Robert G. Ingersoll, to defend her.[1]

Sports fans, deprived of the diversion of a world heavyweight championship fight, had to be content with baseball, college football, bike racing and other tame pursuits. The first U.S. Open golf tournament was held at the Newport, Rhode Island, Country Club; in Latrobe, Pennsylvania, one of the earliest professional football games was played (the Latrobe Young Men's Christian Association defeated the Jeannette Athletic Club 12–0; John Brallier, the winning quarterback, was paid $10).

The heavyweight title fight, however, was never far from peoples' minds or long off the front pages, and there seemed to be no end in sight to the ongoing carnival.

It had been fourteen months since Robert Fitzsimmons first challenged Gentleman Jim Corbett and six months since the Texas promoter guaranteed a title fight in the Lone Star state. So far, all the public had to show for it was a lot of political and religious squabbling, plus a seemingly endless litany of charges and countercharges flying between the two fighters' camps. Now Fitzsimmons claimed he was through with the Florida Athletic Club, and Corbett had not only retired but had presented his title to someone else as his personally chosen heir to the throne.

Could he do that? Was boxing on its last legs? Did anyone care anymore?

Dan Stuart cared. He not only lost a great deal of money on this traveling road show, his reputation was at stake. He had promised the public a fight and, if he had to, he'd move heaven and earth to produce one. Which is how he came to be walking the unpaved, dusty streets of El Paso's notorious tenderloin district in November of 1895.

> El Paso is the biggest little town in all this country and can handle anything from a cowman to a prizefight.
>
> —El Pasoan Col. Will Harris,
> *El Paso Daily Herald,* Oct 21, 1895

A group of prominent businessmen had been trying to land the fight in El Paso almost from the beginning. As far back as early August, the local papers were speculating on the profit to be had if the boxers trained in El Paso. Once prizefighting was officially outlawed at the special session, the *El Paso Daily Times* declared in a headline, "JUAREZ THE ONLY PLACE."

Indeed, one day after the special session, the El Paso agent of the Texas and Pacific Railroad, B. F. Darbyshire, received a wire from the line's agent in Dallas: "Fight cannot take place in Texas. What bonus will El

Paso give to have it take place in Juarez? Quick, united action may take it there."

Darbyshire passed the message on to druggist and ex-mayor A. K. "Doc" Albers. Albers passed the telegram among the town's business leaders. A representative was sent to Juarez to send "red-hot messages to the City of Mexico." By the afternoon of October 3, El Paso had a "carnival committee" that met at the home of Judge Townsend. They appointed gambler and saloonkeeper J. J. Taylor to go to Dallas and secure the fight.

The decision makers of the Florida Athletic Club met with Taylor, but also with others—including Mayor Waters of Hot Springs. Certainly the continued animosity of Mexico's President Diaz to the fight was not helping matters.

Early in October, Mexico City's *Two Republics* newspaper wrote, "The so called manly art has few admirers in Mexico, where it is considered a degraded and brutal sport, a thousand times more revolting than the bloodiest bull fights." The paper argued that "the prejudice against prize fighting is so very much more intense here than it is in the United States that it would take a very bold governor to authorize in a Mexican state a spectacle that is not tolerated in any state of the American Union. Mr. Stuart and his short-haired friends must not suppose for a moment that the fight may take place in any Mexican state." In case the short-haired ones were reading the article, the reporter made it plain that foreigners could expect unorthodox treatment: "The laws of Mexico are very elastic in the matter of maintaining public order."

Despite that, four subcommittees were formed to petition El Paso's businessmen. The *Times* spurred them on by mentioning that the fight could pull "not less than $200,000 in cash" to El Paso.

The *El Paso Daily Herald* hurried to assure the skittish that they had nothing to fear: "The procuring of this fight for El Paso does not mean the filling up of the town with sports, bums and hoboes, but it does mean work for the mechanic, business for the stores, the filling up of all the rooms in the hotels and lodging houses, the feeding of numerous people at the hotels, boarding houses and restaurants and spending of a large amount of money in this section by people from other parts of the country, and in this way every citizen of El Paso and Juarez will be benefitted either directly or indirectly."

On October 16, Dan Stuart received notification that $10,000 had been raised in El Paso. That was the same day Arkansas Governor Clarke arrived in Hot Springs amid rumors of possible militia intervention. Stuart was doing a behind-the-scenes juggling act.

The situation inspired a front page poem from the *El Paso Daily Herald*'s regular columnist, a writer named Whitmyer who went by the curious nom de plume of "Wun Lung":

> From morning till night
> We hear nothing but "fight."
> Do you think it will come off at El Paso?
>> Or where will it be,
>> In a sewer or up a tree?
> I think it will be a grand and glittering
>> fiasco.

Lung continued: "We don't care for the scientific display of the manly art itself, but as has been before stated, we want the samolians that the boys will bring with them."

Speculating on how the county of nearly twenty-thousand souls could absorb the influx of twice that many or more, Lung decided "we would have to put up tents, build castles in the air, utilize the storeboxes, etc., etc. But if Mr. Stuart will bring his physical culture show along we will try and demonstrate that the town is built on the India rubber plan and can stretch like a stick of molasses candy in a hot sun."[2]

After Corbett's initial arrest in Hot Springs, hope was raised anew. On October 21, Fitzsimmons expressed his preference for a finish fight in El Paso to a "pillow-throwing contest" in Arkansas. Things were looking up.

The next day the committee uped the ante, offering a purse of $25,000 plus a cut of the gate receipts to the winner.

The day after the Arkansas supreme court ruled against the fight, the *El Paso Daily Herald* published a dialect poem:

The Arena

> "'Twon't be hour bloomin', blarsted fault,
>> If we don't get that bloody fight,
> For we've heverlastingly 'ustled
>> From hearly morn till dewy night.
> We've put hup the bloody stuff, ye know
>> To pull hoff the bloomin' fray
> And now want bloody, blarsted Jim and Bob
>> To sign and come hour way."

Kipling it wasn't.

On November 2, the *Herald* reported, "Stuart wired this morning that today he will make his last effort to bring the fight to El Paso. Julian says he will sign for El Paso, provided Joe Vendig has nothing to do with it."

As if this were a serial with daily cliffhanger endings, the paper added, "There are liable to be new developments at any moment."

That last statement tended to characterize the whole carnival these days—if nothing else, it provided readers with a lively, continuing story, and helped sell a lot of newspapers.

On November 7, the Associated Press received a message from Dan Stuart. "I leave for El Paso in the morning and I think the place and time for Corbett and Fitzsimmons to settle their difficulties will be found and fixed between now and Sunday. I am making the move individually and alone and intend to offer such purse and protection that neither man can refuse to accept if he intends or wants to fight. The whole sporting world is in a mood to see this championship matter settled in the ring."

Dan Stuart arrived in El Paso at noon on November 9 on the Texas and Pacific train from Dallas. He was met by Taylor and other committee members, treated to lunch at the Vendome Hotel, given a reception at Taylor's Gem Saloon, and shown around town. He said little and looked a lot.

A *Times* reporter called the robust Stuart "a fine specimen of physical manhood and a pleasant, courteous gentleman. There is nothing about him to indicate a sport. He is a man of intelligence and his conversation is entirely free from sporting slang."

He was also entirely free of information. "You must acknowledge that there has been too much talk already," Stuart reminded the committee. "Too much talk ruined us at Dallas and Hot Springs." If he was going to play the hand he was dealt, he would do well this time to keep it close to his vest.

But then came Brady's telegram announcing Jim Corbett's retirement from the ring and once more everything looked hopeless. Except to Dan Stuart who wired back, "Tell Brady that Corbett had better win that belt before he disposes of it."

Dan Stuart was not in the best of moods.

On the night of November 11, Jim Corbett was in a prize ring in Maspeth, Long Island. Not to fight, but to make a speech.

The scene was a scheduled twenty-five-round bout between Peter Maher and Steve O'Donnell sponsored by the Empire Athletic Club. The match drew the biggest crowd the club had ever seen, a crowd that cheered as Corbett made his way to a box seat before the preliminary match. When that ended in the fifth round, the crowd roared for Corbett.

He willingly climbed through the ropes and, noting the voices crying, "Three cheers for Fitzsimmons!" told the crowd, "If I were in England or Australia and acted as Fitzsimmons did in the match I would be chased out of the country." He was cheered lustily.

The ensuing fight was more like a mugging. As the men met following the bell, Maher lashed out with a powerful right to O'Donnell's jaw, and Corbett's sparring partner hit the floor. He got up on the count of seven and again was felled with a stunning right. O'Donnell made it back to his feet by the count of nine. Backed quickly into a corner, O'Donnell took a powerful punch from Maher's left. He stayed down this time and the match was over, sixty-three seconds after it began.[3]

It didn't take long for Maher's backer, J. J. Quinn, to issue a statement over the roar of the crowd: "Maher challenges any man in the world to fight for the championship, and he will not put the stakes so high that no one except a man with three millionaires behind him can accept." In case anyone missed the point, Quinn added, "he is particularly anxious to meet Fitzsimmons."

Telegrams from New York urging a Fitzsimmons-Maher fight began reaching Dan Stuart in El Paso two days after the O'Donnell knockout. Stuart wired Brady for confirmation of the champion's retirement and disposition of his title.

After receiving it, the promoter was still astonished. "Just where and by whom Mr. Corbett was authorized to give away the championship I am at a loss to understand," he said. "Even if Corbett really wants to quit, public opinion will whip him into meeting the Australian and if he refuses to fight him why Corbett will be a dead card."

Stuart still wanted Corbett. He sent a wire to the Associated Press offering a $20,000 purse for Fitz and Corbett to fight, and he was willing to forfeit the whole thing if he could not find a safe haven for the match. This time there was a difference. "I am in this deal alone," he wrote, "and no man can say I ever failed to make good my word."

Fitzsimmons not only agreed instantly but claimed the vacated heavyweight title for himself.

Jim Corbett didn't budge, telling the *New York World,* "When I announced my retirement from the ring I meant it. I would not train again for a great deal of money, and particularly for this bluffing foreigner. If he wanted to fight he could certainly have had one at Hot Springs. If Fitzsimmons expected me to be led into another wild goose chase and bankrupt myself paying expenses he is mistaken. I am surprised at Dan Stuart in taking stock in Fitzsimmons."

Perhaps he hoped that stock would pay dividends. One thing that came out after the Hot Springs debacle was Stuart's plunge into the heretofore unknown field of movie rights.

Pioneer experimenters with film were eager for fresh subject matter with plenty of action, and prizefighting was a natural. Credit for the idea goes to Grey Latham who, after viewing various peepshows with his brother Otway and fellow University of Virginia classmate and engineer Enoch J. Rector in 1894, said, "Everybody's crazy about prizefights, and all we have to do is to get Edison to photograph a fight for this machine and we can take it out and make a fortune on it."

The Latham brothers joined with Rector and Samuel J. Tilden, Jr., to form the Kinetoscope Exhibition Company and filmed a staged prizefight in Edison's "Black Maria" studio in July of 1894 between Jack Cushing and Michael Leonard. The result was put into peepshow machines in New York City. It was a hit.

They next signed Jim Corbett to the world's first exclusive film contract and had him fight Pete Courtney for six one-minute rounds, that being all the cumbersome Kinetoscope could handle. The firm soon dissolved, with Rector and Tilden retaining Corbett's contract and most of the technical expertise.[4]

One of the bones of contention between Martin Julian and William Brady early on was whether or not Corbett had a contract with the Eidoloscope company to film the big fight.

On September 24, Brady claimed no such contract existed. "There will be no Eidoloscope in the building. That has been thrown out altogether. Even Corbett will refuse to let them take his picture." He made no mention of Rector and Tilden.

Julian smelled a rat. Passing through Houston four days later, Fitzsimmons stated their policy on film rights. If any kind of movie camera was present at the fight, "I will refuse to proceed unless I am paid for it. I am one-half of this show and I propose to prove that I am the biggest half. That being the case, I am entitled to something." His stand was inalterable. "I do not propose to furnish any person or syndicate with an attraction which they can peddle to the people of the country and let them reap all the benefits. If they want my share of the fight they must come up with the coin."

It just may have been the first talent holdout for residuals in the history of the movie industry.

That had still been a major dispute during the Hot Springs phase and the *Chicago Tribune* revealed that Stuart had the movie equipment on hand and that even without gate receipts he would stand to make a profit as long as there was enough light for filming.

The paper also learned, after the fight was called off, that all of Joe Vendig's expenses—including the special train Julian said didn't exist—were paid for by the Eidoloscope Company, which offered Vendig a bonus of "a good, fat sum" if he succeeded in pulling off the fight.

Jim Corbett's ego and precedent-setting film contract not only led to this movie of him with Pete Courtney, but provided Fitzsimmons with a guide to the champion's style. Courtesy Museum of Modern Art, New York.

One can understand Martin Julian's suspicions and demands for equal fees.

As for Dan Stuart, there was still a chance of getting his investment back—if not through gate receipts then through distribution of any film made of the fight, so a fight there must be.

The *El Paso Times* described Stuart as "a man who impresses every one with confidence in his ability to do just what he promises to do. He is an earnest and enthusiastic worker and refuses to be defeated in any undertaking." If anyone could turn a profit from this carnival at such a late date, it was Dan Stuart.

Just before leaving El Paso to seek out Corbett, Stuart hedged his bet. "If he positively refuses to do so, I shall then match Peter Maher against Fitz for a finish contest; and I tell you Maher is a hot card in the east just now."

After noting that the New York papers were roasting Corbett ("Corbett cannot play against the press of the country. It is one too many even for the man who knocked John L. Sullivan out"), Stuart hopped a train and headed east on November 18.

He picked up Fitz's signature in San Antonio (where Rose Fitzsimmons was on the verge of having a baby), stopped over at Dallas to send wires to reporters in New York, Philadelphia, and Boston to come and witness his talk with Corbett, and then made for New York by way of St. Louis and Chicago.

While Stuart was en route, his quarry was telling the press that he was definitely finished with fighting.

"I am disgusted with the entire business, and henceforth will confine my attention to the stage. I cannot be induced to again enter the arena," vowed Corbett. "I bestowed the championship upon Maher, because I consider him the peer of any man in the ring, and have no hesitancy in saying that he can whip Fitzsimmons."

Apparently feeling the press needed more spice in the sports pages, Jim Corbett gave a long interview to the *New York World* that Martin Julian called "a cowardly attack upon Fitzsimmons and myself." Julian retorted, "Should Mr. Stuart fail to drag Corbett out of the hole which he has so cowardry [*sic*] crawled into, then Fitzsimmons will only be too pleased to fight Maher or any other man living."

At least some things about this fight hadn't changed.

Stuart arrived in New York on December 2. Corbett said he was on "a fool's errand," adding, "This fellow Stuart has cost me any amount of time and money besides plenty of worry and bother." By now the feeling was no doubt mutual.

The Texan was not put off, and on December 3, though confined to his hotel room with an illness, Stuart remained optimistic. "I have selected a battleground within two miles of El Paso, Texas, but not on Texas soil. The headquarters will be El Paso, which is naturally adapted for reaching the mill. Five trunk lines meet there. One thousand Mexicans alone will attend and I will guarantee no fizzle. The grounds will be under my control."

An arena would not be necessary. "A number of circuses have winter quarters at El Paso and we can use an immense circus canvas with a seating capacity of 25,000. This is going to be a final showdown."

It was not to be, however—not this go-round. A wire from Stuart to Doc Albers on December 4 stated, "Corbett stands pat that he has retired. Will close match with Fitz and Maher tomorrow for February 14 for the championship of the world."

Under the heading, "MILL ON THE RIO GRANDE," the *El Paso Daily*

Times trumpeted the match just made at New York's St. James Hotel. The paper also reminded absentminded fans that Fitz and Maher were not exactly friends. They had fought once before, in 1892, and the result had left such deep bitterness that the El Paso meeting would be more than a mere title fight. For one of them, it would be a deadly grudge match.[5]

Peter Maher was born in 1869 in County Galway, Ireland. He took up amateur pugilism while working at the Guinness Brewery in Dublin. Maher was a good, strong lad and in his first bout laid out a local brawler known affectionately as the "Dublin Terror." It took two hours and forty minutes.

Following that victory, he entered regular competition under the auspices of Dublin bookmaker Tony Sage and continued to best all opponents, eventually emerging as the amateur champion of Ireland.

He turned pro, and his potential was so obvious he came under the management guidance of Billy Madden who, after some successful bouts in England (he beat Gus Lambert in one minute), brought Maher to America.[6] Their goal was nothing short of a match with then-champion John L. Sullivan.

Sullivan declined to face the newcomer until he had proven himself worthy. Maher was willing and made short work of Jim Daly, "Bubbles" Davis, Jack Fallon (who became his trainer), Ike Peckham, Fred Woods, Jack Lynch, Harlem Jack Smith, a black fighter named Joe Godfrey, and "Sailor" Brown. None were considered contenders, and Sullivan remained at a distance.

As a stepping-stone towards Sullivan, Maher looked around and found the middleweight champion, Robert Fitzsimmons.

In January of 1892, Fitzsimmons had run out of opponents; most middleweights were afraid to face the hard-punching redhead. If he was going to continue as a fighter, he had to move up in weight class. Even though Maher was heavier, taller, and was six years younger, Fitz agreed to a match set for Mardi Gras week in New Orleans.

Some of Fitz's unorthodox training ways first came to notice at this time. A *Picayune* reporter visited his camp in Bay St. Louis, Mississippi, and watched him chop down trees and high-jump nearly five and a half feet, run wind sprints of a hundred yards, exercise with weights, and generally "work like an ox" in an apparently unstructured manner.

Maher, in contrast, trained in East Hampton, Long Island, in a far more conventional manner, running for fifteen miles at a time along sandy roads, punching bags and eating "like a horse."

Word came on February 11 that Maher would finally get his chance at

Sullivan. The champ signed for a purse of $35,000 in a match set for August with only one condition: Maher first had to beat Fitzsimmons. It was all the incentive the Irishman needed. Training intensified, with a little creativity of his own: shoveling earth into wagons for farmers.

Fitz too picked up the pace as the date drew near, shoeing horses and repairing wagons for his neighbors, but he ran for only seven-mile stretches.

The one sour note of the training tune-ups came on the night of February 22, when Peter Maher went out on the town and got plastered, something he did far too often.

Jack Fallon finally induced him "to break away from his convivial Irish friends." But back at camp, reported the *Picayune,* Maher "caught Fallon unawares and knocked him down. As soon as he was down Maher kicked and beat him in a frightful manner. He was infuriated with rage and strong drink." Another trainer had to pull Maher off the fallen and battered Fallon.

Among the sports, the fighters were judged to be so evenly matched that professional gamblers were having a tough time with their wagers. Some just gave up and declared they would "flip the copper" the day of the fight.

The fight on March 2 drew the biggest crowd in the Olympic Athletic Club's history. With nearly an hour to go before the fight, carriages and busses snarled traffic on Chartres Street; large numbers of people—including some with tickets—were turned away at the door. Inside, the arena seemed surrounded by a sea of hats, thousands of hats bobbing on an ocean of cigar smoke.

Maher entered the ring first, wearing green tights. His handkerchief—the symbolic prize of the fight according to the rules—was white with a raised silver harp inside a green silk shamrock. Fitzsimmons came in next wearing trunks and shaking hands all around. His trophy handkerchief was white with red and blue borders and featured a kangaroo on the shield of Australia.

Although Maher had tried hard to get the fight date changed, not wanting to box on Ash Wednesday, the gong sounded at 9:15. Everyone later agreed that it very nearly ended in the first round.

Neither man had seen the other before entering the ring and the fight started with cautionary probing jabs and feints. A half-swing, half-push from Fitz sent Maher to the floor. An angry Maher rushed after Fitz who danced away, smiling and jabbing. One jab opened a cut inside Maher's lower lip.

The blood brought out the devil in him that Fallon had reason to recall. He chased Fitz around the ring, swinging viciously. Fitz gave him a hard left on the mouth and then, following a clinch, Maher flailed away. A sharp right to the temple put Fitz onto the ropes and nearly through them. He was dazed, groggy, pale, and Maher moved in to finish him off.

The gong sounded, but no one heard it.

Maher rushed at Fitz like a man possessed. Fitz, sitting on one rope while his head rested on the top one, seemed to be at his mercy. In came Maher with a furious salvo of blows, but he was swinging blindly. Despite his awkward position, Fitzimmons blocked, parried, and dodged with surprising agility, which only made Maher all the more furious and more inaccurate. At last the referee heard the clanging bell and stopped the round.

(Three years later that first round was still being contested in the newspapers, the *Chicago Tribune* reporting that Fitz "was 'all out' in the first round and that, for the kindly office of the late George Clark who struck the gong with his cane ten seconds before the three minutes were up, Maher would have been returned one of the quickest winners on record.")

But the fight did not stop then and both groggy men made it to their corners, Fitz helped over by his seconds, who gave him brandy. When round two began, Maher was still bleeding from the lip, producing a stream that not only filled his mouth but flowed down to his chest. Fitz went to work on the cut and punished it whenever he could.

In the third, Maher continued to bleed profusely while a refreshed Fitz danced and played with him. By the end of round four, Maher was covered with blood while Fitz appeared unscathed.

In the seventh, Fitz slammed his stiffened right arm into the side of Maher's neck and chin, a pivot blow that stunned and confused his opponent. Referee Duffy let it go with a warning not to do it again.

Fitz went back to work on the wounds in the eighth round and kept Maher's blood flowing; the Irishman's breathing was becoming difficult as he swallowed more and more of his own blood.

Maher was disoriented in the twelfth, swinging wildly in pain and rage but missing frequently. Fitz kept out of his way and then, seeing an opening, slammed another left into his mouth. Maher's whole body quivered like a tuning fork. After reeling about the ring, he told Fitz he'd had enough. The bell rang.

. After a brief exchange in the corner and with the referee during the break, Maher's seconds threw in the towel. Fitz took his brandy bottle over to him, and the victory celebration began.

In his dressing room, dejected and looking "like a slaughter pen,"

Maher waved away questions about his physical condition. "I lost because Fitz was too clever for me."

The bitter reaction from the Irishmen who dominated American boxing at the time was swift and scornful. Charley Mitchell condemned his countryman, saying, "Maher is the dirtiest cur that ever stepped into a ring. He ought to be ashamed to own himself an Irishman, and Irishmen generally should be ashamed to own him as a representative of their nation. He can't fight and he won't fight."

Frank Slavin agreed. "Maher is a coward and knows nothing about fighting." Referee Duffy added, "Maher lost because he is a quitter."

Fitzsimmons came away from the bout with a swollen thumb he had dislocated in the first round and gave due credit to Maher. "He is a much better man than people seem to think," said the man who ought to know. "There is a good deal to be said for his gameness too."

But the Irish weren't buying it. The label of "Quitter" had been permanently affixed.

Charley Mitchell was still not finished blasting him in the papers. "Maher, I think, is a horrible cur, quitting before he should have done so." Mitchell declared, "I consider him a disgrace to Ireland." Further, "the ordeal bursted his vaunted reputation, by the sheerest cowardice, into a thousand fragments."

Fred Gallagher of *London Sporting Life*, termed Maher "a cocktail," referring to a half-breed horse who cocks his tail and quits in a pinch during a race.

One reason for the abuse might be that in New York alone it was said that at least $100,000 was lost on Maher by gamblers. The *Picayune* reported that "all the Maher men are swearing to-day and say that Madden should buy a steerage ticket and send his world-beater back to Ireland."

Despondent, humiliated, branded as a quitter and coward by his fickle supporters, Peter Maher tried to kill himself on March 5 by jumping from a northbound train traveling at forty miles per hour. It took five men to pull him back from an open window. He had been on a "crazy drunk" ever since the fight and witnesses attributed his "wild dash for death" to that.[7]

Fitz's then-manager and trainer, Jimmy Carroll, tried to stick up for Maher, calling him "a man of good judgement." By the time Maher gave up, said Carroll, "he was so choked with blood he could hardly be understood. Maher is a far better man than some boxers who are roasting him for a quitter."

Fitz agreed, adding that he would be "only too happy to give him a benefit, at any place he may select, and give him the whole proceeds." It was a tradition to help the loser. "I stand ready to spar with him or anyone else to assist him."

Jack Fallon, the trainer Maher beat during a drunken rage, was conciliatory. "Maher is a good man, however. He acted like a fool this time, but he said to me on the way home that he would follow instructions after this. If he can be made to do that you will hear from him yet." He was right.

Time healed more than Maher's facial wounds. Eventually the Irish community accepted him back into the fold, and he returned to boxing. After another loss in December (he was knocked out by Joe Goddard in three rounds), he took on and whipped all comers, including Bob Marshall—"the alleged English champion heavy weight"—in just forty-five seconds.

He did his homework too. Admitting Fitz once "outscienced" him, the *El Paso Herald* remarked on Maher's rebirth as a fighter since that 1892 disaster. "He bided his time and went extensively into the generalities of the art, the last two years having been sufficient to steep him in depths beyond any other man in the mysteries of fistiology."

In October of 1895, Maher came to Texas by invitation for Stuart's fistic carnival just as that began to unravel in the legislature. He went on to Hot Springs with Corbett and was ready at ringside on October 31 to step in against the champion if Fitz didn't appear. His manager, J. J. Quinn, had $10,000 in his coat for that purpose. But Corbett didn't show up either.

Instead, Corbett gave him the title and bowed out.

Then came the O'Donnell rout and Dan Stuart's plan for a rematch with Fitzsimmons, the man who humiliated him. This time, Maher was far more experienced, better trained, and, noted the *El Paso Daily Herald,* "as a two-handed fighter the Irish champion is thought to have few if any equals. His left is almost as effective as his right, and he has learned how to punch straight out instead of swinging in the old windmill fashion."

He had come a long way since 1892, and now he was eager to prove it.[8]

After the contract was signed by both fighters, Fitz and Julian balked at the reduced purse—halved somewhere between Texas and New York. An angry Fitzsimmons told W. K. Wheelock, "If Maher wants to fight for the middleweight championship at 158 pounds, then I'll fight him for the $10,000." Julian added, "Fitz whipped Maher once and where is the use of fighting him again?"

Ruby Rob then demanded a purse of $20,000, and the championship belt. "The Police Gazette champion belt I will not fight for. I will not dirty my hands with the thing. The original belt, which they claim mysteriously disappeared, is in the hands of James J. Corbett. The substitute belt, which cost only $250, they can keep."

He concluded his ultimatum with, "I can make a living making horseshoes: I am not above doing it, and I'll not fight a championship battle for a purse of $10,000." That had to be a feint; in addition to his wife and son and lion, Fitz now had another mouth to feed, Rose having given birth to a boy—baby Bob—in late November.

Corbett, naturally, was soon heard from: "My sympathies are heartily with Maher. I hope he'll beat the Australian's brains out. But if he does not I'll make Fitzsimmons fight for any amount of money he pleases or for a shoestring." He then took his new show, *The Naval Cadet,* on the road.

While the details were being worked out, things moved forward on other fronts. Jimmy Carroll, Fitz's trainer for the 1892 fight with Maher, was now living in Mexico City and wanted very much to switch sides this time and train Maher. He still harbored some resentments toward Fitz and booked passage to El Paso hoping to be in on the redhead's fall. He wrote that he'd bring his new protege, "Australian" Billy Smith, with him.[9]

Dan Stuart hit Dallas on December 15, and then met with Martin Julian. Whatever arm-twisting was done, the $10,000 purse became acceptable. The new contract was signed on a tug floating outside of Galveston Harbor the next day.

Dan Stuart commented, "I am sure that nothing but an earthquake can disturb the men this time." The Houston papers called Dan Stuart "the impresario of the prize ring" and he was quoted as saying, "It is a go this time and they could fight with meat axes if they wanted to."

The El Paso committee immediately began arranging training quarters for the men while the manager of the holiday fiesta going on in Juarez— originally scheduled to run from December 8 to January 1—began planning additional bullfights and more monte games for the expected high rollers. El Paso was about to start a two-month party.

Within days, letters of inquiry were pouring into El Paso from all over the country; gamblers in New York were taking bets and making Maher a slight favorite. Joe Donovan was so impressed that he gave Dan Stuart some tongue-in-cheek praise:

"There has been no other in the annals of the ring to hold on to things like this 'Dan' Stuart of Texas. It is becoming evident that we or our children, or our children's children at sometime or other are going to have

A "beautiful creature of modern civilization" is how Martin Julian referred to
downtown El Paso. This scene of San Antonio Street taken in 1900 is little
changed from when Julian saw it five years earlier, complete with mule-drawn
streetcar. Courtesy El Paso County Historical Society.

a heavy weight championship glove contest, to be staged through the everlasting perseverance of Stuart or some of his descendants. Stuart simply won't quit at all till there's a fight. Others in the business come and go, but Stuart goes on forever."

Martin Julian came in early and approved Fighting Bob's training quarters on the west side of the Juarez plaza, in a building that once housed the local lottery concession. He also arranged for a Christmas evening exhibition at the Myar Opera House and predicted that Fitzsimmons would beat Maher in six rounds.

"The fight is going to be a good one," assured Julian, "and will be fast and furious while it does last." And it wouldn't stop there. "Just as soon as we finish Maher we are going after Corbett again. We have run him out of the ring and we intend to make him fight or run him off the stage."

And since Fitz wasn't around to object, he added that he'd be going back to New York soon to see his wife (Fitz's ex-wife) and new little one, "for I have a prettier baby than Bob's."

Fitz, Rose, baby Bob, and Nero the lion were scheduled to arrive on Wednesday morning, Christmas day, on the western flyer. In anticipation, the *Herald*'s overworked Muse produced this:

> When Bobby Fitzsimmons comes,
>   Hurrah, hurrah!
> When Bobby Fitzsimmons comes,
>   Hurrah, hurrah!
> When Lanky Bob comes on the run
> Followed by Peter Maher, we'll have some fun
> And we'll go and see the fight
> When Bobby and Peter come.

Yes, this time it was all locked up. So, OK, John L. Sullivan was going around saying that when Corbett retired the belt should have reverted back to him, and that this drawn-out wrangle between Corbett and Fitzsimmons was "responsible for killing the boxing game." And, yes, on December 24, Peter Maher nearly got arrested in Chicago when the police broke up a sparring exhibition at Sam T. Jack's Opera House.[10] So what? That was Illinois. He should have known better.

In a border town like El Paso, things were done differently and virtue was reserved for Sunday mornings. It was a wide open city, holiday fiesta fires lit up the mountaintops at night, all were happy, and Dan Stuart was going to pull it off at last.

Give round four to Stuart on points.

Was it his fault the carnival hit town in the middle of a purity crusade?

ROUND FIVE: El Paso, Part One

Nothing short of lightning or the destruction of the earth by fire or flood can stop the contests we have arranged to pull off.

—Dan Stuart,
El Paso Daily Herald,
January 7, 1896

WHEN MARTIN JULIAN ARRIVED in El Paso on December 21, 1895, he pronounced the city to be a "revelation" to him.

"Back in the east," Julian explained, "El Paso is considered as located in the wild and woolly west, on the extreme outpost of civilization. And I naturally expected to find here a border city, something like we read about in border literature. You can imagine then my surprise on finding El Paso a typical American metropolis—a pretty substantial well built city, equipped with all the modern conveniences and in fact a beautiful creature of modern civilization; stylish and full of dash and energy, and thoroughly cosmopolitan. I like El Paso and I like her people."

While some of that can be written off as public relations boosterism, Julian's surprise at finding the city's reality so different from eastern impressions was undoubtedly genuine. But perhaps "metropolis," "modern," and "cosmopolitan" were not quite the right words.

The Rio Grande was not yet completely tamed for purposes of irrigation, and there was still the feeling of being an oasis in the midst of a hostile desert. It was not uncommon to see articles in the local papers telling readers what to do if they awoke to find a poisonous centipede on their necks ("don't get excited and grab at him, because he might sink his claws into your flesh and poison you. Just sit still, and let him crawl. If he should decide to take a promenade down your back and come up via your chest, just keep calm and let him perambulate. . . . A centipede is a peculiar insect and he don't like to be interfered with when he is taking a stroll").

El Paso's fire alarm system consisted of citizens firing guns into the air—and sometimes into each other. (If there was gunplay in town, someone had to go tell the fire department it was a false alarm.)[1] The city payroll for the month of December, 1895, was a whopping $2,363.88. The "new woman" in bloomers was still considered shocking, though not illegal, especially when spied riding racing bikes around town.[2]

(Yet, local women could shock even jaded Easterners. In November, the *Daily Herald* had observed: ". . . to a stranger who blows in on us from the effete east, it is a novelty to see a young woman parading along a principal street puffing gaily away at a coffin nail, just as though it were the usual thing for women to trot along and smoke like men.")

It was not totally out of a sense of civic pride that the *Herald* could relate this little tale: "A man in town said the other night he dreamed he was in heaven and then awakened and found himself in El Paso. He said that the difference was so slight that he had no kick coming."

Yet El Paso was not so long removed from its days as a frontier trading post and village of small adobe houses. Spanish conquistadors and missionaries marched through in the late 1600s but the first house on the north side of the Rio Grande was put up in 1827.

The U.S. Army first encamped in 1849; the post—named Fort Bliss in 1854—served as protection for both settlers and emigrants heading for California. Raids by the original land owners—mainly Apaches—tended to make travel hazardous to one's health. Stagecoaches started bringing mail and passengers to the outpost in 1854 (the fare from San Antonio was $100, but that included meals). Four years later the Butterfield Overland Mail Company built a major depot and rest stop in town—as the trip to California took twenty-four days, a layover was most appreciated.

El Paso got its first mayor in 1873, and by 1879 could boast of six lawyers, five stores, three saloons, three hotels, and one school.[3] Gunfights in the street were what passed for prime-time entertainment, along with horse races, public hangings, and, of course, bullfights across the river in Juarez—they were not for the squeamish.

The horses in the bullring were unpadded, blindfolded and often gored. One account in the *Times* described an encounter where "horse and rider went down in a cloud of dust before the mad bull, whose horn was buried in the horse's neck making an ugly hole from which the life blood gushed."

There were outlaws and rustlers, but only scattered, renegade Indians to worry about. The last Indian battle in the area occurred eighty miles away at Guadalupe Peak on January 29, 1881; Geronimo was captured nearby in 1886.

The first transcontinental railroad link was completed at Promontory, Utah, in 1869, but the second track-laying race set out for El Paso. The Southern Pacific, pushing from the west, beat the Texas and Pacific on May 19, 1881; suddenly the village became a boom town and a major stop for cross-country travelers.

Completion of the railroad line left a lot of laborers—mostly Chinese coolies—unemployed and stranded and they formed their own community along with the Anglo and the Mexican. Four years later the *Herald* could report that "there are more Chinese gamblers in El Paso to the square inch than there are white ones," adding, "when some of them lose they look as if they had smoked fourteen pipes of hop and were just recovering from the effects."

Such a melting pot also produced curious news items, like this one in the *Herald*: "I see that Charlie Sue, the Chinaman, got hitched up yesterday to a dark-skinned, dark-haired senorita, who looked as if she were about half a dozen of one and six of some other. This match vividly recalls to me that beautiful Sunday school song, 'What Shall the Harvest Be?'"

(Not all mixing was officially approved, however. In late October of 1895, a black porter at the Pierson Hotel by the name of King Tatum was arrested by El Paso police for miscegenation. He had married a Mexican girl six months before up the road in Las Cruces and that was all right, being in New Mexico Territory, but when he brought her to Texas he ran afoul of the state law that made the marriage of a black with any other race a felony.)

Those addicted to cocaine and morphine satisfied their cravings by a simple visit to the local drug store, for neither drug was illegal.[4]

The first bank opened in 1881, and the city got electricity and telephones in 1883. For public transportation there was the mule-driven streetcar, established in 1882 by Gen. Anson Mills and Judge Joseph Magoffin (the line conveniently ending at the judge's house).

The Myar Opera House, where Fitz was to put on an exhibition, opened in 1887 to bring culture to the city—you could tell because "public prostitutes" were barred from the good seats and limited mainly to the rear and the gallery.[5]

Oh, there were prostitutes aplenty, most of them paying for licenses disguised as fines. The railroad had proved to be a mixed blessing, bringing growth, prosperity—and sin. The trains indiscriminately carried businessmen and ranchers, gamblers and gunfighters, ministers and farmers, "daughters of joy" and outlaws, sports and pugilists—something for everyone.

El Paso's Myar Opera House, where Fitz and Maher sparred and John L. Sullivan emoted. It was built in 1887, and the upper two floors were used as a hotel, part of which eventually evolved into a well-known brothel. It burned down in 1905. Courtesy El Paso County Historical Society.

Gambling dens ran twenty-four hours a day, brothels almost as long; El Paso's sordid reputation rivaled those of Frisco's Barbary Coast and New Orleans' Storyville as the nation's steamiest towns—and that didn't refer to the weather.

Most of the sin palaces clustered along Utah Street downtown, forming their own tenderloin of saloons, fleshpots, "sporting houses," and games of chance. This did not go unnoticed by the Puritan element. An early reform movement was started in 1883 by newspaper editor S. H. Newman, the Citizens Reform League being primarily aimed at political corruption in the city council; even saloon keepers joined that one.

Vice became the main target in 1889, when the Law and Order League sought to regulate—if not stamp out—gambling. In 1890, a *Times* reporter detailed "the chaos of debauchery" to be found in the sleazy part of town, while a Baptist labeled Jim Burns' Red Light Dance Hall "a plague spot, a dreadful disgrace," and characterized its owner as "the wickedest man in El Paso." Given the impressive competition, Burns may have felt proud of the title.

Reform politicians were unpopular, however, and seldom got into power until 1893, when one, Will Burges, became city attorney and several others made it to the city council. They started harassing and closing the houses of sin.

Burges found the taking of fines from prostitutes little better than organized bribery. "By taking money from these women, we are giving tacit approval to violating the state laws against prostitution," Burges lectured, "and until the hypocrisy ceases, we must consider the 'fines' as, yes, a form of licensing."6

Virtue, however, proved to be something of a passing fad.

The League's mayoral candidate went up against Robert Campbell, accused so vehemently during the campaign of being nothing better than a poker player that ever afterwards he was known as "Poker Bob." The sobriquet ensured Campbell's win. Not without influence, the League bypassed the city's officials and asked Governor Culberson to send the next best thing to the wrath of God to clean up the city—the Texas Rangers.

On July 31, 1895, District Attorney W. C. McGown wrote to Culberson saying that forty-five to fifty conspirators regularly violated the anti-gambling ordinances.

Further, he emphasized, "Although the laws ARE OPENLY VIOLATED ALONG THE PRINCIPAL STREETS OF THE CITY, the police of the city have made no effort to prevent the violations of the laws of Texas." Rather, the peacekeepers actually "REMONSTRATED WITH THE CITIZENS FOR PROSECUTING THE OFFENDERS." McGown attributed this—not without some justification—to official corruption and lamented, "NO ASSISTANCE CAN BE LOOKED FOR FROM EITHER THE CONSTABLE'S OFFICE OR THE POLICE FORCE."

McGown told the governor of threats and attacks by the gambling bosses and that the lives of decent citizens were "IN CONSTANT DANGER from this lawless set of men, who have no interest in this community, except to violate its laws and to plunder its people."

Sheriff F. B. Simmons concurred, and Will Burges added a note with his own capitalized hysteria that said, "VIOLENCE HOURLY THREATENED."

Their case wasn't hurt when, nineteen days later, the gunfighter-turned-lawyer John Wesley Hardin was gunned down in the Acme Saloon by Constable John Selman. It was a personal squabble, and Hardin was shot from behind.7

The Rangers were duly ordered in, and the episode drove a wedge in relations between Austin and El Paso to the point where the words "Ranger" and "Culberson" were close to being considered profanities by many citizens. El Paso was at the isolated, far-west end of Texas and, in most matters, wished to be left alone.

The Rangers were gone—and the anti-gambling court injunctions temporarily lifted—when Martin Julian arrived; but the reformers were still in place.

On December 30, columnist Wun Lung complained of a local minister who figuratively jumped onto cardplaying and dancing among young folks as a means of enjoyment. "It seems to me ministers of the gospel would discover in this enlightened age, that they are wasting time and breath in discoursing against these two popular forms of social amusement, and that the more they rail against them the more popular they become. If you want to make a broth unpalatable don't add spice to it."[8]

But with a nationally advertised prizefight coming to town, the preachers were guaranteed to do a lot of discoursing.

Among the first was a circuit-riding evangelical named Kilgore who preached a revival at El Paso's Trinity Methodist Church nightly through most of December. He generally stuck to religious matters but toward the end of his stay shifted to current events. It was soon reported in the *Evening Telegram* that Kilgore publicly prayed for the Fitzsimmons train to smash up before reaching El Paso.

The preacher quickly corrected the story by saying that he wished the train only to be "hindered" on its journey, adding that every Christian man should try and prevent the fight. That pretty well set the tone for things to come.

The GH & SA train bearing Fitzsimmons and party arrived unhindered on Christmas morning. He found a large crowd and a Mexican band waiting to greet him, the latter provided by Señor Daguerra, manager of the Juarez fiesta programs. They formed a parade for the pugilist and led him through El Paso and on to his quarters in Mexico.

It was a full day for Fitzsimmons, starting off with Nero the lion deciding to eat his bicycle and "getting away with the best part of the front wheel." In the afternoon the gringo was seated in the judge's stand at the bullring, where he watched one picador get gored in the knee and faint from loss of blood, and another get tossed in the air. Despite the festivities, Fitz was the center of attention. In the evening he hit the opera house.

A *Times* reporter sought him out at the theater and found him "in a bad humor" because some minor pieces of equipment had been left in Juarez and Julian declined to fetch them. Fitz blew up. He rushed out to the box office where, in front of the waiting crowd, he angrily informed Julian there would not be a show.

Opera house manager McKie, showing more business acumen than sense, rushed from his office and shouted at the heavyweight, "Yes, there will be an exhibition, too. I have a contract here calling for an exhibition and it is going to take place."

This lively and unrehearsed exchange, though entertaining, did not show promise of anyone coming to blows. Consequently, several hundred potential paying customers turned away and sought amusement elsewhere. So did Martin Julian, who quit on the spot.

The articles were sent for and the exhibition was held, though the paper reviewed it as "very tame."

When Fitz appeared on the stage—one that had seen everything from Madrid's Grand Spanish Opera and minstrel shows to Edwin Booth in *Julius Caesar*—he was given an ovation that shook the building. The highlight of the show—not counting the outside tantrum—was his demonstration of bag-punching, ending with a solid right that broke the bag's moorings and sent it flying into the audience.

As this was the way Fitz always ended his bag exhibitions, one may suspect prior tampering.

Fitz's outburst before the show had a sharp and immediate impact within his own family circle. His mother-in-law, perhaps not used to his temper, declared she had been rudely treated and was leaving. Beside her was her son Martin, who hotly announced that he was finished as Fitz's manager.

"I shall have nothing more to do with the ungrateful lubber," railed Julian. "After all I have done for him, then for him to act as he did tonight." He then gave his side of things.

"Just before time for the curtain to go up tonight he notified me that he had neglected to bring over his suspensory and other necessary articles." Being close to show time, Julian suggested he used Roeber's gear. Fitz exploded. "He came rushing through the audience with his suspenders hanging down and ordered me to close the admission doors." For the man most concerned with profit and loss statements, this was too much. "So I just quit. There is not a spark of gratitude in the man's composition and I do not intend to move another finger for him. He can take the money he makes out of this fight and go with it. I do not like to use strong language in the presence of mother, but I must say—"

The *Times* declined to repeat what Julian's mother, "a fine, motherly soul" (and ex-acrobat), heard, but noted, "the angry young manager used words that fairly burned the atmosphere and were not at all complimentary."

It's possible that neither the words nor the tone would have been unfamiliar to some others who had previously parted company with the man from Down Under—such as ex-manager Captain Glori, ex-trainer Jimmy Carroll, and ex-lawyer Emanual Friend. Fitz tested very high on volatility. But this time he was about to be left in El Paso, less than two months before a championship fight, without a manager.

When asked if this would upset his plans, Fitz said he was sorry Julian got "huffy" for no reason, but assured everyone he could "paddle his own canoe." He may have been up the creek, but he still thought he had a paddle.

Fortunately, cooler heads prevailed—Doc Albers's among them—and by midafternoon the next day, both men had been brought together and made to talk things out. Julian agreed to stay on.

As in Dallas and Hot Springs, Fitz had little to say about Jim Corbett that was printable. "Corbett is a blankity, blank, blank, blank," he told a *Herald* reporter who valued his job enough not to quote him exactly.

And when he was told Maher would be given a benefit before leaving New York, Fitzsimmons—the man who once offered to throw him one personally—was derisive: "They all have a benefit but me. Those eastern Irish are boosting Maher up, but it will do them no good." Reminded of his own roots, Fitz said, "Yes, I'm half-Irish, but I don't go on my stock. I'm banking on my own abilities and not on my nationality. And I intend to bank that way to the end."

The sermons continued but to no avail. Wun Lung even took the preachers to task in a front-page editorial, his theme being money laundering on a spiritual level.

Expressing cynical disbelief that anyone "could be so heartless and inhuman to pray that a train bearing a party of sporting people to El Paso, would be wrecked before it reached here and the people destroyed," he admitted to hearing other "very un-Christ like assertions" from the ministers about the fight. Regardless, the columnist felt it was all wasted energy.

"What brings money to the town and puts it in the pockets of our business men and church members, benefits the churches. Of course, it may be claimed that the money comes from sinful sources, but if a man can be cleansed of his sins cannot money also? No doubt the biggest part of the cash the minister is paid with, has paid poker debts and seen much service on the faro-table, but it is not to be—or at least, isn't—despised for that."[9]

As the eventful (but fightless) year came to an end, things seemed relatively quiet for a change, all things considered.

Julian left for New York to attend to business, promising to return on January 7 (he took the ailing Roeber with him); Fitz settled into his training facilities, built a cage for Nero, and occasionally came over the river to shoot pool at Phil Young's Cafe or take in the sights. Ruby Rob was persuaded to play right tackle on the El Paso football team in their upcoming New Year's Day game against the Albuquerque Indian Industrial School (Billy Smith got to town in time to play left tackle).

New Year's opened with a bang in El Paso. Quite a lot of them, if the *Times* was any indication: "Judging from the number of pistol shots that were fired at 12 o'clock last night it would seem as though every inhabitant of the city had been saving up their ammunition for the event."

At three in the afternoon nearly a thousand people gathered at Sportsman's Park by the Santa Fe depot to witness the "hottest game of football ever played in the west," one pitting a team of long-haired Indian students against a mismatched and unpracticed team of short-haired, mustached Texans, some of whom looked as if most of their training occurred in saloons. It was certainly one of the West's most disorganized games, and Wun Lung decided to play sports editor for a day:

"Football is a rough and tumble game and the players expect to get used roughly and they can claw each other, they can 'mug' each other and they can break arms, legs and skulls, as long as it is done ligitimately [*sic*] and not intentionally." He did think, however, that "when a game of football is played ropes should be stretched along the lines and the spectators kept outside. At times yesterday one could not tell whether the ball was over the goal or in some spectator's pocket."

He also complained that "there was too much chinning about the decisions, and there was too much mixing up of the police with the game. It was the general opinion of people who knew all about the game that no officer had a right to interfere with the players as long as they did not fight each other."

Of course, with Bob Fitzsimmons and Billy Smith on the line, one could never be sure a prizefight wouldn't break out between downs.

One witness was heard to say, "I think them there fellers' heads gits punched more'n the ball." Another commented, "They just look like a lot of hungry dogs fighting for a bone." A third analyst noted, "Them's the doggonest scrappers I ever seed." It was that kind of game.

The closest thing to a brawl came when El Paso's center, McCoy, started shoving one of the visiting Indians and Chief of Police E. M. Fink

This was not a forerunner of America's Team, but El Paso's motley gang of footballers, here augmented by Bob Fitzsimmons, fourth from the left, and Billy Smith, second man in from the right. Courtesy El Paso Public Library's Southwest Collection.

went out to break it up. The spectators indignantly rushed onto the field, and the chief quickly retired.

Fitz was a little slow catching on to the game; twice within a few seconds, a young Indian's block sent the pugilist spinning to the turf. The crowd roared when another brave, by accident, hit Fitzsimmons on the chin with a right cross. Accident or not, *that* was a game he understood.

Once he warmed up, things went differently: "One of the copper colored lads thought to throw Fitzsimmons, but the prize fighter coolly caught the visitor by the nape of the neck and the bosom of the pantaloons and presto the youth was sprawling on the ground ten feet away." When a spectator shouted, "Give them 'ere Injuns a clip!" Fitz hollered back, "What would I want to hit them poor little ducks for?"[10]

Albuquerque scored first but missed the two-point kick, making the score 4-0. El Paso scored its first touchdown just prior to the half when the Indian team rushed over to a referee to protest a call before time was called. In the confusion, the Texans calmly picked up the ball and walked into the end zone with it. The goal was good, making the score 6-4.

No, it wasn't the least bit organized.

The Indian team played better than the short-hairs, but was kept out of the end zone by superior size and weight. After scoring one more touchdown fluke via an Indian fumble, El Paso hung on to win 12-4. Not bad for a team that hadn't played together before.[11]

The first week of the new year saw the usual goings on about town, as duly reported in the press: "El Paso is just now infested with several tough characters who are making their presence felt by their depredations," went one report. "They are a brutal outfit and seem to delight in beating Chinamen nearly to death"; "The police say the town is full of confidence men. They do their 'steering' on this side and finish the work in Juarez"; "A runaway on San Francisco street last night created some excitement, but no one was hurt"; "Two disciples of Oscar Wilde were jailed last night by Deputy Constable Farrell"; Lillian Lewis played Cleopatra at the opera house as part of her national tour, including the "sensational novelty" of a barefoot ballet in the third act.[12]

Then there was the case of the over-protective father. "Pastor Tom Grigsby, of the African M. E. church, distinguished himself this morning by shooting Walter Williams, also colored, in the head." The motive was simple: "Williams has been hanging around his house on Tays street paying surreptitious attentions to his daughter."

There was bad news for saloons that week: "The El Paso Womens' Christian Temperance Union, has been finally organized for active local work with twenty-seven members," all of whom were connected with churches and not apt to be caught drinking anyway. The pledge was: "I hearby solemnly promise, God helping me, to abstain from all distilled, fermented and malt liquors, including wine, beer and cider, and to employ all proper means to discourage the use of and traffic in the same."

The fiesta south of the border was still rolling merrily along past its scheduled end date and picking up some heavy bettors. The *Herald* reported seeing a table piled high with as much as $25,000 on the night of January 8, and the game's manager said $100,000 wouldn't be a surprise when the out-of-town sports and plungers began flooding in.[13]

(The *New York World* was somewhat scornful of the fiesta. On February 2, 1896, the paper wrote, ". . . bull fights are held daily in the amphitheatre and the plaza is crowded with gambling booths, for everybody gambles in Mexico—men, women and children, and the fiesta of 'Our Lady of Guadalupe' is nothing more than a big gambling carnival.")

So far, Fitzsimmons was the only member of the fistic carnival on the scene.

Dan Stuart was in Dallas, but he wasn't idle and kept in touch by telegram. One wire at year's end read: "The prospects are now that I will have five first-class events and wind up the last day with a double bill. I am determined to make this El Paso carnival the biggest on record. I am in Dallas at work on railroad rates. Everything looks propitious for an affair of much greater magnitude than was at first contemplated."

Peter Maher was in New York, where his benefit exhibition drew six thousand people at $2 a head; not bad travel money. It was denied that Jimmy Carroll had been hired as Peter's trainer.

Martin Julian was also in New York trying to lift the attachment on Fitz's stake money, $5,000 of which belonged to Stuart and Joe Vendig.

Locally, an itinerant faith healer named Francis Schlatter was said to be due in town just in time to handle any wounds suffered in the carnival.[14]

As the only star attraction in town, hundreds of people trooped over to Juarez each day to watch Fitzsimmons train (at twenty-five cents each). He started the day with ten-mile runs after breakfast. Afternoons saw him sparring and wrestling with trainer Jack Stelzner and taking an hour's bike ride around the cities.

As he paused in his riding to buy some raw meat for Nero, a reporter asked if it was true that Fitz once entered a cage of three wild lions. He confirmed it, but modestly said, "It only takes grit to do that."

Back across the border in El Paso, there was some trouble developing over money. Dan Stuart had been promised a bonus from the local fight committee, and the money had not yet been raised. It was understood that without the bonus, the carnival would pack up and move to Phoenix.

The *Herald* urged committee members to pry open their wallets and "lay aside all bickerings and jealousies and go to work with zeal and vim. Remember that El Paso's reputation is at stake financially and that only by united effort can anything be accomplished." It was hoped that Dan Stuart's return and personal supervision would revive interest and apply some leverage to those uncooperative billfolds.

Stuart detrained at the El Paso depot on the morning of January 9. He brimmed over with confidence: "Nothing short of lightning or the destruction of the earth by fire or flood can stop the contests we have arranged to pull off. It is a cold 200-to-1 shot that they will come off as advertised, and it will be the grandest carnival of sport ever witnessed in the United States."

Five hundred comfortable chairs for ringside would be shipped soon from Dallas, and local ticket sales would begin in six days—$10 and

$20; more for the comfy seats. Two hundred box seats would go for $40 each.

The carnival card was now set, including two matches between fighters "of the ebony hue": Joe Walcott and Scott "Bright Eyes" Collins for the welterweight championship, and George Dixon against Jake Marshall for the featherweight championship. In addition, Jack Everhart would fight Horace Leeds in the lightweight division championship, and bantams Jimmy Barry and Johnny Murphy would mix it up, also in a title fight.[15]

The somewhat ironic date for the heavyweight fight was set for February 14, Valentine's Day.

The committee members who met the train nervously made small talk, assuring Stuart that Fitz was training hard—when not running around the cities he was punching the bag; a *Herald* reporter watched him work the bag for an hour and a quarter straight, then start a wrestling match and punch the bag between rounds.

When it couldn't be put off any longer, Stuart was told of the bonus delay. He wasn't exactly thrilled. "I have just received today a telegram from Joe Vendig in New York, in which he says that there is $12,000 worth of advertising ready to be delivered and scattered throughout the world. This will give El Paso $12,000 worth of advertising and as yet El Paso has done nothing to help the cause along." He also produced a wire from the Western Passenger Agents Association agreeing to a special excursion fare to the carnival and back, with the New Orleans Mardi Gras thrown in.

To a *Times* correspondent he complained, "I have arranged for El Paso one of the most interesting fistic carnivals ever held in this or any other country, and it will draw a large crowd to this city. I have, in fact, done more than I promised to do, for instead of giving you one event that would hold the people here one day, I have listed already four events and count on keeping the crowd here a solid week."

Needless to say, Stuart felt let down. "El Paso is tonight being discussed in every hotel, barber shop, railroad station, club room, saloon, restaurant, and on every train in the north, east, south and west. El Paso literature decorates the walls of nearly every city in the United States, and yet your people appear to be indifferent to this work being done for them."

When he regained his usual composure, Stuart expressed confidence the city would come through for him.

There was, fortunately, other fight news of a brighter and lighter nature. The brighter one, for Dan Stuart at least, was a new contract with Enoch Rector to film the great championship carnival using his modified Kinetoscopes.

All the fighters were said to have a piece of the action, with Fitzsimmons having worked out a royalty deal. The film was expected to be worth "a large fortune," and other cameras would be banned. "No snapshot pictures will be allowed and the man who draws a pocket Kodak is likely to be fired from the ringside." The royalties, however, would not be forthcoming until after a film was successfully produced.

Dan Stuart, sport, gambler, and fight promoter, was now Dan Stuart, movie agent.[16]

On the lighter side of pugilism was the case of the John L. Sullivan knockdown by one Dan "Billy" Goat in La Salle, Illinois. Sullivan, Paddy Ryan, and troupe were expected to hit El Paso four days before the fight—they were "following the money" with their latest show, *The Wicklow Postman.* Their road show included a goat named Dan that Sullivan enjoyed slapping and teasing; after a while, Dan grew tired of having his whiskers pulled.

Dan, a lightweight, was unintimidated by the heavyweight's size or reputation. Spying Sullivan in his La Salle dressing room, Dan charged, snapping his rope and plunging headlong into the ex-champ, knocking him off his feet and sending him crashing into a corner.

When he tried to get up, Dan rammed him again. As Sullivan lay gasping on the floor, Dan turned and laid out another actor with a solid butt to the stomach.

At first there were threats of goat stew for dinner, but after calming down, Sullivan said Dan could whip any goat on earth and offered to back him in a finish fight.

(Sullivan had been claiming that Corbett's vacated title should have reverted to him. If that was so, then it was now the property of Dan "Billy" Goat, and Fitz would have an opponent with a battering-ram punch to face. Of course, they'd have to change the Queensberry rule against butting.)

There must have been an even bigger laugh heard in Juarez when Fitz read that retired Jim Corbett was now offering to fight him—for a $20,000 forfeit. The man was unbelievable.

Peter Maher, ardent fistiologist, arrived in El Paso on Saturday, January 11. He came, he saw, he left.

The El Paso committee did all it could to keep him in town. He was met by a large, cheering crowd even though the train was ninety minutes late. The quiet fighter and his entourage (including fighter Jerry Marshall) took a hack to the Gem Saloon to see Dan Stuart, then checked in to the Vendome Hotel, snubbing the training quarters arranged for him at Mesa Garden.

Committee member, saloon owner, and fellow Hibernian Si Ryan engaged several carriages, put plumes on the horses, and drove everyone to the Juarez bullfights on Sunday afternoon.

Maher said he was fit but was otherwise uncommunicative. The *Times* observed, "He looks as tall as Corbett, is as straight as an arrow, with broad shoulders and an admirably proportioned figure all around. He carries himself with the easy grace of a healthy athlete."

Come morning, the healthy athlete carried himself forty-seven miles north to Las Cruces to train. Manager J. J. Quinn decided it was safer there than to risk antagonizing Governor Culberson. New Mexico was a territory and somewhat freer than states. (The move did not, however, cancel an opera house exhibition set for the coming weekend.)

So El Paso would not play host to either of the heavyweights, but could still count on the money-laden crowds to take up residence in the city.

That Saturday's train was a full one. In addition to Maher and Marshall, W. K. Wheelock was also aboard. He immediately set up headquarters with Stuart across from the post office in the Sheldon Building, the city's principal business site. As a precaution, tickets would be sold in Juarez, but buyers could conduct their business downtown. Stuart was already "overrun with letters and telegrams" from all over the country.[17]

Someone else who would not be training in El Paso was the Texan Scott Collins, set to fight Walcott. It was learned that this "apple of the average Dallas colored man's eye" would remain in Dallas until at least the first of February.

Meanwhile, Marshall—"the colored boy who is to fight Dixon"—was at hand and seen by the press as "a wiry, determined looking negro [*sic*] boy and his friends say that he will make Dixon put up the fight of his life."

Everhart was also staying in town for a while, having located his quarters in a hall directly behind the Gem Saloon; the great John L. would certainly have endorsed the choice.

Opinions on the fight were not hard to find—as Stuart said, it was being talked of from coast to coast. One frontier authority on the subject, and a man whose name was bandied about as a possible referee, was an ex-lawman and now a popular Denver sport, William Barclay "Bat" Masterson. The bringer of law and order to Kansas and one-time crony of Wyatt Earp was a fight fan sure to be on hand in February and expressed his feelings of the coming carnival in a letter to a friend.

"Maher is the most improved man in the business today," wrote Masterson. He attributed the earlier loss to Fitz to one main thing: "Maher was a drunken sot at the time."

Things were different now. "Now he can feint, can side-step, put his head out of harm's way, cross with either hand, and, what not one fighter in a thousand can do, can uppercut with either hand and knock out with either hand."

Turning to Fitzsimmons, Bat admitted he was good but had not improved much in the past three years: "Everybody has hit him, and several have nearly laid him out. And no one has ever hit him that can hit like Peter Maher can today, and no one who has ever hit him can hold a candle to Peter from a boxing standpoint."

Masterson the renowned gambler wrote, "I would like a wee bit of money on Maher against any man living but the 'Pompadour.'" He had also backed Maher in 1892.

If powerful hitting was what Fitz needed to train against, he wasn't getting it from his most visible sparring partner—Nero.

The *Herald*'s sports reporter watched some of their bouts and was suitably impressed: "The lion waits until Fitz's back is turned and then makes a spring and the two then get down to hard work. Then they go after one another over adobe fences and on top of out houses. In this way Fitz keeps himself actively employed and never quits until the lion is tired out and wants to stop. The lion is as gentle as a house cat, but it is strong."

Maybe, but he couldn't punch worth a fig.[18]

Fitz and Maher were not the only ones planning on a knockout. There had been rumblings from the El Paso Ministers' Union, and rumor had it that a resolution was in the works, complete with battle plans. Taking the offensive, W. K. Wheelock told a fight committee meeting on January 13 that the kind of fighting being protested was old-fashioned, that the ministers were out of touch by twenty years.

Wheelock insisted modern boxing would not bring a blush "to the cheek of the most refined lady in the land." Of course, ladies were not usually admitted to fights.

The next day, as committee members were making the rounds of all those who had pledged bonus money, the Minister's Union put forth its manifesto. It was headed, "An Appeal to the Citizens of El Paso," and appeared inside the *Times*.

"We ask our citizens to refuse to have any part in raising the required bonus and to decline giving the carnival any moral support." They cited the poor reputation the town would get and argued that business would suffer rather than increase, at least in the long run. "Among those who come will be many who by gambling will intend to take away money."

And, of course: "In the trail of the crowds will likely come many prostitutes. Will their traffic leave or take away money?" They labeled all who assist the fighters as "criminals in practical contempt of law."

The choice was obvious: "Shall the keepers of saloons, gambling dens and houses of prostitution dictate the business policy (to say nothing of the moral question) of El Paso, or shall it be the sober sense of our own business men."

The appeal was signed—"In behalf of the Evangelical churches and ministers of El Paso"—by A. M. Elliott, Adolph Hoffman, and Charles J. Oxley.

On the same page, quite by coincidence, was this blurb: "The Times has been requested to again warn the merchants of El Paso to order ahead plenty of fish, oysters, eggs and butter to feed 20,000 people six days. Give our visitors plenty to eat."[19]

The contrasting views worked wonders on the pursestrings of the merchants. In one day $6,000 of the bonus was collected, and the remaining $4,000 was picked up by late evening. To businessmen, money talked louder than prayers.

W. K. Wheelock was not quite done with the ministers, however. "We do not dictate what church people should attend," he said, "why should they or anyone try to dictate which style of physical sport we should enjoy?" Wheelock opened a drawer containing, he said, ten thousand letters asking for seats and claimed, "there is not twenty of them from sporting men. The bulk of them are from the presidents of banks, railroads, express companies, insurance companies, large mercantile establishments, and men of that character."

Stuart's right-hand man assured the populace, "There is absolutely nothing brutal or offensive seen or allowed" in modern prizefights. "If there was anything more offensive to be seen at these contests, as conducted with gloves as large as pillows, than at a Sunday school social, or picnic, I would not say anything. I do not make the comparison with either base ball, foot ball or polo, as they are so brutal and dangerous that a comparison would not be fair. This opposition is simply a fad—born from ignorance or desire for notoriety."

He was even receiving requests that "permission and space be given for the fair sex to witness the glove contest." Though it was not customary, he was confident that would be arranged. If the women had proper escorts.

His considered advice was fitting for wide-open El Paso: "More physical culture and less six-shooter is my idea."

The ministers retorted in the *Herald,* this time joined by a Baptist, the Reverend Leander R. Millican (known in later years as the "Sky Pilot of the Range").

"We are convinced that it is fully as brutal as ever," they stated. "Besides the $10,000 they ask as a bonus, it will cost the city five times that amount in the way of extra police force, prosecutions, losses by burglaries, robberies, to say nothing of unpaid bills to merchants, caused by the inability of victims to pay, who have been drawn into betting and carousing by the element that follow in the wake of those who pose as public benefactors."[20]

The response had no discernible effect, and El Paso continued to look forward to the fight, as the *San Antonio Express* put it, "like a young maiden in a state of delightful expectancy."

Julian had returned on the 16th (bringing with him a supply of souvenir books titled *The Life and Battles of Bob Fitzsimmons,* cover price twenty-five cents) and at noon on Saturday, January 18, he, Quinn, Stuart, and Fitz met in a back room of the Gem and agreed on a referee. It would be George Siler, sports editor of the *Chicago Tribune.* Stakeholder was to be Houston hotelier James Lawlor.[21]

Peter Maher, his big mustache shaved off for the fight, came in from Las Cruces that evening on the Silver City Special for an opera house engagement. While he sparred with trainer Peter Burns, the most intent member of the audience was Fitzsimmons. (And a reporter who could not help noticing that "Maher has a magnificent figure and muscles stand out like cords all over him.")

"Bright Eyes" Collins arrived early on Sunday, and the paper noted that "Colored sports are all agog."[22]

Jimmy Carroll made it to town that weekend still hoping to catch on with the Maher camp. He did not underestimate his old boss, calling Fitzsimmons "the greatest fighter the world ever knew. He is a wonder in the ring and no mistake." But when the two former friends passed one another in Si Ryan's Astor House saloon and gambling emporium, no word was spoken.

Carroll felt that Maher had "improved wonderfully" since his fight in New Orleans. "One of his blows will knock Fitz out if he can land, but that is a difficult matter. I am here for the purpose of getting Fitzsimmons licked, and if anyone knows just how to go about it, I do. I know all of Fitz's strong points and I know also his weak and vulnerable points."

Maher, however, was satisfied with Burns and did not hire Carroll after all. Jimmy hung around town to train Billy Smith against Burns, and waited for the opportunity to see Ruby Rob take a fall.

Meanwhile, the scope of the fistic carnival kept enlarging: Dan Stuart was now a procurer of bulls. Señor José de Moreno of Madrid was bringing six Spanish bullfighters to the fiesta (at a fee of $1,500 a day).

THE GEM BAR, EL PASO, TEXAS.
JOSEPH L. KOPF, PROP.

The Gem Saloon, frequent gathering place for fighters and journalists, some of whom stayed in rooms out back. It was a tourist attraction—a relic of the Old West—until torn down in 1910. The interior featured marble columns, cushioned booths, and a bar built for serious imbibing. The image is from a turn-of-the-century postcard. Courtsy El Paso Public Library's Southwest Collection.

Stuart was going to provide, free of charge, all the bulls necessary for a five-day corrida. Also set for the carnival now was an international cattle roping contest with cowboys from across the Southwest—the kind of "Cowboy Carnival" that eventually became known as a rodeo.

One attraction Stuart declined was a novelty act offered by a Houston man. Clad only in trunks, the man would catch and kill a dozen rattlesnakes within twenty minutes. Stuart's position was that if the spectators wanted to see reptiles in the arena, they could drink their fill of mescal prior to the fights.

The promoter was as confident as could be. "There is not the most remote chance for interference of any sort," Stuart said. "It is costing me about $1,000 a day now to perfect the minor details of the carnival, and I am not sufficient of an imbecile to continue in this outlay without something akin to an iron-clad guarantee that I am right."

All signs pointed to his being more than right. Tickets were going fast, and nearly every train brought new visitors to town. The morning paper gleefully pointed out that "parties are being formed all over the country, and any number of Pullman cars have already been reserved for the trip." No doubt about it, the money-laden crowd was on its way: "From Boston, Philadelphia, Washington, Baltimore and Norfolk seats have been called for, while St. Louis, Chicago, Minneapolis, St. Paul, Omaha, Denver and San Francisco already have written and wired for blocks of seats."

On January 24, Dan Stuart opened bids for four thousand feet of lumber to be used in the construction of a stage, site still a secret, and Fitz, in a jolly mood, made a four-pound horseshoe for Sen. John Dean, the only man in the state senate to vote against Culberson back in October.

Publicity photos were taken on January 24, though at first both Fitz and Maher balked, their managers wanting to sell their own photographs. Stuart said these were free for publicity purposes, and when both camps were certain they weren't being cut out of anything, Mr. Burge, a local photographer, was allowed to do his job. The *Chicago Record* thought the incident demonstrated "how the commercial spirit has grown among prize-fighters."

Well, money *was* one of the key incentives of the carnival, and the cost of everything in town seemed to have skyrocketed. While other children of the town were content to follow and emulate their new fistic heroes in droves—"El Paso kids have contracted the sweater craze since the arrival of the pugilists. To be sporty and look tough it is proper to wear a sweater"—the hoopla and temporary inflation caused young Ethel Goodwin, a student at Franklin School, to write a poem for the *Times:*

> ### After the Prize Fight
>
> A little lad climbed an old man's knee,
>   Begged for a story, do Uncle please,
> Tell of El Paso, that wondrous town,
>   With its adobe buildings,
> They're world renowners.
>   Soon the great prize fight
> Will be at its height
>   Prices of all things will go out of sight,
>   They'll charge for everything but the air,
> Oh! what a difference after the fight.
>
> After the fight is over
> Just watch the rents come down,
>   When all the sports and hayseeds,
> Have skipped away from town.
>   Many a man will be broke,

People will keep out of sight,
  Juarez will be dead and buried,
After the fight.
  When you go there,
Take your own lunch,
  For you can't afford
To buy things to munch.
  Frijoles cost one dollar,
Chile con carne costs two,

  They've got you in these,
What will you do;
  If you get tired of walking around
You'll find seats in the plaza
  To sit down.
They'll charge ten dollars
  For one night,
That is the way they treat you
  Over at the fight.

. . .

After the fight is over,
  After the fight is done,
What will the people of El Paso do
  With their furnished rooms?
Hack fare will still be a quarter,
  Mr. Campbell will still be mayor,
That will be some consolation
  After the fight.

Directly below the poem was this ad: "Fitzsimmons' Favorite: Won the belt. Best cigar on record. For sale only at No. 35, Main St., across the river. Watch the number." Another ad, taken out by W. H. Tuttle and made to look like a news item complete with headline, read:

Arrested!
Fitzsimmons, Maher and Stuart as they
were passing the Masonic building BY THE
FINE DISPLAY of picture mouldings and frames,
from the following well known firms. . . .

Clearly the businessmen of El Paso were prepared to face tomorrow only when tomorrow came. A fraudulent "Carnival Edition Guide and Sporting Directory" put out for the big event listed not only hotels, saloons and restaurants, but the addresses of several prominent madams—Gypsy Davenport and Etta Clark among them. Supply-side economics and free enterprise at their best.[23]

All the hotels were filled by January 25, two weeks ahead of the Valentine's Day fight date. And they weren't all filled by the appearance of William Jennings Bryan at the opera house—bimetallism just wasn't that big a drawing card, though the speech was a rouser nonetheless.

And no one, it seemed, was paying attention to the preachers. They sent their manifesto to newspapers around the country, trying to discourage visitors to no avail. They wrote to New Mexico's Atty. Gen. Harmon asking him to keep the fighters out of the territory; Harmon replied the authorities would make their own decisions on the matter.

Which made Dan Stuart even more amiable. "Enemies of the carnival can go ahead interviewing all the officials in Christendom but that will not interfere with the carnival events taking place as advertised."

The ministers' dire predictions were gradually being dissipated like smoke. Stuart arranged for a corps of northern detectives at his own expense to watch over the crowd, but it hardly appeared necessary. Anyone with an unbiased eye could see things were as peaceful as ever.

One local man asked the *Herald,* "Where are all those bums and thugs that were so much talked about a short time ago? I expected to see a lot of tough mugs here by this time and have been burying all my silverware and sending all my gold watches to a safety deposit vault." He looked around and decided, "If there is any great amount of drinking going on it seems to be done by our own citizens." Obviously, "somebody must have made a mistake."

It wasn't Dan Stuart, that much was certain. In other towns, mass meetings connected with the fight always denoted fierce opposition voiced harshly in the flickering torchlight. When a mass meeting was called for El Paso's courthouse on January 29, it was not to protest, but to discuss ways of lobbying the railroads to reduce fares so still more people could join the carnival.

Wun Lung commented on the feeble protests by writing of the ministers: "They might as well have gone out and written their resolution on a board fence with a piece of chalk and then turned a stream of water on it, for all the good they will do. It is queer that some people won't attend to the business they are paid for, and go out of their way to try and make it unpleasant for other people." Giving his own theological view on the matter, the reporter said, "I believe if praying will stop that fistic carnival it would move Mt. Franklin."

Nearby Mount Franklin didn't budge. And neither did Dan Stuart, the undisputed winner of round five.

ROUND SIX: El Paso, Part Two

Yes, you may announce to the world that the carnival will take place . . . and that all doubting Thomases may pack their grips and come right on to El Paso if they desire to see the greatest glove contests the world has ever known.

—Dan Stuart,
El Paso Herald,
January 29, 1896

This bill will undoubtedly put a stop to the whole business. . . . There is no doubt whatever but that the president will sign it.

—Thomas B. Catron,
El Paso Times,
February 6, 1896

IF THE MINISTERS' PRAYERS were working, it was with a scattergun effect.

Peter Maher's train into El Paso was, in the Reverend Kilgore's amended terms, "hindered" on its way by wrecks on other roads. Fitz's traveling companion, the wrestler Emile Roeber, came down with pneumonia and returned to New York. The high altitude was adversely affecting Maher's roadwork, and at one point his training was put off due to a painful boil in the small of his back. Late in January, Fitz broke Stelzner's nose while sparring.

The spring-like weather enjoyed through December turned to thunder, lightning, and heavy rain late in January—it was the area's worst rain in seventeen years and left the streets a muddy quagmire for horses, wagons, and pedestrians. The *Chicago Record* reported that "some adobe huts seem ready to melt" in the downpour.

Then one muggy night, the thrashing Fitz had a dream.

"He dreamed that he whipped Maher in nine rounds," said the *Chicago Record,* "but that Peter was so hard to finish that in the ninth round Fitzsimmons had to sit on him and bump his head against a stump in order to put him out." A bad omen?

As if a Mutual Hostility Society meeting had been called, Fitz was rapidly being surrounded by people with grudges against him (or vice versa). Joining Jimmy Carroll in town were fighter Jim Hall, who had a beef against Fitz going back several years, the Australian's bitter ex-manager Captain Glori, now managing Horace Leeds, and Joe Vendig was due in any day.

The only thing missing from this prayerfest was a plague of locusts, or, as in *Julius Caesar,* lions in the streets.

Actually, there was one lion loose in the streets. He went by the Roman name of Nero. Or, as Theseus says in *A Midsummer Night's Dream,* "Here come two noble beasts in, a man and a lion."

Big cats were not unknown in the southwest. Mountain lions still hunted the arid landscape and *barrancas* of Mexico and were justly feared. But a two-hundred-pound, African male lion was something altogether different.

"Fitzsimmons' lion is the terror of the Mexican town across the border," reported the *Chicago Record.* Nero was now large enough "to tear a man to pieces if he wanted to," but so far had refrained from doing so. Martin Julian was said to live in terror of his boss's pet. The local labor pool was not notably filled with "Housekeeper/Lion Tamer" applicants and a number of respondents fled for the hills on sight of Nero. They eventually hired a Mexican woman, who spoke little English and was "always on the verge of hysteria through fear of the lion."

The playful pussycat wasn't satisfied with trying to eat Fitz's bicycle for Christmas dinner. A month later he tried his paws on a punching bag—a "crazy bag" fastened to both floor and ceiling. The *Herald* found it more amusing than the kitty:

"He sat up on his haunches and swiped the bag a blow with one paw and then with the other until the bag came back at him and hit him square in the mouth. Nero did not like this and made a dive for the bag with his mouth, but that only made matters worse, as every time he touched the bag it would fly back and hit him harder. Nero at last lay down and looked at the bag and seemed to be studying out a plan by which he could get the best of it."

Wun Lung visited Fitz one day and was introduced to the household's mascot. Nero "jumped upon my back several times and almost knocked me down," he reported, until the lion got used to him. "We became pretty well acquainted, and I didn't feel like he would chew me up for a meal; I wasn't meat enough." The visit enabled Lung to see a performance that rivaled Sullivan's tussle with Dan the goat in La Salle.

Fitz was sharing an adobe wall with a nanny goat named Princess, who supplied milk for Bob junior. Nero spied the goat and leaped onto the wall. Lowering her head, Princess "shot into the lion with such a whack that Nero was knocked clear off the wall, and looked as if someone had been treating him in an ungentlemanly manner." The victory gave Princess enough confidence to set her sights on the ex-blacksmith. Taking a run at him, she butted Fitz off the wall as well.

A week later the two animals had another get-together that roused the whole town. Nero was again loose in the yard when he encountered the belligerent Princess, once more atop the wall. Perhaps remembering their first bout and desiring a rematch—though having posted no stake money— the lion leaped.

They met head on and Princess knocked him off again. With blood in his eye, Nero went after the goat a third time, and Princess made a bleating retreat for the street, the lion in hot pursuit.

This produced pandemonium. Women screamed, men shouted, bare-footed children yelled, and all ran for their lives as the goat and lion raced through the dusty streets, Fitz, Julian, and Stelzner coming fast behind them. A shortcut through a vacant lot enabled Fitz to intercept Nero and drag him home.

The authorities had a little talk with Fitz after that and Nero was put on a good stout chain, though he still had the run of the house. No one knew that better than Dan Stuart. He was having a pigeon potpie dinner with Fitz one evening when the lion, responding to a call from the fighter, leaped onto the dinner table with a roar, nearly toppling Stuart over backwards.

Something else the Juarez authorities did was cite Julian and Fitzsimmons for operating an amusement—that is, charging admission to the training—without the proper license. Rather than pay the fee, the facility was closed to visitors.

The ill effects of all that antagonistic praying for hindrance appeared to reach as far as Illinois, where John L. Sullivan lost another fight—this time with a train.

The first reports made light of it. Said the *Herald:* "Poor old Sully has many ups and downs in this life, but night before last he got lower in the ditch than ever—he stepped off the hind end of a moving train. He picked himself up and offered to fight any man that put hands on him."

The *Times* wrote, "John L. Sullivan has been boozing again. He walked off the rear platform of a moving train night before last and was not injured."

In fact, the matter was far more serious.

It happened between Rock Island and Peoria, when the train was going forty miles an hour. Officially, no one was saying Sullivan was drunk but that the train "gave a sudden lurch" while he was getting some air at the rear. He missed a grab at the railing and "in an instant he was hurled to the ground and rolled about thirty feet."

When his absence was noticed three or four minutes later, the train was stopped and put in reverse. They found him two miles back, lying unconscious on his face. His clothes were on fire, matches in his vest pocket having been ignited by the fall. The ex-champ's face was badly cut and there were knee and shoulder injuries as well. He did not regain consciousness for forty minutes. He was told to stay in bed a week to avoid possible "fatal complications."

Game trouper that he was, Sullivan went on stage that night.[1]

That scattershot praying seemed to be affecting nonfighters as well. Mrs. George Darrow, a shooting gallery operator, took offense at the *El Paso Tribune* hinting she was attracting married men to her place of business. Mrs. Darrow declared, "I am an honest, hard working woman," and as for the local newshounds, "I do not intend to allow any person to try and besmirch my reputation." She resolutely showed up at the *Tribune*'s office and proceeded to horsewhip editor J. B. Fitch on the front steps. Fitch, the ponderous ex-chief justice of the Arizona Supreme Court, managed to get hold of the quirt after being struck three times and crashing through a glass door.

(The irony was that freelancer George Speck wrote the story, and Fitch, it was said, "had no authority to overlook his copy." Mrs. Darrow horsewhipped the wrong man.)

That was the kind of year 1896 was turning into—crazy. And if a plague of locusts wasn't readily available for the ministers to use, perhaps a new blast from Jim Corbett would suffice:

"Yes, it is true that I shall re-enter the ring and that I will challenge the winner of the Maher-Fitzsimmons fight." It was the shortest retirement on record, almost three whole months.

The man who once said he'd fight Fitz "for a shoestring," for a five-dollar bill, for glory, or for fun, reiterated his insistence on a $20,000 guarantee that Fitz would show up. "I am disgusted at Fitzsimmons' actions in the last match and I will not again chase him all over the country and lose time and money in an effort to fight him."

Apparently preferring an opponent nearer at hand and smaller in size, Corbett reportedly attacked a Philadelphia fireman who accused him of smoking in his dressing room at the National Theatre. A. M. Murphy claimed Corbett first shoved him from the room and then struck him twice. Murphy responded by punching the champ in the mouth, drawing blood. In the struggle that ensued, the fireman claimed to have thrown Corbett down the stairs. Mounting the stairs in rage, Corbett again attacked the official, but the two were quickly parted.

Corbett later denied the whole thing and said that Murphy exaggerated to make himself look important. Following that episode and the one in Green's Hotel in August, one thing should have been clear: Corbett ought to stay out of Philadelphia.

Nobody in El Paso was paying much attention to the antics of the unretiring champ anyway. He was yesterday's (and maybe tomorrow's) news. All eyes now were focused on the Irishman, Peter Maher (the "a" in his name, El Pasoans were told, was pronounced the same as the "a" in "at"). His training regimen was scrutinized closely for signs of strength and weakness.

The people of Las Cruces had provided a house and an Irish cook for the fighter. A cook of whatever nationality was indispensable, as Maher loved to pack away the food: a typical dinner consisted of two broiled chickens, baked potatoes, homemade bread and tea, plus whatever else was handy.

Mornings were for roadwork; the afternoons were taken up with sparring, wrestling, and bag punching, though the challenger showed little enthusiasm for formal training. The *Herald* said Maher "believes in taking life easy, joking with all that call to see him and guying the life out of his training companions."[2]

J. J. Quinn was hard put to dispel that lazy image, and the one about Maher being presented the title by Corbett.

"Richard K. Fox [of the *Police Gazette*] offered Peter Maher the championship belt at the suggestion of Corbett," explained Quinn. "Maher declined to accept it on the grounds that he had not won it by fighting, and that he would not take it any other way."

According to Quinn, the Maher master plan was to whip Fitzsimmons, whip Corbett, then take to "whipping all others as fast as they come to him." Unlike Sullivan and Fitzsimmons, "Peter bars no color, and they can come at us in all shapes of physical fitness or infirmities."

Someone was indeed coming to do battle, though as yet little notice was being taken beyond a short, jokey paragraph in the afternoon paper:

"The report comes from Dallas that the adjutant general will come to El Paso in a few days. He is probably coming to select a seat to an event that will occur in other territory."

It was openly speculated that the fight would take place in either Mexico or New Mexico. In the latter territory, the *El Paso Herald* had so far found only one positive editorial comment about the fight, that written by a New Mexican editor who "has been pummeled with clubs, guns and brass-knucks with periodic regularity during the last three years." (Being an editor was tough work in those days.)

Without naming the man or his paper, the *Herald* quoted the opinion on February 1: "To the editor it seems there is no more harm in a prize fight than in a sermon if it is properly conducted. Men who object to prize fighting frequently carry a big six-shooter for defense. . . . Men are occasionally killed in the prize ring but they also drop dead in pulpits about as often and with as much cause."

The *Herald* thought Stuart should send the man a free ticket.

At the rate tickets were selling, both in person and by mail, he'd have to do it quickly.

Along with requests for tickets and information, the *Times* reported that carnival headquarters received everything from crank letters (like the reptile roundup offer and pleas for money and free souvenirs) to fight challenges. One of the latter came from a heavyweight named Denver Ed Smith to take on the winner of the main event. He was backed by Harry M. Wildon, sporting editor of the *Cincinnati Enquirer*.

Wildon was yet another name crossed off of Fitz's Christmas card list and the fighter bristled indignantly at mention of the man's name. "That man Wildon is the fellow who said I would be tarred and feathered should I ever visit Hot Springs." Typically, Martin Julian exploded: "Let Smith place the money in some gentleman's hands and we will consider his proposition." It was as if he could still smell the bubbling tar.

As February came and the fight date grew ever nearer, the Minister's Union became desperate and sought reinforcements. The populace of El Paso being unimpressed by cries of doom and gloom, and rumors spreading of the fight being held outside the city, they again appealed to New Mexico's Gov. William Thornton to stop it. This time the reply was so much to the point that the ministers did not release it to the press—El Paso heard the general contents only after the governor's own newspaper, the *Santa Fe New Mexican,* gave the gist of it.

Thornton's letter to the ministers said he was powerless, having no statute against fighting, no money for his territorial militia, and no chance

El Paso's "moral element" was righteously led by the Ministers' Union, many of whom were still on hand when this photo was taken two years later. *Back row, left end:* Rev. C. J. Oxley, Trinity Methodist Church. *Back row, right end:* Rev. Adolf Hoffman, First Methodist Church. *Front row, left end:* Rev. Leander Millican, First Baptist Church. *Front row, center:* Rev. Hallam, First Christian Church. In a 1930 newspaper article, Hoffman wrote that their effort in 1896 was "one of the most history-making actions ever taken by ministers of El Paso" and that the ensuing fight was "a classic in the history of pugilism." Courtesy El Paso County Historical Society.

of his "helpless" deputies getting military help, as there was an Act of Congress forbidding it.

The New Mexico legislature had a chance to pass an anti-prizefight law the previous winter but declined to do so. Understandably, as living in the wild territory was not exactly a church social. Even the governor was not above duking it out. Early in January he came to blows with his tax collector, a man named Sharmon. The *Herald* commented: "Both are rather old and out of practice, so no harm was done."

Now this same governor was upset by the public disclosure of his earlier, "personal" letter, feeling it would only encourage fighters to invade his territory. Through his newspaper, Thornton expressed his displeasure with the clerical tactics: "From the manner in which the El Paso Ministers' association has managed its opposition to the pugilists it would seem that a more appropriate title for their organization would read: 'The El Paso Ministers' association for promoting prize fighting in New Mexico.'"

Now that must have stung.

Which is probably why the Union next turned to the pastors of Las Vegas, New Mexico, for help. Spurred on by their Texas colleagues, the Vegas pastors sent their own letter to Thornton on behalf "of all the righteous people of New Mexico." They called the fights "immoral and pernicious influences," expressed their sympathy with their besieged brethren, and beseeched (if not bedeviled) the governor to stand as firm as the Rock of Ages.

"An opportunity is yours such as few men ever enjoy," wrote the pastors. "You have the power as our executive. Will you use it and bring to yourself honor and the approval of a righteous people and of Almighty God upon you?"

Dan Stuart didn't quite know what the fuss was all about. "Neither Governor Thornton, the Minister's Union nor any federal official can prevent these contests and they need not worry their brains over the matters."

Which must have made someone in Mexico City uneasy because that same day the Associated Press carried this item: "Secretary of the Interior Cozio has wired the state government of Chihuahua that no prize fight must be allowed at Juarez. Five hundred rurales (rural troops) will be sent there to prevent a fight. The rurales are composed of the hardest fighters in the Mexican army." Joaquin Cortazar, the vice governor of Chihuahua, assured Señor Cozio that "energetic measures have been directed to prevent its taking place" in Juarez. Meanwhile, Juarez authorities put a temporary halt to the "surfeit of gambling" that had dominated the fiesta.

Things were definitely getting stirred up.

As if to show that all religious-minded folks were not in agreement, fighter Horace Leeds hit town and announced that Stuart would have to rearrange his fight card. Leeds was a Sunday school teacher and would not fight on Sunday the 16th as scheduled. Stuart held firm.

Dan Stuart was getting a mite testy. "I am over $25,000 out of pocket by reason of the Hot Springs affair and pride myself of a sufficient amount of ordinary intelligence to have profited some by that experience. Every dollar of the purses offered for the five fights scheduled is up. This money goes to the fighters whether they get into the ring or not. Think you, do I look like a fool? Would I tie up all this money on a gamble or a chance?"

It is, he declared, "an absolute certainty that all of the fights will take place. This is final and irrevocable."

Fighters, managers, trainers, newspaper men, sportsmen and fans continued pouring into town—ten to fifty on every train. The police were complaining—not of rowdiness, but of such orderly deportment; there was no one to arrest.

Joe Vendig arrived on February 1 along with Maher's biggest backer, the flamboyant Michael "Buck" Connelly, who was immediately taken to Las Cruces by John J. Quinn.

Rumor had it that Connelly was heading a syndicate that had $25,000 to bet against Fitzsimmons' admirers from New Orleans. When asked about the matter, the cagey Connelly replied, "We are not after New Orleans money especially—anybody's money will suit us." Then he went searching for Joe Vendig to see how much cash "Circular Joe" was carrying.[3]

Members of the working press were billeted at the Lindell Hotel and runners were standing by to rush fresh copy to the Western Union office. The press corps itself did a lot of its background work in the tenderloin saloons. One group went on a fact-finding trek with police Capt. Frank Carr as a guide. Afterwards, Carr was impressed with the reporters' professional tenacity in digging up depravity and going where even angels feared to tread; he said they found out more in one night than he had in several years. Journalism was thankless work.

On February 2, the *New York World* covered more than half a page with pictures of the ten fighters lined up for the carnival and wrote, "the eyes of the entire sporting world are turned Southward and all roads lead to El Paso. It is the promised land for the dead-game fraternity."

It was the *World*'s opinion that this "feast of fighting" would take place in the Juarez bullring. "A few years ago Juarez was a city of adobes, but now its principal business street is lined with brick buildings of modern architecture." The bullring in season was said by the paper to be "a scene of enchantment" for Americans, a place where society ladies from New York and even London rubbed elbows with señoritas, Indians, and cowboys.

The *Chicago Record*'s correspondent, future humorist and playwright George Ade, instructed readers on the mystique of bullfighting. "The bullfighter here in Juarez occupies the same relative place as the matinee actor in the states. He devotes most of his leisure time to fascinating the young women, and it is clearly fixed in his own mind that he is irresistible."

Bullfighting did not appeal to the youthful Ade, who thought "it is a sad commentary that the 'sport' gives the bull no chance to save himself from death." He did not expect the spectacle to appeal to visiting Americans, "but they are expected to attend out of curiosity."

Ade noted that bullfighters were paid well—Morena, from Madrid, would get $500 a fight. He also mentioned that the fiesta's manager Daguerre "holds the gambling concession for the state of Chihuahua and pays $60,000 a year for it, and even at that his profits are said to be very large."

Which might explain all the gambling at the fiesta.

Back in October, the Mexican consul in Laredo told the Associated Press, "We do not need money and if we did we should not sell Mexican dignity for any amount of it." L. Lamedax Diaz made his position clear: "I am officially authorized to state President Diaz will not permit the fight to take place on Mexican soil."

Despite the strong condemnation of boxing by Mexico's president during the Dallas and Hot Springs phases of the carnival, it was still widely assumed that the fight would be held south of the border. Dan Stuart continued to send representatives to Mexico City, hoping to work out a concession, and that fueled the rumors. The expected arrival in Juarez of Gov. Miguel Ahumada and other state officials on February 6 appeared to signal a victory.

The carnival continued to move forward, progress not even slowed by a blaze in the training quarters of Scott Collins that brought out half the town and the entire fire department. The building was saved and no one was hurt. More errant prayers?

Bat Masterson left Denver with five other men—reputedly seasoned gunfighters—to take charge of Stuart's security arrangements and keep order at ringside.

And the church ladies of El Paso were outraged that women would be permitted to attend the fight. A resolution was circulated saying, "We, ladies of El Paso, hereby protest against having the fair name of our city and our characters so besmirched. We wish it understood that we consider the carnival a disgrace to the city and the invitation to ladies to attend an insult to every true woman of El Paso and womanhood everywhere."

What they thought of Mrs. Darrow's horsewhipping of editor Fitch went unrecorded.

Jim Hall was already helping to get Maher into shape and, not too surprisingly, working on his animosity toward Fitzsimmons. Their contretemps went all the way back to their days together in Australia. The two fought for the first time in 1888, for four rounds and no decision. The same thing happened later in the year. They met again on February 10, 1890, and Fitzsimmons knocked him out in one round.

As Hall was a leading contender for the Australian middleweight title at the time, this was not good. They fought again just two days later *for* the title. The match was fixed.

"I was a green country boy," Fitzsimmons later said by way of explanation. "They said if I would let Hall whip me he would be the champion, and they would take me to America and England and France and Germany, and I would dine with dukes and get four pounds a week boxing." Seduced by such largess, "I consented to lay down."

It was put in the record books as a fourth-round knockout by Jim Hall. Fitz had his first fight in America three months later. Ruby Rob had the American middleweight title and had already whipped Peter Maher when he was again matched with Hall. This time it was in New Orleans, March 8, 1893, (by coincidence, the same day Fitz became a naturalized citizen).

The $37,500 purse was then the largest ever offered, so big that after the bout the *New Orleans Picayune* predicted, "The day of extravagent purses ended last night." (In a prescient commentary that foreshadowed the Corbett-Fitz affair, the paper said that "the story of how often they were nearly matched, what they said of each other, and how their matches fell through would make a book of reasonable proportions.")

Hall was favored but the odds vacilated greatly during the day of the fight. When the gong finally sounded, the old bitterness sent both men flying at each other savagely.

It was over in the fourth when Hall left himself unprotected for just a second, which was all the opening Fitzsimmons ever looked for or needed: Hall went down like a dead weight, "felled and whipped by the cleanest knockout blow ever seen in the local ring."

Fitzsimmons, the new citizen, felt vindicated. "This fight is the first opportunity I have had to get square," he said afterwards. Hall wanted a rematch but didn't get it.

So it came to be that Jim Hall was now in Maher's camp, trying for a proxy retribution. He said, perhaps with a certain amount of malice aforethought, "I don't believe that Fitz will last more than four rounds with him. And it wouldn't surprise me much if Peter whipped him right off the reel."

Maher was still playing at training, kicking a football around and raising large clouds of choking dust. Hall just shrugged. "We let him do about as he likes. You couldn't hurt that big fellow; besides, he doesn't need any more training."

And unlike Fitz, wrote the *Chicago Record,* Maher "never cripples any of his trainers." A low blow, that.

Fight news was temporarily pushed off the local front pages with the disappearance of Col. A. J. Fountain, a prominent Las Cruces lawyer, and his nine-year-old son. Posses were formed, and the armed men gave the crew at Maher's training camp considerable anxiety. Marshall, Murphy, and Burns were all training with Maher, and the fighters commented that they wanted no trouble out West because "a man with a gun has too long a reach."[4]

More people arrived, including Joe Walcott and Bat Masterson. The *Herald* described Walcott as a "low, chunky built fellow and as black as the ace of spades, but he is strong, gritty and a good fighter."

The *Times* said the Barbados welterweight was "tar-black" and "FAT like unto a possum," but was unafraid of Collins, though "Bright Eyes" towered over him by eight inches. George Dixon was on the same train, and the *Herald* took to calling the two "Little Chocolate" and "Charcoal Joe."

The suave Masterson was "welcomed by all the visiting and local fancy." El Paso's party was well under way.

The ministers were not laying down on their self-appointed task of stopping the carnival. They tried Governor Thornton again, and this time he seemed to have found a loophole. "In the absence of a special law," wrote Thornton, none too enthusiastically, "we are therefore compelled to seek for a remedy under the rules of the common law adopted in this territory. By the provisions of this law, every person engaged in prize fighting is guilty of having committed an assault and battery, and can be arrested and punished for this offense."

Thornton dutifully passed this reading of the law along to all authorities close to the Texas border and tried to wash his hands of the whole affair.

It wasn't good enough for the El Paso ministers. Reverends Hallam, Oxley, and Millican, on behalf of their Union, next wired El Paso's congressman in Washington, J. V. Cockrell: "Undoubtedly prize fight in New Mexico. Neither territorial nor federal law prohibiting. Can't congress prohibit immediately."

This tactic did not set well with local businessmen. The *Times* quoted an angry "merchant and church man" as saying, "Only two or three preachers are doing this mischief. They floated in here and have no interest in the town outside of the salary paid them by their congregations and if we are bankrupted by their doings and El Paso becomes too poor to support them they can float away to some other town. I think the people who own property here should have something to say as to what they want."

This time, however, the ministers were barking up the right tree, for in Washington their pleas found an able and willing ally, delegate Thomas Benton Catron, a man who, according to the *Times* of El Paso, "enjoyed an unsavory reputation in New Mexico for morality and political intrigue."

The territory of New Mexico was a hotbed of special interest groups, called "rings," whose primary motivations were power and greed. The biggest was based in the capital and known variously as the Santa Fe Ring and the Land Grant Ring. It was organized by Catron and another shrewd attorney, Stephen Elkins. Elkins went east to become secretary of war under Benjamin Harrison, but Catron stayed in the wide-open territory and carved out a spectacular chunk of it for himself.

One method of extending the boundaries of his power base was to defend native land grant cases in court and take part of the land in fee. Catron was beyond doubt the biggest gobbler of land in the business—by 1883 he had accumulated well over 800,000 acres and was one of the biggest landowners in America.[5]

Strong-arming and bribing voters were just small parts of Catron's bag of tricks, and he dominated territorial politics for over twenty years. Governor Thornton was a one-time partner in Catron's law firm, but now the two men were sworn enemies.

Catron's reputation was such that, when he was nominated as congressional delegate in 1895, the *Durango* (Colorado) *Democrat* wrote: "Catron has a record that would stink a Ute out of his tepee."[6] Which doesn't say much for Catron *or* Utes.

Catron was a brusque man, easily Dan Stuart's rival in rotundity, and one both respected and feared. He was a staunch advocate of statehood for New Mexico, not least of all because it would nearly double the net worth of his massive land holdings. It's likely that Catron saw prizefighting as an obstacle to statehood, since the sport was so universally outlawed. That would have been more than enough motive to take up the gauntlet of the El Paso Ministers' Union. But there was the added incentive of being able to badger Thornton.

What became known as the "Catron anti-fight bill" was introduced on February 5, a Wednesday.

"The New Mexico line is within about three miles of El Paso," Catron explained to those House members not up on their geography, "and can be reached on the Southern Pacific Railroad from that city. The governor [Thornton] has stated that he knows of no law in New Mexico by which these prizefights can be stopped. I believe they could be stopped if the governor desired to stop them; but it seems that he has no such disposition. The Congress of the United States can control these Territories."

He told them how: "The bill I have prepared is an exact copy of the law that has lately been adopted by the State of Texas at a special session of the legislature of that State." The only change he made was to increase the penalty to a five-year minimum sentence. Citing the lack of time, Catron urged that the bill be passed without lengthy committee consideration.

The only objection that morning came from Massachusetts Representative William Knox, who disliked the stern punishment for those aiding and abetting fighters. When told that spectators too, regardless of age, could be jailed for five years, Knox retorted, "It might as well provide for capital punishment."

No further objection was raised and the bill was sent to the Committee on the Judiciary which unanimously approved it by mid afternoon, at which time it was returned to the House. Catron was elsewhere, but the bill had another strong advocate.

David B. Henderson of Iowa presented the rewritten bill for unanimous agreement. He defended the increased penalty by declaring that "the sentiment of the country is absolutely against this barbarous practice." The bill would also put an end to amateur boxing in colleges.

A member named Sherman provoked general laughter when he said, "Let me ask the gentleman from Iowa whether this would cover fights between the bulls and bears in the bucket shops of Washington?" Henderson retorted, "I will have to leave that to someone who is more familiar with that branch of the subject than I am. I have no acquaintance with the bucket shops of Washington." (A bucket shop was an unsavory brokerage house that would make a profit by taking an order at a set price, buy at another, and keep the difference. This was later made illegal.)

When Representative John Dalzell of Pennsylvania wondered aloud if this would stop dueling, Henderson said, "Oh, no; not at all. We can not afford to stop that."

The bill, with a softer penalty (not less than one year or more than five in prison), was passed and went to the Senate.[7]

Back in El Paso, reported the *New York World,* Dan Stuart "only smiles. No matter what happens Dan Stuart smiles." The gong and ring ropes were now in Stuart's office, and his terse comments were upbeat:

"You can say for me that so sure as the principals are alive and in condition to get into the ring on the date set for the contests, so sure will they fight, and fight to a finish. If anybody evinces any sort of doubt as to this, I will lay them four to one for any part of $50,000."

He mentioned that Bat Masterson had arrived "and he will have much to do with the protection that will be accorded visitors." Whether from rowdies or from the law, he did not specify.

The Senate passed the bill in three readings and sent it to Pres. Grover Cleveland to sign. This had a discouraging effect in El Paso, and one wag commented that there'd be a grand ball at the Gem Dance Hall that night—provided Congress didn't object. Stuart remained publicly optimistic, saying there'd be a fight if he was the only spectator and the reserved seat cost him $10,000.

The *World* had no trouble affixing blame for the depressing turn of events: "It seems that the action in Congress was due to the efforts of the Ministers' Union. One week ago last Sunday they stopped praying against the carnival and began writing the authorities." Still, the desert around them was huge, and "the sports declare it will be strange if Dan Stuart does not find a battlefield somewhere in this vast wilderness."

The action in Washington also produced a response from President Diaz of Mexico: "I have a force of cavalry out scouting along the frontier, and I have ordered them to arrest anyone entering Mexico to take part in a prize-fight."[8]

Governor Thornton rushed to offset the remarks of Tom Catron by saying he was not only in sympathy with the bill, but that it was written at his suggestion. Which was hotly denied by Catron.

The livid Catron even charged conspiracy: "I believe Governor Thornton, while pretending he would like to stop the fight was actually acting in collusion with Dan Stuart in order to have the fight come off."

Thornton's reply was characteristic: "Catron reminds me of a boy with his first pair of boots; he has got his first bill through and he is strutting around with a chip on his shoulder snapping at every one."

In New Mexico, this was called politics as usual.

At the war department, authorities told the *Chicago Record* they had "an ample force of troops in New Mexico and adjacent to the border to take care of any number of sports who would likely be there to take chances of arrest."

On the day the Catron bill passed the Senate, pioneer moviemaker Enoch Rector arrived in El Paso. Five of his best men and all of the cumbersome apparatus ($15,000 worth of it) were already on hand to meet him. Despite everything, the plans were going ahead.

"El Paso still believes that Dan Stuart has something up his sleeve," the

Record told its Chicago readers, "and knows what he is talking about when he says he will pull off the fights no matter what happens in Washington." It attributed his "magnificent calm" to twenty years of poker playing. Still, with a week to go, Stuart's sleeves would have to hold a magician's entire repertoire of ready aces.

"Stuart's friends," reported Ade, "say that he has reached a point in the rugged path of management at which he is willing to drop all his money rather than to lie down and admit defeat." The fighters were ordered to go on with their training.

Snow was falling in El Paso when Grover Cleveland signed the bill outlawing prizefights in the territories on February 7.

While Dan Stuart merely smiled at the news, businessmen began striking their names off of church rosters and taking ads out of a church newspaper—the publication soon folded. The Ministers' Union was cursed in the streets.

By coincidence, that night was the coldest all winter.

The *Times* printed a heartfelt poem by "Mrs. W. F. H." which pretty well summed up the town's attitude toward its clergy.

The Prize Fight

"Someone" and his precious crew
Suddenly very pious grew,
And for the reputation great
Of El Paso and the state,

Straightway raised a din
Commenting on the sin
Of Fitzsimmons and Maher
And their followers there.

Church and religion are all right,
But to meddle with the fight
Is not their business now,
So why this awful row?

There are other things to do,
Deeds noble, good and true,
Let the pugilists alone
And seek work nearer home.

Daily, hourly, sinners fall,
Go and help them one and all.
Men and women need your care
More than this pugilistic pair.

The notoriety you sought
Was very very dearly bought.
Do you know how much is lost,
Did you count the financial cost?

If you have nothing more to do,
Seek green fields and pastures new,
For your work is now complete,
Shake El Paso's dust off your feet.[9]

The *El Paso Telegram* echoed the sentiments in an editorial: "If the carnival is defeated by the efforts of two or three men in this city they will occupy very unenviable positions as long as they dwell in El Paso. . . . There is a deep feeling against the ministers, which bids fair to result in a situation so warm for them that they will have to seek some other place to earn a living unless they can live on the interest of their money."

A disgusted Martin Julian received a telegram from Britain that read: "Should the contest not take place and there is no chance to pull it off, the National Sporting club of London will post five thousand pounds for a 20-round fight. Wire acceptance or declination to A. Lumley, New York."

Julian crumpled the wire and snarled, "Here we are fighting to a finish for a cheap purse and taking chances against soldiers when we might pull this off in the best sporting club house in the world and get a lot of money out of it."

The intensity of the praying must not have been turned down because misfortunes continued to plague the battlers. On the night of February 7, Billy Smith was approached by a drunk named Jack Shea, who demanded twenty dollars. Smith was tapped out, having just lost $200 at a keno table. He tried to get past Shea without being charitable and Shea pulled a knife. He swung at the boxer's face.

Smith dodged the blade and slugged Shea, staggering the would-be mugger. Shea came at him again; Smith ducked but the knife cut through his overcoat and drew blood. Furious, Smith tore into his assailant and was punching him vigorously when the police arrived and carted Shea away.

Four nights later Joe Walcott was in a saloon with "One-Eyed" Connelly and Captain Glori, when he was approached by a man "weighted down with six-shooters and bowie knives." The big Texan looked down on the 5'1½", 140-pound fighter. Without preamble, the stranger said, "So you're Walcott, are you? I'd like to kill you."

When ex-police chief Glori attempted to outline the rules governing barroom etiquette to the man, he was threatened with having his brains splattered about the room. Things became real tense, then two of the man's friends pulled him away.

Walcott took advantage of the moment and, with a reporter puffing alongside, "started to break all short-distance records in a wild dash for his training quarters." He was quoted as gasping out, "If I ever get in the house, I'll never come out again until the train is ready to carry me north." Under the circumstances, one could hardly question his attitude.

Maher no sooner had his boil cut out then he came down with a painful carbuncle. And for him the worse was yet to come.

Wun Lung felt the Muses calling and penned this:

> Says Dan, "the preachers make the claim
> We can't have that fight on earth,
> And as they own the whole shebang
> We'll hunt another berth.
>
> "Now on the quiet, I'll tell you,
> We're going up 'mong the stars,
> And you bet your boots we'll draw a crowd
> Up on the planet Mars."

Always above the fray, if not the stars, Dan Stuart worked on, assuring everyone he never had any intention of invading New Mexico. To be sure of that, and to save his political neck, Governor Thornton arrived in El Paso with Sheriff Ascarate of Doña Ana County and some deputies. They came to keep watch on the fighters' movements.

Stuart was not fazed—not nearly as much as when a couple of coots named Cactus Mason and Greasewood Ike, somewhat in their cups, ventured into the carnival office one day with a proposition.

Ike had heard tell of the Houston man's offer to kill a dozen rattlers in the bullring. He topped the offer by saying he could wipe out twenty in ten minutes, while his dog took on twenty-five rats in the same pit. And he only wanted $35 for the entire act. Tempting as it must have been, Stuart turned them down.

On the night of February 8, the lumber for the stage was loaded into a freight car standing alone on a siding. The circus tent and movie gear were also in the car. There was enough film in the car, at forty frames a second, for two hundred minutes (or roughly fifty rounds) of fighting. The car was located in a place where it could easily be attached to any line leading out of El Paso. It appeared as if a quick getaway was being contemplated.

Fitzsimmons, Maher, and the rest continued their training, Fitz running behind a buggy with Julian whipping the horse along El Paso Street.

Julian said the only thing that could save the Irishman was for Fitz to drop dead in the ring.

Congress or not, there was still a lot of interest in the fight. Betting around the nation was heavy and the *Chicago Record* reported that "perhaps never before in the history of fighting tournaments was there such an opportunity for 'combination' or pool betting. With five contests scheduled there are no less than thirty-six possible combinations on which the odds should range from 12 to 1 to 150 to 1."

The favorite line was: Fitzsimmons, Everhart, Walcott, Dixon, Barry. Fitz was the favorite now among the gamblers, though "Maher may give Fitz the surprise of his life."

A *Chicago Tribune* headline read, "NEW YORK IN A PUGILISTIC FEVER," and reported, "It is talked of in the cheap bar-rooms and it is discussed in the gilded Hoffman buffet. A sporting editor of a great New York paper had his head punched the other night because he expressed too freely in a saloon dedicated to Maher, the opinion that 'Lanky Bob' would crow on his victim before the carnival ended." On the morbid side, "the wife of a prominent New York pugilist had dined off rat poison all because she could not accompany her husband to the carnival."

The paper noted that "with Congress arrayed against the fight on the one hand and Mexican troops with loaded guns ready to interrupt" on the other, Stuart had but one chance: "It has dwindled down to a case of pure luck."

Referee/newsman George Siler arrived and talked with both heavyweights. Siler was doubtful. He filed a somewhat downbeat report to the *Tribune* in which he wrote, "There is no chance whatever of any of the fights . . . coming off in public."

To the local El Paso readers Siler was more optimistic. After a talk with the carnival's chief executive, the ref told the press, "I asked him how things were going and his reply was, 'We will pull off the fights.' That was sufficient for me. When Dan Stuart stands fronting an emergency and says it is all right, [he'll] make good what he says."

Bat Masterson was also satisfied, wiring friends in Denver to come on down to Texas. The situation seemed well in hand.

After a meeting with the principals, Stuart released a statement: "We are satisfied, first, that there is no possible danger of interference in any of the glove contests booked. The arrangements are perfect, and the battles will be fought out to finishes and under conditions which preclude all danger of interference from any source."

Ever the confident promoter, Stuart reassured doubtful fans by saying, "The fights will take place, and those who contemplate a journey here to witness them, can come on without the most remote misgivings or fear."

The fast action of Catron and the Congress should have delivered a knockout punch. But Dan Stuart, perhaps a little groggy, was still on his feet, bobbing and weaving.

Call round six a draw.

ROUND SEVEN: Rangers

*He said he would shoot the principals first and
fire on the spectators after he had settled our hash.*

—Bob Fitzsimmons

THE BUREAUCRATIC NOOSE being fitted around the carnival started
growing tighter. The first real pinch came from the south.

The *New York World*'s correspondent in Mexico City reported that
local papers "are vowing with intense impressiveness that the bellicose
Gringoes shall not stain their territory with gore. Here in the capital there
is even more excitement than down along the Texas frontier."

The excitement was such that the nation's highest political figure
issued some bellicosity of his own: "President Diaz himself declares that
he will hurl a big part of his army against the invaders the moment they
pitch the ring this side of the Rio Grande. The army is in daily practice
for such a direful emergency."[1]

Two companies of Mexican national infantry were moved to the Juarez
barracks to guard against, as rumored, a prizefight breaking out inside the
blood-drenched bullring.

An anonymous fight fan came up with a solution, however. A line of
stone monuments spaced six miles apart helped delineate the border
between Texas and Mexico (flooding sometimes shifted the riverbed and
caused jurisdictional confusion). One monument larger than the rest
stood straddling the three lands of Texas, Mexico, and New Mexico. Why
not move the marker and construct the ring so that the confluence of the
three territories hit smack dab in the center?

The *Chicago Record* cottoned to the idea and imagined what the news
flash might look like: "Maher rushed Fitz into New Mexico, but the
Australian dodged away and escaped into Texas. Maher led with his right,

but Fitz took it over his shoulder and countered with his left on the neck, staggering Maher and sending him into Mexico."

If only it were that easy. Still, Dan Stuart was not publicly showing any strain and opinions on the fight were being given just as if nothing untoward was going on.

Bat Masterson was cornered and predicted "a fierce, quick fight" that would go to whichever fighter struck hardest first. "If Maher lands one of his heavy blows on Fitz, the kangaroo can not recover. On the other hand, if Fitz gets in one of his knock-out punches on the Irishman it is good-bye Peter, and so it goes."

John L. Sullivan, on the mend and heading for Texas, agreed. "I think it will be a short battle, possibly not over four rounds." Sport that he was, he noted that the betting was now at ten to seven in Fitz's favor, and observed—somewhat wistfully, "If I had $15,000 or $20,000 I would like a whole lot of the short end of that betting."

That was assuming, of course, there would be a fight at all. The odds changed dramatically on February 9, and for the first time there was real fear in the fighters' camps.

It was that morning, the *El Paso Herald* reported, that fourteen "stalwart, bronzed and determined looking men" got off the train and entered the nearby Pierson Hotel for breakfast. Nobody dared approach "the resolute looking strangers."

Then one was recognized—Capt. John Hughes of the Ranger detachment ten miles to the north in Ysleta. Soon the identities of the other men became known: Adjutant General Mabry, from Austin; Capt. J. H. Rogers, of San Antonio; Capt. J. A. Brooks of Valverde. Plus "ten solid looking Texas rangers." And with that information, a chill went down a lot of El Paso spines.

It was not amiss that Adj. Gen. Woodford Haywood Mabry went unrecognized. On more formal state occasions he would array himself in his formidable dress uniform with its brass buttons and fancy epaulets, then mount his molasses-colored charger, every inch the military man. When he took to the field, he dressed much more plainly.

A native of Jefferson, Texas, the forty-year-old Mabry had attended the Virginia Military Institute and became adjutant general for Texas in 1891, under Gov. James Hogg. Mabry was kept on when Culberson became governor. Mabry was the man most credited with making the Rangers synonymous with swift, no-nonsense law enforcement. He personally led two companies against Mexican rebel Catarino Garza along the southern border.[2]

No one ever referred to Texas Rangers as a "happy-go-lucky" bunch, and this grim group of determined law enforcers demonstrates why. Adj. Gen. Mabry is at the left in the front row; then come Capt. John Hughes, Capt. J. A. Brooks, Capt. Bill McDonald, and Capt. J. H. Rogers. They and their stalwart men were charged with stopping the great fistic carnival during the El Paso phase. Courtesy El Paso Public Library's Southwest Collection.

The *Herald* described him as "a well built man of the average size, with florid complexion, flowing flaxen hair, and of few words; and what he does say is straight to the point." Contrary to earlier stories, Mabry and his men were not in El Paso to procure fight tickets.

And more were coming.

Opinions on just what or who the Rangers were or represented varied. The *New York World* said, "The rangers of Texas correspond to the militia of any Northern State, except that the men are mostly graduated cowboys, sheriffs and deputy marshals who are in active service all the time, and whose principal duty is to protect the border. The twelve who rode to town this morning wore big white hats and long revolvers and had lariats tied to their saddles."

The threat of using the Rangers to stop the fight had first been raised during the Dallas phase. At that time, the *New Orleans Picayune* said the Rangers were men "controlled by special laws, who know nothing of military red tape, and who quietly and secretly, as cowboys, move about and swoop down upon offenders and all who propose infractions of the law."

In September, when the *Chicago Tribune* interviewed the Dallas official identified only as "Jim," he voiced a guarded respect for the Rangers as "a sort of little standing army" entirely controlled by the governor. "They make a specialty of going it blind and shooting up everybody and everything the Governor tells them to."[3]

Culberson, through playing games, was sending in the most dreaded Ranger of them all. Arriving on the Texas & Pacific train from Amarillo just a few hours after Mabry, with another troop of men, was one who epitomized the tough, feared breed known as a Texas Ranger: Captain Bill McDonald.

Bill McDonald was a legend in his own time, a man who, it was said, "would charge hell with a bucket of water,"[4] and could "pick cherries with a rifle."[5]

He was born in Mississippi in 1852, coming to Texas with his family when he was fourteen. At sixteen he was tried for treason and acquitted— by Judge Dave Culberson, Governor Culberson's father. McDonald became a grocer at Brown's Bluff on the Sabine River where he palled around with the local justice of the peace, James Stephen Hogg. He became a Wood County deputy sheriff and soon established himself as both fearless and deadly.

McDonald moved around Texas a lot, changing occupations frequently, but behind a badge was where he was most comfortable—his exploits against train robbers and rustlers along the Cherokee Strip were near mythical. When Hogg became governor, he made McDonald captain of Company B, Frontier Battalion.

(It was a thinly stretched but busy battalion, responsible for scouting over 173,000 miles of wilderness. In two years the four companies accounted for the arrest of 676 criminals and the recovery of 2,856 head of stolen livestock, among other duties.)

In the Texas panhandle town of Amarillo, he had but eight men to help uphold law and order in one of the most lawless parts of the state. For a manhunter like McDonald, it was enough.[6]

The lean, mustached McDonald's favorite saying was, "No man in the wrong can stand up against a fellow that's in the right and keeps on a-comin'."[7]

There was no question that McDonald was one who kept a-comin'. And now he was in El Paso, and the fellas who were in the wrong were Fitzsimmons, Maher, and Daniel Albert Stuart. Something had to give.

Mabry met first with Governor Thornton, who promptly returned to New Mexico to arrange for more deputies to guard his border. Two days later Attorney General Harmon said, "If they fight on any territory of the United States we will follow them to the ends of the earth if necessary to bring them to justice."

Next Mabry met with Stuart at the Vendome Hotel. The adjutant warned the promoter that if any of the fights came off on Texas soil, the governor "would never rest until every person connected with them had been arrested and punished."

During their long talk, Stuart maintained that the sacred honor of Texas was in no danger of being violated. Not quite convinced, Mabry announced he would remain in El Paso for a spell. The company at Ysleta was moved closer to town. He had at least forty Rangers in town and perhaps thirty more at the ready. McDonald was assigned as Dan Stuart's personal watchdog.

With physical reinforcements in place, the Reverend Oxley took to his pulpit that night to soundly castigate Stuart, Thornton, the fighters, and anyone else with whom he disagreed. The Methodist Church was packed, mostly with women.

Pleadings for more divine hindrance were apparently answered when Peter Maher next took to his daily roadwork. Green and boggy Ireland had not prepared him for a Southwestern desert sandstorm, walls of blowing dirt hundreds of feet high that mask mountains and blot out the sun. The local weather, shifting again, quickly dried the mud, baked the earth, and kicked up the dust into a swirling ocean of grit. Maher ran right into it.

Alkali dust lodged in his eyes. Rubbing only made it worse. By day's end, what with more dust filtering down from his adobe quarters, and more rubbing, the sore left eye closed. The grit was removed, but the eye remained bloodshot and partly shut. Then the right one grew inflamed.

The fight was four days away.

"The whole enterprise," reported George Ade, was "done up in a fog of uncertainty." He said the Ranger force had increased and was camping close to the depot. Mabry "goes about in plain citizen's clothes and does not adopt the buckskin breeches, with white hat and big gauntlets of his fighting terrors."

Ade induced Bat Masterson, a budding sportswriter, to submit an article to the *Record.*

"That all this commotion has been stirred up because two men are going to box with five-ounce gloves seems to me to be utterly ridiculous," wrote Masterson. He figured Congress ought to have better and more important things to worry about and added, "There has been a good bit of four-flushing since this crusade against glove contests commenced, and any liberal-minded man has good cause to kick that so many sports should be ruined."

There was in fighting, he said, "less danger, indeed, than that jockeys will be killed, football players mangled and professional bicyclists maimed."

Dan Stuart, "an honorable sportsman," was a friend of Bat's. "To be sure, he has been up against it . . . since he launched his canoe on the tempestuous waters of the sea of pugilistic enterprises, but Dan is here to stay this time and if it comes down to cases will pull the fights off just to show that a Texan is not to be bluffed and hang the expense."

Just so long as the expense was the only thing hanged.

The *Las Vegas* (New Mexico) *Optic* agreed with Masterson, though in a backhanded way: "It does indeed seem that we are straining at gnats and swallowing camels when the whole power of a nation is put in motion to put down a fist fight between two fellows, both of whom deserve to be mauled anyhow."

The *El Paso Herald* thought this whole bizarre business would end up in school history books, if only because no one would ever see the like again: "The indications are that the fistic carnival that Dan Stuart says he will surely bring off will be the last of the kind that will ever occur. The tightening of the lines around prize fighting are being drawn so close that the death rattle can be heard. . . . The calling out of rangers and United States marshals, sounds in no uncertain tones the death knel [*sic*] to the prize ring in the United States."

Sullivan, on the Texas & Pacific train and just a day away from the action in Fort Worth, also thought pugilism was as good as buried. "The governors and the fighters who fought their big battles through the newspapers have killed the business. The day of the big purses is gone. Ten thousand dollars will be about as large a sum as we shall ever see hung up again."

Gen. Miguel Ahumada, governor of Chihuahua, arrived in Juarez with a secretary and interpreter on February 11, three days before the fight, to be one of its pallbearers.

Downtown Juarez, Mexico, decked out for a fiesta in 1891, just the way it looked to the later fight crowds. In the background stands the mission established by the Spanish conquistadors in 1650. It is still in use today, though it now stands beside a modern cathedral. Courtesy El Paso County Historical Society.

Ahumada stepped off the Mexican Central at nine in the morning. He was an imposing man, over six feet tall, balding, and sporting a mustache whose ends were twisted into sharp upward points. A goatee adorned his chin. A seasoned military leader, Ahumada had fought against the French in the time of Maximilian and later led a campaign against the Yaqui Indians in Sonora. He was named commandante of Chihuahua in 1886 and governor six years later. Banditry in his provinces was being eradicated under his stern policies. This was not a man to be trifled with.

The governor was lavishly greeted by a large crowd and a group of army officers. Mayor Tito Arriola of Juarez was on hand with an orchestra. Following the ceremonies and a tour of the city, the governor seated himself at a large table adorned with cigars and bottles and began receiving delegations.

The first to reach him was a committee of El Paso businessmen. Their talk was uneventful and did nothing to change the highly charged situation. Next came the Ministers' Union, led by the Reverend Millican. The governor had a statement ready for them concerning the fight.

"I came here personally to stop it, and will not under any consideration give permission for it. If the national territory be trespassed, or our law be violated, I decidedly resolved to inflict punishment on the offenders."

The mayor of Juarez said they'd have six hundred troops available by the day of the fight. The ministers departed, satisfied that his promise was "unequivocal."

The *New York World* illustrated the latest fight news with a cartoon showing a downcast Maher and Fitzsimmons being kept apart by a mustachioed caricature of a pistol-wielding, rifle-toting bandido wearing a sombrero with a large knife sticking through the brim. The figure was labeled "ranger," but was obviously a composite of what easterners imagined Rangers and Mexican soldiers to be like.

George Siler had an audience with Governor Ahumada and the *Tribune* published it on February 12, two days before the fight. Ignoring bullfighting and cock fights, both of which were highly popular in Mexico, the governor condemned prizefights without hesitation, though he had never seen one: "We understand it is brutal and degrading. None of the United States have permitted the pugilists to meet and pound each other, and if the pastime is so disgraceful that the Americans will not permit it to be practiced it is hardly likely the Mexicans will ever give it any countenance."

Would he arrest only the fighters?

"Everybody concerned in the breaking of the peace will be apprehended. This, of course, would include the spectators, for by their presence do they not encourage the pugilists and induce them to defy the authorities?"

The man designated to be in the center of the ring was undoubtedly worried at this point, for he asked, "Suppose they resist?" He reported the answer this way: "Then (with a shrug of his huge shoulders and a peculiar smile) I suppose they will be treated as soldiers usually treat lawbreakers who resist authority."

No further elaboration was necessary. As for fighting on one of the river's bancos, once mentioned by the Austin and Dallas papers, Don Miguel said, "Whichever country's officers or soldiers are nearest the lawbreakers at the time of the breaking of the peace will for that particular occasion have jurisdiction over the land in dispute." Prisoners would be tried by the arresting officers' country of origin.

The governor added, "We are a peace-loving and law-abiding people, and, being such, we certainly would not permit an exhibition in this country which will not be permitted in yours."

When told of the interview and the various moves against him, Dan Stuart never flinched. "I have given my word to all my friends that the fight will take place, and I have not yet asked to be excused. All I can say is that the fight will take place."

Not to be upstaged by a mere governor, Fitz gave an exhibition at his Juarez training quarters that afternoon and invited Ahumada. The governor accepted but sent a representative in his place. That night he watched Dixon and Walcott spar at the opera house and commented, "I do not like it as well as I thought I should from what I have heard about it."

Official resolve was not softened by the report of a prize ring death in Philadelphia—Frederich Schleichter was knocked down and his skull was fractured when he hit the floor. An ex-policeman named Henry Pluckfelder was jailed for murder.

The only public change from carnival headquarters was the announcement that James Lawlor was ill and could not make it to El Paso. Consequently Tom O'Rourke, the manager of Dixon and Walcott, was now the official stakeholder. He immediately placed the money in the State National Bank.

The unflappability of Stuart and his crew puzzled the *Chicago Record.* "Either they are impelled by blind courage, or else they are now relying upon one or more Mexican officials to willfully fail in the performance of duty," wrote George Ade. "There is nothing else to be figured from the situation."

Nonetheless, speculations were rampant. When it was suggested (by Ade) that a quick fifty-mile train trip would outdistance the cavalry of both countries, a Ranger told him why it wouldn't work. During the hunt for Geronimo, said the veteran Indian fighter, troops crossed the river from either side at will. The same cooperation could be expected this time:

"I'll tell you that if President Cleveland and President Diaz get it fixed between 'em all the armed men on both sides of the river could be put on the trail of those fighters to follow them up and arrest 'em, no matter where they attempted to fight. What's more, the whole thing is liable to be fixed up at any minute by telegraph. With the two countries on the proposition to prevent the prize-fight, the boundary line won't cut any figure."

If one looked west towards the territory of Arizona, there was no relief in sight. Governor Hughes, himself facing charges of misuse of his office, nepotism, and favoritism, was determined to follow in the footsteps of

Culberson, Clarke, and Thornton, and went overboard doing it. The militia companies at Phoenix, Tempe, Mesa, Yuma, and Tucson were all put on alert as of February 11, just in case that trainload of lumber headed for the Arizona border, the San Simon station being just four hours away from El Paso.

Hughes also asked the Interior Department to send a strong force of deputy marshals to help block the border. (When Hughes wired Mabry collect for an update on the situation, Mabry, the good bureaucrat, told the key operator, "Let Hughes pay for it.")

Dan Stuart was surrounded—armies to the left of him, the right of him, the front and the back of him. And the question everyone was asking two days before the fight was, "*Where?*"

The Carnival

Where shall it be? Up in a balloon or on the desert bare,
On mesa or in river bed, the echoes answer 'where?'
Some say it shall not be at all, but one stands undismayed
Altho' the powers of heaven and earth against him are arrayed—
    Dan Stuart says, "it shall be!"

The government vows it shall not be in Texas or in New Mexico,
And Diaz vows within his bounds the boxers dare not go.
But preachers may preach and rave and rangers may scour the plains,
The hero of the carnival treats threats with cold disdain,
    Dan Stuart says, "it shall be!"

From east and west and north and south the crowds are pouring in,
For there are wise and honest men who think such fights no sin,
El Paso men stretch forth their hands and welcome one and all,
They trust the word of that cool man whom nothing can appall,
    Dan Stuart says, "it shall be!"

These are no vulgar fights, but scientific tests,
Keeness of eye and strength of arm each dangerous blow arrests,
And rugged is the fighter's health and strong his arm and muscle;
Nigh scathless even the vanquished comes from out the fiercest tussle,
    Dan Stuart says, "it shall be!"

There's money in the game some say and doubtless it is true,
But empty plate would even make a minister look blue.
It seems this carnival must "go" as safe and sure as fate,
For notwithstanding all the vows yet made by church and state,
    Dan Stuart says, "it shall be!"[8]

For the Chinese inhabitants of El Paso, February 12 was New Year's Day and 1896 the Year of the Monkey. The "Celestials," as the local papers patronizingly called them, started the celebration on the night of

February 11, then held a joyous parade through downtown, complete with firecrackers and plenty of noise.

Despite their depression over the state of the carnival, now seen to be near collapse, the city's Anglo businessmen joined the party with a loud band and some noise of their own. The whoop-de-do helped distract attention from some monkey business of a more down-to-earth nature. Even forty rangers couldn't watch everything.

No one could find the railroad car with the movie equipment. Stuart and his associates had been playing a shell game with the Rangers—now you see it, now you don't. The car was shifted around on various sidings, shuffled in among other cars, always one step ahead of those who thought they had it cornered. Just when they were sure they had the right car's number, it would be opened and found to be empty of camera gear.

Late on the night of February 11, when the firecrackers started popping, Enoch Rector and his photographers vanished. It was said they had boarded a train and were headed for the battleground. But which train? Which direction?

The Rangers were beside themselves. When two railroad cars suspected of containing carnival equipment were attached to a westbound freight, the train was halted by Captain Hughes. It was 2:30 A.M. He placed four of his men on board, and they stayed there until reaching the state line. It was a false alarm.

"The Texas rangers," wrote the *Times*, "are a manly looking set of men and they are holy terrors to evil doers." But right now, they were growing frustrated.

When Fitz showed up at the depot the day before the fight and actually boarded a train, there was a near riot as rumors spread and people flocked to the platform—in a matter of minutes a thousand people had gathered, along with half a dozen Rangers. Some boarded the train. As it pulled out, Fitz hopped off—he had just been saying good-bye to some friends heading west. People muttered under their breath and Fitz returned to Juarez, feeling like the mouse who just made the cat chase his tail.

Mabry was not amused. He called in Julian and Fitzsimmons and told them precisely what would happen should the ring be pitched on the soil of Texas. This was no laughing matter to him. When they left, both men looked pale and very worried.

Fitz later related how Mabry told them "to keep out of the power of the United States Government," and that if they fought in his jurisdiction, "he would shoot to kill first and do the arresting afterwards."

A sobering thought. Asked if he believed this threat, Fitz said he had no doubt at all. "And to cap it all [Mabry] said he would shoot the

principals first and fire on the spectators after he had settled our hash."
The redhead announced that if the ring was set up in Texas, he'd rather
forfeit than be shot down. "I am not stuck on fighting," he said, not
totally for Mabry's benefit. "I can make my living in several other ways. I
can make horseshoes or go on the stage."

Mabry put more fear into Julian than did Nero.

Next, the adjutant general tried to put the squeeze on Stuart for his
train tricks. "I'm going to board that train of yours with my men at all
hazards," he told the promoter.

Said the sanguine Stuart, "All right." He offered to pay their fare as
well. This no doubt caused Mabry and Bill McDonald to exchange
glances, so Stuart explained. "You fellows are usually good company, and
I'll be glad to have you with us. Your duties will not amount to much,
though, for we are not going to violate any Texas law. I should like to
have you as my guests at the ringside."

What could he have up his sleeve?

All agreed, Mexico was out. Across the border a squadron of Mexican
cavalry had spread its squads north and west along the river; it looked like
preparations for a war were underway. Governor Ahumada ordered a halt
to the gambling and bullfights until the carnival ended, and said, "If the
fighters are found in Mexico my troops will at once open fire on them."

No one doubted him.

The commander of Fort Bliss, Colonel Parker, restricted all officers to
the post after 6:00 P.M.; this was seen as a sign that the troops might be
mobilized at a moment's notice.

Up in Las Cruces, seemingly out of harm's way, Peter Maher continued his training. Like his opponent, Maher was now a naturalized American citizen. "It is not in any spirit of egotism that I predict that I will
conquer the big Australian," Maher told reporters.

He looked back at their 1892 match and admitted he hadn't been
ready. "I was a big, strong fellow, to be sure, but a mere novice in the art
of boxing. I was hardly more than a boy and had but the most elementary
knowledge of the game of stop, hit and get away."

Looking back, he could only shake his head at his own inadequacies at
the time. "Even at that I had Fitz nearly out in the first round, but did not
know enough to take advantage of points I had gained. I also made the
mistake of sparring him at long range after that round instead of getting
in to him and fighting at close quarters."

This time, things would be different. "Fitz will have to knock me out
to win. I will fight while breath and senses remain."

He made no mention of his irritated eyes, but did take a figurative swipe at Sullivan, Corbett, and Fitz: "Of one thing my friends and the public can rest assured. I will never go on the stage, never become an actor or lecturer, but remain a fighter as long as youth, health and strength remain with me."

Governor Hughes of Arizona, meanwhile, was getting more and more hysterical as fight day approached. When Maj. R. Allyn Lewis reported from Bowie, just across the New Mexico line, that he had positive information the fight was heading straight for him, Hughes ordered three militia companies to Bowie to form a reception committee and warned the Southern Pacific Railroad Company not to participate in such a scheme.

Hughes's overreactions set off a number of rumors and stories about the state of things in Arizona. In one, his distraction was so acute that one morning he failed to notice when a waiter had dumped a plate of ham and eggs in his lap at breakfast. Then there was the nightmare, as reported in the *Herald*:

"[Hughes] would start up from a troubled nap every once in a while, and scare the wits out of his better half by leaping in the middle of the floor and calling loudly for United States troops and ordering the militia of Arizona and southern California under arms immediately if not sooner, to repel the threatened invasion of Dan Stuart and Bat Masterson with their mythical 100 armed Pinkertons."

Dan Stuart was so tickled by the daffy doings of Governor Hughes that he immediately sent Arizona's chief executive a telegram: "You may, like Horatius attempt to hold the pass, but with my ten thousand Pinkertons I will beat down your sorried columns and by forced marches reach San Francisco and hold my carnival before you can arrive on the scene."

Tweaking governors was becoming a full-time occupation.[9]

"He has 'come,'" wrote Wun Lung, "the only great John L. Can anything be added to our cup of happiness?"

He may have meant that ironically, but there was no denying the big, warm reception that greeted Sullivan and company at the depot—the ongoing Chinese New Year's festivities were completely overwhelmed by the brass band and open carriage ride to his quarters with "half the town staring at him."

The ex-champ's head still carried a turban of bandages and he kept to his room most of the day, uncharacteristically avoiding a welcoming bash at Si Ryan's place. But that night, woozy though he might have been, Sullivan hit the stage at the Myar Opera House.

He was greeted with loud and long applause. "With all his faults," noted the *Chicago Record,* "there will always be a warm spot in the hearts of all free Americans for the man who for twelve long years proved himself a fighter and a defender of his title. Not one stain rests against Sullivan that he ever 'laid down' until the ravage of time compelled him to succumb to a younger man."

The next morning's train brought two-hundred more fans to see the fight—what they found were steeply inflated prices (hotel rooms worth seventy-five cents a night a week before were now $5 a night) and Rangers. Lots of Rangers.

While the papers were gloating about the well-behaved crowd (with only a few notices of annoying conmen, muggers, and pickpockets), Adjutant General Mabry's view was slanted in favor of the ministers. The city, he informed state officials, "was full of desperate characters looking for spoils from whatever sources." His subsequent report charged Stuart with controlling the press coverage.

Mabry told his superiors, "two reporters informed me that Stuart exercised a kind of censorship over all dispatches; that he demanded they be colored in his favor, with a threat that unless it was so worded they could not see the fight."

There is no evidence of this. Most of the correspondents, being sportswriters, favored the fight before they ever arrived. As the big day approached and it was announced that the press would have to buy tickets, there may have been some hearty grumbling among those who expected free ringside seats.

Mabry lauded the Ministers' Union, "who represented a large class among the best citizens approving the Governor's action and upholding my methods," and questioned Stuart's integrity. "He had the dispatches to quote him as saying he would never violate the laws of Texas. If he does not do so every day in some of his gambling establishments, then common report has woefully misrepresented him."

Mabry's methods included placing "a close and constant espionage" on the principals, as well as "on the passenger depot and the cars loaded with paraphernalia of the ring." Nobody was going to pull a fast one on him.

Although the site of the match was still a secret, the *Times* reported that "those most directly interested have an abiding faith in Dan Stuart's ability to do what he says he will do. There is nothing to do but wait."

Those waiting were far from lonely. One day before the fight there were an estimated 1,500 visitors in town, with more to come—including a crowd from Mexico City. Along with the sports, troops continued to pour into Juarez, their strength expected to be up to five hundred men by the time of the bout, two hundred of them Rurales.

If that wasn't bad enough, the Las Cruces contingent was no longer being spared the attention of the authorities.

James Conroy, Murphy's trainer, looked outside on the night of February 12 and found their quarters "surrounded by as hard a looking set of men on horseback with rifles as I ever saw. They patrolled the house, that is within fifty yards of it, all night and had the life scared out of everybody." The situation was nerve-racking. "Neither Maher nor anybody in our camp is ready to die with his boots on, and unless Stuart can guarantee protection neither Maher, Marshall, nor Murphy will get in a ring."

Matters became worse. The alkali dust Maher got in his eyes earlier in the week had made him so blind that two days before the fight he couldn't see his hand in front of his face. J. J. Quinn moaned, "It must be these ministers prayed the blindness of Peter. They are a lot of disgusted sports in El Paso tonight."

The Irishman was brought to El Paso and ensconced in a room above Doc Albers' store. Dr. Alward White was summoned. After careful examination he pronounced Maher the victim of acute opthalmalia. He would not be allowed to enter the ring on Friday. Perhaps on Monday. A week for sure.

Which brought up the question of the $1,000 forfeit. Quinn argued that letting his fighter enter the ring in this condition would be "manslaughter." He asked for a week's postponement. It was taken under advisement.

Troubles continued to mount. Jimmy Carroll declared Fitzsimmons had owed him $900 for a long time and he filed suit to attach the stake money turned over to Tom O'Rourke. Stuart said none of that money legally belonged to Fitz.

At the same time General Mabry crossed the thin line between "espionage" and declaring a state of martial law. When he heard Maher was in town, two Rangers were dispatched to stand guard. When Fitz, Rose, and Rose's mother showed up at the opera house to watch Sullivan and Paddy Ryan emote, Mabry placed two more Rangers on either side of him, like bookends.

Doc Albers was incensed at the "indignity" of having his house watched, calling it "an act which is frowned down upon in our enlightened civilization even in the eastern monarchies," and vowed, "I do not intend to let this outrage go by unnoticed." He dashed off an angry letter to the editor of the *Times,* where it was printed the next day. His rage was

MAHER KNOCKED OUT BY A TEXAS SAND STORM IN FIRST ROUND.

Peter Maher found that a West Texas sandstorm packs a powerful punch. It delayed the fight and signaled the break-up of the carnival. From *Chicago Tribune,* February 15, 1896.

evident. After proclaiming that Mabry was trampling on the U.S. Constitution, he denounced the governor in no uncertain terms:

"The sick man in my room has no idea of rendering asunder any of the pet enactments of our infantile executive. Neither Mr. Maher or the undersigned have the most remote idea of becoming felons. . . . It is also an insult to the intelligence of a community when such indignities are heaped upon it, be they born of the fevered apprehensions of an overzealous demagogue or the children of a man who parades about in mock heroic epaulettes [*sic*]."

(The ex-mayor's letter was referred to in Mabry's later report as an "outburst of virtuous (?) indignation.")

The subsequent action of the city council was not so easily dismissed. They still bore a grudge for the last time Culberson had invaded the town with Rangers. At the next day's council meeting, Alderman Roberts introduced a resolution blasting Mabry, the Rangers, and the governor. After denouncing the latest "high-handed proceedings" as "violative of every law and principle of liberty," it called Culberson's actions "an outrage and insult to this entire community" as well as to all the "liberty loving people of Texas," and a "shameful attempt" to "gain cheap notoriety under the guise of enforcing the law."

Siding with E. C. Roberts was Alderman James Clifford, who labeled the present situation one of martial law that treated the people and their officials as lawbreakers; he said the only time Culberson noticed El Paso was "when occasion offered to humiliate her people."

"Poker Bob" Campbell, the mayor, thought the resolution a mistake and judiciously called the Rangers "good men, brave and efficient officers." He did not vote.

The resolution passed with only Aldermen G. W. Davis and J. F. Kachler opposed. But all the outrage and resolutions in the world couldn't make the fight come off as scheduled.

Valentine's Day dawned bright and clear, a perfect day—the movie people would have loved it. But there was no prospect for a fight in sight.

Peter Maher was back in Las Cruces sitting quietly in a darkened room, a green shade (and sometimes a bandage) over his swollen and encrusted eyes, regularly applying cocaine to his eyes to kill the pain. Outside and standing off about a hundred yards were the ever-present Rangers in their white hats, holding "short ferocious Winchesters." They escorted managers and trainers everywhere.

After having viewed Maher's eyes, Julian and Fitz agreed there was no fakery and postponed the big fight for the weekend.

But even that was too long for most people to while away in El Paso. They had businesses and families elsewhere. The hoard of sports began heading home—not in groups as big as when they arrived, but the transient population of paying customers was definitely thinning.

Meanwhile, someone found the boxing ring.

And another ring.

And Dan Stuart laughed. Under the noses of the alert, sleepless Rangers he had managed to move out enough lumber and men to build not one but two dummy rings as decoys! One was north of Juarez near the New Mexico line; the other was three-and-a-half miles down river in Mexico. "Each of the rings," reported the *New York World*, "is now being carefully watched by Mexican soldiers concealed behind as many clumps of sage bushes."

But with the carnival now delayed, and the plan exposed, the decoys were no longer useful. And there was little to do but sit, wait, gamble, wait, drink . . . and wait.

By any standards, it was a strange week, beginning with word from the heavens that Peter Maher was going to win.

Two astrologers with national reputations and known as Astor-Hazelridge made charts on both combatants. While Fitzsimmons clearly had greatness fixed in his stars, Maher's zodiacal signs were better, "for a new star is emerging above the horizon upon whose brow the gods are lowering a diadem which in appearance looks suspiciously like the championship belt."

In February of 1896, according to the soothsayers, the moon had entered the tenth mansion in his chart, that labeled "honor and preferment." Therefore, said the team, "we have no hesitancy in proclaiming Mr. Maher as the logical victor."

One of them was going to see stars, that much was certain.

The participants in the ridin' and ropin' carnival perked up the town with a brass band and parade; the saloons, dance halls and gambling houses did a lively business; and Governor Ahumada came across the bridge to split a pint of champagne with John L. Sullivan. (When the official's greeting was translated as "Pleased to meet you," Sullivan responded with some French that sounded like "Mercy Bocoop.")

The big thespian said afterwards, "You can bet your life that guy is too much of a sport to stop a fight."

No one was willing to place that high a wager on the matter.

The *Arizona Citizen* took up the case of Governor Hughes and found it to be "a ridiculous farce" and an act of "tomfoolery" to send militiamen "to chase jack rabbits up and down the San Simon valley." The paper felt it was a waste of tax money, adding, "If the brutes cross the line let the sheriff arrest them or, better yet, let them fight if they want to. They will not hurt one another and if they do what difference does it make to anybody in Arizona?"

Visitors continued to drift out of town.

General Mabry was suspicious. He was convinced Maher's sore eyes were a ruse and would become miraculously healed as soon as a safe fighting ground could be found. His report to Austin said he spoke with a Dr. Yandell, who supposedly diagnosed the fighter. Dr. William Yandell, quite truthfully, told him he never saw Maher, so the general assumed it was all a hoax. Apparently no one bothered to tell him it was Dr. White and not Dr. Yandell who treated Maher.[10]

To pass the weekend, the platoon of pugilists crossed into Mexico on Sunday to watch the reinstated bullfights. Most of them went home ill—even Sullivan left saying he didn't want to see any more of that kind of sport.

Fitzsimmons, who had been a regular at the arena, never did get used to it. "Fighting is golf to this blooming, bloody game," he commented after watching a bull disembowel a horse. As the dying horse ran around the ring with its entrails hanging out, Fitzsimmons turned to Governor Ahumada's interpreter and asked what the official thought of such a sight. Don Miguel said he saw nothing bad about it and declined to compare it to prizefighting.

It was Sunday evening when all the lesser fights were canceled. As the men picked up their forfeit money and started to make other plans— Walcott and "Bright Eyes" to meet in Long Island City on March 8, Marshall and Dixon in Boston in a month—the crowds began to leave town in droves. The fistic carnival was busting up.

On Monday, February 17, a conference was held in Dan Stuart's headquarters. It was not a friendly get-together: Julian had decided to claim the forfeit. Buck Connelly said the new agreement was for next Friday, and fighting a blind man wasn't very brave. Julian said Fitz was ready now. Connelly said he was to be told of the site twenty-four hours in advance. Stuart calmly injected, "The battleground's ready."

The room was packed with newsmen anxious to know more, but Stuart would not divulge the location.

Fitzsimmons, fresh from a morning exhibition for Governor Ahumada, blurted out, "You want to fool the public, your man don't want to fight. He's afraid. The whole of you are curs. The fight is off!" Storming out of the meeting, Fitz announced to the throng outside, "I will fight that old stiff James J. Corbett or any other man in the world."

Julian and Connelly then tore into one another. Julian wanted his forfeit *and* the fight. He challenged Connelly to pick five people at random from the crowd to decide the validity of his claim. Connelly deferred to Stuart who quickly selected a five-man jury. Their verdict was that Fitz was not entitled to the forfeit yet. A resigned but angry Julian agreed to a new fight date of Friday, February 21.[11]

Wanting, as always, the last word, Julian told the waiting crowd, "Fitz is going into the ring for business. He will whip Maher in short order Friday and will be ready to take Corbett on Saturday. And I mean what I say, too. Pompadour Jim is Bob's meat if he can be enticed into a twenty-four-foot ring with Fitz."

In Chicago, Corbett was dubious. "If they pull that fight off every one of them will go to jail. I learned my little lesson at Hot Springs. I never thought from the first that the fight would come off. Why if it had, I would have been there fighting instead of Maher, but I'm not going to chase around the country testing law any more."

Just the same, Corbett sent Fitz a wire that day: "Read in tonight's papers that you said I was a cur. The first time I see you I will make you take it back as I did before."

Martin Julian wired back: "All right, chappie. Get ready. Put yourself in better condition than you were in Hot Springs and get down here. Fitzsimmons will put you out of existence the day after he puts Maher among the has-beens."

That night the cast of *The Wicklow Postman* was to be augmented by "all the notable sporting men, rangers and notables in the city" appearing on stage as spectators at a prizefight. It was "the great London crib club scene," where Paddy Ryan and Sullivan staged a mock bout—the way things were going, that looked to be the only fight anyone was going to see.

It didn't go quite as scripted. The *Times* reported, "Last night, John L. Sullivan was loaded to the gunnels with booze and he went to the hotel in a carriage after trying to give an exhibition at the opera house." They were kind enough not to give details.

Doc White's son, eighteen-year-old Owen, later recalled "the great John L., downed by the bottle, and lying prone on the sidewalk in front of the Grand Central Hotel." Impressionable youngster that he was, Owen was proud of the Gem's bartender, Danny Creelan, for having "scored a knockout on a national hero."[12]

If boxing was dead, Sullivan was going to be the chief mourner at the wake. He drank immoderately all week. The ex-champ was sharing a rooming house next to the Gem with a number of correspondents, George Ade among them. The unlighted hallway had a number of sharp turns and one night during a bender Sullivan mistakenly let himself into Ade's room.

"I was awakened by a deep rumbling sound," recalled Ade. "Between me and the window I saw a vast bulk." Sullivan, undressing, was talking to himself and heading for the bed.

Years later, Ade pondered his choices. "I could have told around, for all time, that John L. Sullivan and I once slept in the same bed." It was the thought of Sullivan waking to find another man in his bed, and the fact they were one flight up, that caused him to speak out, lest the fighter "not be in any mood to receive laughing explanations."

Ade rolled away just in time and haltingly explained his presence to the foggy ex-champ, eventually succeeding in getting him to his own room, speaking gingerly all the way. Once there, the man from Boston insisted on showing Ade his wound from falling off the train. The stitches were ragged and ran across the top of his head; he'd been sewn up with piano wire.[13]

Sullivan and Ryan left town on February 19, booked for a show in Albuquerque. Charles "Parson" Davies, their manager, stayed behind to act as timekeeper for Maher. They were far from the first to hightail it— there were fewer than five hundred visitors still present. Leeds, Dixon, Walcott, Barry, and company had departed on the seventeenth. Others soon joined the disappointed exodus. Among the fighters only Jack Everhart stayed—he would be in Fitz's corner as a second.

Fitzsimmons remained in a temper, once offering to bet Tom O'Rourke $1,000 that Maher wouldn't show up on Friday. Julian refused to give him the money. Fitz was calling everybody a "cur" these days and worked off a lot of steam pedaling his bike furiously around town.

Maher got progressively better and predicted he'd win the fight in less than ten rounds. He was well enough to give a couple of his shadows a brisk workout on the eighteenth. Peter boarded the Silver City train as it passed through Las Cruces and then hopped off at Mesilla Park outside of town and jogged back. Two Rangers who scrambled on board with him had no choice but to jump off and run back, weighted down by armaments.

And so the time was passed. Correspondents sat around Dan Stuart's offices rehashing everything, chuckling over rumors and filing virtually the same copy each day. Governor Ahumada returned to Chihuahua City.[14] Governor Hughes was reported suffering from "nervous prostration." Major Lewis, who caused the militia to be sent to Bowie, came to town to get a fight ticket for himself. And, of course, the Ministers' Union was still expressing what it called the sentiments of the people.

The Union's latest broadside was a catalogue of local sins deserving of hellfire, or at least repression:

"We respectfully call the attention of the city and county officers to the open and flagrant violation of the law in the following particulars:

First—The violation of the Sunday law; business houses open; saloons open all day; Sunday games and races where admission fee is charged.

Second—Violation of the gambling law; gambling runs night and day.

Third—Shameless prostitution in the heart of the city; indecency paraded in the streets; the city conniving at, by collecting fines, which amount to license, and renting property which is used for that purpose.

Fourth—the dance house nuisance; prostitutes and bad characters carrying on these things week days and Sundays to the annoyance and scandal of those who live in the neighborhood.

The ministers were as unrelenting as, well, as a fighter stalking his opponent in the ring. The cancellation of four fights, the unequivocal actions of Governor Ahumada, the scattering of the vast flock of fans, all pointed toward an ecclesiastical knockout, regardless of the new agreement and optimistic pronouncements. The round was theirs, and they did not expect to go another.

Rumors blew through town like tumbleweeds. One had the movie company paying all expenses for the fight to take place on a barge in Galveston. Another had the high-strung Governor Hughes building an amphitheater for the bout in Yuma.

Wun Lung quoted an eastern paper as saying the arena was "located in a spot in the mountains where the foot of man had never before trod and which could be held against a regiment of soldiers by a few men, as there was only a narrow pass leading to it."

Idle journalistic minds at play.

None of the rumors mentioned the fight coming off in or near El Paso. Through it all, Dan Stuart remained placid, saying just one thing to the curious:

"The next round is mine."

ROUND EIGHT: The Main Event

Never has any town been host to a finer collec-
tion of pugs, thugs, and assorted camp followers
and hangers-on than was El Paso. . . . I learned
that the right way to promote something is to
prohibit it.

—Owen P. White[1]

"SEVERAL MONTHS AGO," wrote the *Times,* Stuart, Wheelock and Vendig "promised that the largest congregation of noted sports ever brought
together in this country would be in El Paso for the carnival." They had
kept their word.

But that was last week. No inducement could hold the crowd an extra
seven days.

The word spread quickly. From the gambling halls of the Juarez fiesta
to the bordellos along Utah Street, from the one-room adobe homes along
the river to the wooden barracks out at Fort Bliss, the word was carried by
men in serapes and sombreros, cloth caps, derbys and business suits, by
little barefoot boys in knickers, silk-clad painted ladies, journalists with
ink-stained fingers, sports with coins clinking in their hands, ministers of
every cloth, and maybe by the wind itself. The word was heard in English,
Spanish, Chinese, and a few Indian dialects, slipping into the saloons,
boarding houses, parlors, churches, stores, and banks as swiftly and resolutely as a thief in the night. And the word was: the fight is off.

With just two days to go, the town looked deserted. Bedrolls and cots
no longer clogged hallways. No one was spending the night under or on a
keno, faro or pool table, or atop a saloon's bar. The city seemed to be
nursing a hangover with nothing to show for it.

The Reverend E. R. Hallam was close to spiritual ecstasy when he
told an interviewer, "We exerted our best efforts to stop the prizefight

and you can see what we accomplished." He ridiculed the upbeat pronouncements of Dan Stuart. "It seems to me now that they are only making a puny pretense to hold the fight, without any chance of ever doing so unless they privately go to some point where they will be able to evade the officers."

More out of boredom than anything else, reporters and Rangers alike visited Fitz's gym in Juarez. Captains McDonald and Hughes, as well as General Mabry himself, watched the impromptu exhibition while waiting for Dan Stuart to either make his next move or throw in the towel.

When they weren't watching a lot of bag-punching, the press corps milled around a display case at the Lindell Hotel—it contained the pen used by Grover Cleveland to sign the anti-prizefight bill. The local band and music society, called The McGinty Club, stood guard over the souvenir.[2]

Fitz exercised more than his muscles when he sent a telegram to the *New York World* saying he was ready to fight.

"Although I have been subjected to inconvenience and compelled to resume training after I had once prepared myself, my condition has not suffered. I am in first-class shape and fit for battle."

Peter Maher also sent a telegram.

"I feel splendidly to-day, as well as I did before the sand storm struck me. I shall be in the ring Friday morning and, unless my calculations are away off, it will be Fitzsimmons the has-been, instead of me. This man Fitzsimmons is a funny fellow. He is not satisfied with one fight at a time, but wants to bring poor Corbett down to wallop him. He must think he is a holy terror, but if I get a wipe at him he'll wish he had remained in Australia, he and his boasting manager."

Dan Stuart was not unpacking any towels: "There are but two sure things in the world—death and taxes. Next to these two I don't know of anything as sure as that Maher and Fitzsimmons will fight on Friday, if both men are ready and willing to go into the ring."

Where that ring would be was still a secret known only to Dan Stuart, and perhaps the Western Union operator, though diligent efforts were being made to track it down.

Over in Juarez, the remaining troops were now under the command of Señor Manuel Bauche, Collector of Customs. He had a hundred and fifty cavalry, thirty rurales, and a dozen of his own Custom House guards and mounted police to call on. He just didn't know where to send them.

"I have located every point along the river which can be easily reached from the railway," remarked Bauche, studying a map. "I will have a company of soldiers at each point. Even with my small command I can guard the river for sixty miles and intercept the fighters unless they travel ten or fifteen miles overland from the railroad."

Bauche confided to a reporter that his heart was not in his work. "If they can arrange to fight somewhere outside of Mexico I should like very much to be present as a spectator. I should like so much to see it. Come to me on Saturday and tell me all about it."

On February 19, Stuart went to General Mabry with some bad news— due to the lack of paying customers and dearth of fighters, the profit margin was going to be too small to accomodate freeloaders. The Rangers would have to pay regular fare.

"When I had my own train, I offered to carry you, but now, if you insist on following us, you can fight it out with the railroad company."

Presumably he kept his poker face immobile during this little conference. Then, to help make Mabry's work easier, Stuart informed him that three freight cars would head off in three different directions that night, and that two were decoys.

"I just want to tell you that you may follow all those cars if you wish, but that no matter which one you follow you won't find any ring pitched in Texas."

Mabry's response went unreported, and perhaps it's just as well.

· E. J. Rector reappeared one day as mysteriously as he had vanished. He said he and his Kinetoscope were ready to go whenever Stuart gave the word. The Rangers must have thought they were guarding ghosts.

In the dead of night, two Rangers watched a flatcar of lumber being hitched to a westbound train and climbed on the engine. The engineer took one look at Ranger Ed Aten and brusquely declared, "You're not going to ride on this engine. If you try it, I'll knock you off with the shovel."

The Ranger was in no mood to debate according to *Robert's Rules of Order*. Aten pressed the muzzle of his .45 into the engineer's stomach and told him to pull out.

The lumber went as far as Strauss, New Mexico, then came back, picked up some carpenters, and continued east. Aten stayed with it.[3]

Thursday morning started with a crises. Fitz awoke, looked outside, and found his house surrounded by men in buckskins with silver buttons down the pant legs and red sashes over their shoulders. Each wore a silver-trimmed sombrero. *Rurales.*

Fitz and Julian left the house and cautiously made their way to the bridge. The men followed but let them cross. They picked up an escort of Rangers on the other side.

Shaken by the close attention and worried about creditors—not just

The eastern view of border life along the Rio Grande included this strange hybrid of a *bandido* and a Texas Ranger deciding the big fight in his own favor. From *New York World,* February 12, 1896.

Carroll's suit, but the many unpaid bills piling up in Juarez and El Paso— Martin Julian asked that the purse be brought to the ring in cash. (All of their valuables were already in El Paso "as a guard against the rude attachment laws of Mexico.")

Stuart objected, and Tom O'Rourke nearly had apoplexy.

"Not in a thousand years," exclaimed the stakeholder, "would I carry that much ready money on a trip of this kind. They might as well ask me to carry the purse in Mexican silver."

J. J. Quinn was satisfied to trust Stuart and get on with it. "Fitz has been calling us curs, but I think before we get through people will find out who has been on the level in this thing."

The pair returned to Mexico, promising to be back for a noon conference. At the bank, the money was switched to an account in Siler's name; O'Rourke was given two certified checks to carry.

Peter Maher and his cadre came down from Las Cruces on the noon train but, to avoid the growing crowd in town, got off at the smelter station. A waiting carriage took them to the Astor House, trailed by the vigilant Rangers. The Irishman had a bath, then joined his friends at the National Kitchen for a late breakfast.

"The streets were full of people," reported the *Herald*, "especially near the corner of San Antonio and El Paso streets and in front of the Gem, all afternoon, and it was guess this, and guess that and guess the other thing." The chief rumor now placed the fight in Mexico opposite Fort Hancock, forty-five miles to the southeast. They were *way* off.

When the train carrying the lumber came to a stop, it was not fifty miles downriver. It was not a hundred miles downriver. Much to the surprise of the Rangers, they were 389 miles from El Paso! Forty-two Mexican laborers were waiting at the depot and immediately swarmed onto the flatcar. They were supervised by Jim Bates, president of the Dallas Athletic Club.

Ranger Aten stepped down and surveyed the landscape. It was bleak. Desolate. Nothing to the north but flat scrubland for miles. To the south he could hear the roar of the Rio Grande down below in a canyon, and beyond that was the Mexican state of Coahuila, one-time capital of Texas before the war of independence. If this was their final destination, it was unlikely any Mexican troops could arrive sooner than two or three days, at a gallop.

There was a depot, of sorts, a very small town of fifty inhabitants, and a saloon named "The Jersey Lilly." If Aten didn't know where he was at first, the saloon was all he needed to see.

As the workmen unloaded the flatcar and began hauling the lumber down a rocky slope towards the river, the Ranger stepped into the telegraph office and sent a message to General Mabry, who was in for a shock. The secret site of the fight looked to be Langtry, Texas, presided over by that infamous justice of the peace, Roy Bean, the self-described "Law West of the Pecos."

This was going to raise some eyebrows.

Neither Fitz nor Julian showed up for the noon conference. Stuart waited, then went ahead with his plans.

General Mabry and his men took the news of their destination calmly. In the afternoon he, McDonald, Hughes, and the rest lined up on the courthouse steps and let Mr. Burge take a couple of photographs for posterity, the group bristling with rifles. Perhaps he was envisioning a caption reading, "The men who prevented the Maher-Fitzsimmons prizefight."

At 5:00 P.M. Dan Stuart placed a sign in the window of carnival headquarters: "Persons desirous of attending the prize fight will report at these headquarters tonight at 9:45 o'clock. Railroad fare for the round trip will not exceed $12."

He might just as well have fired a starter's gun for a land rush. The *New York World* described the effect: "The men who wanted to see a battle were flying around packing up hampers of provisions and getting bottled goods ready and making general preparations for a long ride by rail with lunch stations five hundred miles apart." Not all the bottled goods contained water.

As the time approached, a company of thirty Rangers passed double-file by Stuart's office on their way to the Southern Pacific station. Each man carried a revolver and Winchester.

When there was no sign of Fitz by 6:30, George Ade was sent to Juarez to find him. (Ade had developed a rapport with the fighter, having found his soft spot: "Bob Fitzsimmons thought he could sing. If you wanted a good interview with him, all you had to do was praise his rendition of 'Sweet and Low,' which was his favorite.")[4]

The reporter was greeted by Martin Julian, who announced, "Fitz is not going into the ring until George Siler, referee, has $10,000 in hard cash in his pocket ready to turn over to the winner as soon as a decision is made. How do we know but somebody would beat us out of the purse if we simply depend on the stakeholder?"

Fitz came out in a white shirt and suit and began to pace about, psyching himself up, saying of Maher, "If I ever meet that fellow, there will be just two hits. I'll hit him and he'll hit the floor. That is all there will be to it." He also voiced the opinion that the train had no fixed destination—they were just going to ride the rails until a likely spot was found.

Fitz and Julian finally crossed the bridge at 8:00 P.M. in a closed carriage. The street in front of fight headquarters was jammed with people and the men had to push their way through. In the crowd were at least a dozen Rangers "with long guns and big cartridge belts." They contended themselves with peering in the windows and waiting. No one was going anywhere without them.

Several hundred people gravitated to the depot at nine. Three ticket windows were opened at 9:30 and remained busy for the next two hours.

Not all of the carnival's pickpockets had left town and they made quite a haul on the platform that night. The train from the west was late as the result of a derailed freight near Tucson, and the extra time was beneficial to the light-fingered fraternity. One of Bill McDonald's Amarillo Rangers,

Sgt. W. J. L. Sullivan, told a reporter that at least twenty people were relieved of valuables while waiting for the train—one claimed to have been fleeced of $900. No one was arrested.

The people most taxed at this time were Trainmaster McNeal and Yardmaster Scott. They had not been let in on Stuart's plan and consequently were not prepared for such a rush of passengers. There was a lot of scrambling, and by the time the eastbound train pulled in with five cars, McNeal and Scott were ready with five more. The fight train now included four Pullmans and two tourist sleepers (both fighters were given sleeping compartments in separate cars); once those were filled the passengers had to settle for the day coaches.

The through passengers coming from the west must have thought they were being commandeered by desperadoes as two hundred people suddenly invaded the cars.

Some of the passengers climbing aboard—even onto the car roofs— were considered "hoodlums" and undesirables. Bat Masterson and his men settled on a plan of clearing the cars at a point about twenty-five miles to the east; Bat ventured the observation that some impecunious sports would have a long walk back.

Two troops of Rangers were on the platform during the rush for tickets and the long wait for the train. When the line of coaches and the original engine were attached to freight engine 807, a big ten-wheeler, General Mabry and twenty-six of his men joined the party.

They took up a lot of space in the day coaches. The conductor asked for their tickets, and Mabry produced something better: a letter from Governor Culberson telling him to stay with the fighters no matter what. The state, explained Mabry, would pay the fares. Considering the armaments facing him, the conductor did not argue.[5]

Those who had tickets (either purchased or picked from a pocket) found the name "Langtry" on them and this caused a lot of talk. As the train crept slowly out of the station just before midnight, the cars packed tight, few people believed that Langtry was the final destination. It had to be a false clue, like the decoy rings. The fighters would surely get off somewhere before Bean's notorious and distant burg.

Langtry? *Langtry?* Who'd ever stop willingly at Langtry?

There was plenty of time for speculation as the train chugged along the cloudy, vacant Texas border, the passengers on this Southern Pacific odyssey suffering from an "uneasy feeling that it was a mighty hazardous excursion." No Cyclops or Minotaurs awaited, but there might be worse things.

One "facetious individual" kept saying they would all be inducted into the Mexican army for five years if caught crossing the border. This information did little to lighten the feeling that this was a train of fools heading for disaster.

Another helpful passenger felt that the Rangers were just along for the ride. "When the crowd crosses into Mexico the Rangers will go over too, as private citizens and spectators. And I want to tell you the boys would not object to a little rub with those Mexicans." A popular Ranger captain named Frank Jones had been murdered three years ago in Mexico, and relations were still strained.

Quinn was sure his man would win, but admitted Maher "is not in good condition, by any means." Peter denied that and said he was ready at any time. "I understand Fitzsimmons characterized me as a cur a few days ago. He would never have dared to talk that way if I had been present. Wait till I get a crack or two at him tomorrow, and we will see who is a cur. He is a great big bluffer, but bluffs don't go in our argument. My friends have no fear of the result."

Both fighters used water stops to sprint up and down the tracks, and each mentioned the higher altitude having an effect on his wind, especially at Paisano, the highest length of track between El Paso and New Orleans. There were crowds at every stop along the way. At Alpine, "designated the toughest town in Southern Texas," at least three hundred people were on hand to meet the train—most of them cheering for Peter Maher.

At the Longfellow stop, everyone got out to stretch and pick flowers, a fine breather from the cars choked with cigar smoke.

When not predicting victory, Fitz spent much of the morning playing cards. Maher sang a medley of popular songs, sometimes in a trio with Peter Burns and Jim Hall, his seconds, with a special liking for "My Best Girl's a Corker."

Later in the morning the train stopped to take on water at the town of Marathon, just before heading into a barren stretch aptly called Hell's Half-Acre. Fitz, "the big bluffer," was one car in back of Maher. Glancing out a window, he saw an irresistible sight: a big black bear chained to the corner of an adobe house some five hundred feet from the tracks. How could a wrestler of lions miss such an opportunity?

On impulse, Fitz hopped off the train and grappled with the bear. The bear ran as far as his chain permitted, no doubt wondering what the hell was going on. George Ade later told astonished friends that Fitz scared the bear half to death.[6]

Anyone game enough to tackle a bruin was ready for Maher.

All along the tracks, whenever there was time to get off and find a telegrapher, the newshounds relayed updates back to El Paso. Stephenson, the *Herald*'s regular sports editor, wired from Alpine: "Two engines and ten coaches going east. All pugs aboard, and cars crowded. Two hours late. Weather threatening."

At 1:00 P.M. there was a lunch stop at Sanderson, and about two-hundred people jammed into restaurants as Stephenson sent this: "No special dispatches will be accepted by the Western Union from the scene of the fight. The Western Union will send out bulletins to sell in El Paso and other cities first by rounds, and give press associations preference afterwards over special correspondents. The fight will occur near Langtry at 4 o'clock. Everything O.K."

He was wrong. Everything was not okay. Since the train was behind schedule, the lunch break was cut to just ten minutes. There was a frenzied stampede of hungry people for the town's few restaurants, resulting in what the *Chicago Tribune* called "a battle royal between the sports and a lot of Chinese waiters."

Maher put off eating in favor of stretching his legs on the platform, where he encountered a group of Bostonians heading west. An elderly woman came up to him with a fight program, then made as if to pin it on his back "so these other people will know who you are." Nonplused by the attention, Maher retreated at a run, with the woman in laughing pursuit. The crowd found it highly amusing.

Things weren't going well in one of the restaurants either. During the meal Bat Masterson decided an overworked Chinese waiter was too slow and started to get his attention by conking him with a table castor. His arm was checked in midswing by the iron grip of Ranger Bill McDonald.

"Don't hit that man," the Ranger requested, not letting loose. He apparently didn't believe in the customer always being right.

Masterson glared at the tough Ranger and said, "Maybe you'd like to take it up."

The man who could pick cherries with a rifle calmly replied, "I done took it up."[7]

The two veteran gunmen faced each other, and the hush of a sepulcher fell over the crowded room. Both men had guntoting friends to back them up. This was not the sort of fight anyone had planned to see— innocent spectators could get hurt whenever bullets started flying. If there was any sound, it was made by men preparing to dive under tables.

Then Bat smiled, and both men relaxed. The moment passed, and everyone climbed back aboard the train, with great relief.

It began raining while they were in Sanderson, and the train pulled out in a heavy downpour. The passengers stared gloomily out as they passed a drenched chain gang working on the roadbed. It was not a cheery moment, and the next stop was Langtry.

Judge Roy Bean was a large, robust man with a long, unkempt gray beard. He looked like a degenerate Santa Claus. He was born in Kentucky in 1825, and hit Chihuahua as a trader at age twenty-three. Over the years he held a variety of jobs, from dairyman to butcher, but seemed most taken with being a saloon keeper, a line he pursued in San Antonio for nearly twenty years.

As the railroad pushed west in the early 1880s, Bean went along, operating a tent saloon for the track layers, and settled near the town of Langtry.

Langtry was a railroad town, one of many that dotted the transcontinental railway set up for the relief of workmen and train crews. Legend has it that the town was first named Vinegaroon after a particularly ugly, eight-eyed member of the scorpion family and that Bean renamed it for his favorite pinup girl, English singer Lillie Langtry. Other sources, not so romanticized, say the two towns existed separately and that Langtry was named for a railroad construction foreman long before Bean and his obsession arrived.

In any case, he set up a more or less permanent establishment near the border in 1882 and, on the recommendation of Texas Ranger T. L. Oglesby, was appointed justice of the peace. He was in and out of office but remained a fixture of the area, thanks to his unorthodox reading of the law.[8]

The saloon was his court—that *was* named for Lillie, though the name was misspelled. The bar served as the judge's bench, and the butt of a six-shooter made a perfect gavel. Bean would plop himself down on a beer keg and commence with dispensing justice. Or, to put it another way, justice was dispensed with.

When a good customer was accused of killing a Chinaman, Bean became a stickler for precise wording and dismissed the case on the grounds that the Texas statutes did not specify that killing a Chinaman was illegal.

In Texas one could carry a revolver while traveling, so another customer was found not guilty of carrying a gun because he was moving when arrested.

Bean much preferred fining felons than locking them up (the town did not have a jail) or stringing them up (the area did not support trees of a sufficient sturdiness), and when Governor Hogg complained that the fines

A mounted Judge Roy Bean poses for posterity in front of his infamous court-house. Fitzsimmons found the critter cage on the right irresistible. Courtesy Western History Collections, University of Oklahoma Library.

weren't finding their way into the Texas treasury, Bean answered, "Governor, you tend to things up there at Austin and I'll look after 'em out here."

When trains stopped for water, the passengers would rush into the Jersey Lilly for some overpriced beer. As the train didn't stay long, there were few arguments about the price. One man who did register a complaint with Bean was an easterner who laid down a twenty-dollar gold piece and only got nineteen dollars back.

Bean called his court to order on the spot and found the man guilty of public profanity, disturbing the peace, and contempt of court, each charge carrying a fine of $6.66 2/3. The judge reverted to bartending and graciously said, "The beer's on me."[9]

Roy Bean was a frontier character of the first order, a rude, cantankerous, dangerous, belligerent, dishonest scalawag who made a career of bending laws to suit his own purposes. The idea that such a reprobate could be involved with a genial, worldly, and accomplished man like Dan Stuart was hardly credible. So while the train tickets said "Langtry," there were a lot of doubters.

Seventy-three miles from Sanderson, all doubts were dispelled. Engine 807 hissed to a stop in Langtry at 3:35 P.M. Stuart had both fighters getting ready since Sanderson, and Fitz was the first person off the train. The passengers, stiff, sore, bleary-eyed, and not a little inebriated, were slower to disembark.

A special train from Eagle Pass had already deposited some two hundred fans at Langtry, so a good crowd was assured, though it was a mere fraction of what Stuart had once envisioned for his Dallas amphitheater. That must have seemed like a long time ago.

The sports from El Paso were welcomed by Judge Roy Bean personally, but before anyone could ask about the ring, Mabry had assembled his men—lined up as if for inspection, weapons at the ready. They were joined by some U.S. marshals and other duly sworn upholders of the state's dignity.[10] The old judge may have considered himself the only law in this wasteland, but at the moment he was considerably outnumbered.

It was a standoff somewhat grander than the imbroglio in Sanderson, and the stakes were higher. If the ring was anywhere in Texas, things looked to become lethal.

Bean, Stuart, and Vendig conferred, then the spectators were herded into the Jersey Lilly for some liquid nourishment (at a dollar a bottle). Bean pulled Mabry aside.

The ring, the judge explained, was "down the street and down the bluff. And on the bottom there's a bridge to the island—and that's in the State of Coahuila, Mexico."[11]

Island? Mexico? Bean's reputation for deviousness was not unknown to the state's adjutant general. The Rangers adopted a wait-and-see attitude.

That problem settled, more or less, the boisterous and well-lubricated crowd of fistic sojourners hit the makeshift trail, journalists scribbling as they scrambled. They were led down the rocky, winding path to the beach by Jimmy White, a boy who had come all the way from Toronto to see the great carnival.

The beach was about two hundred feet below the canyon's rim. Three hundred yards farther along the river could be seen a topless tent and an improvised pontoon bridge leading to it. The "pontoons" were small boats lashed together.

"The battle-ground was a sandy flat upon a big bend in the Rio Grande River, on the Mexican side," reported the *New York World*. "The

Part of the hasty yet sturdy bridge leading to the Rio Grande sandbar, with some of its proud builders. Courtesy Western History Collections, University of Oklahoma Library.

ring was protected from outsiders' view by a canvas wall. The board floor was covered with canvass [*sic*], over which resin was sprinkled." There was even a compartment meant to house the Kinetoscope equipment and two small tents to serve as dressing rooms.

Jim Bates had done a quick and thorough job building the Langtry Amphitheater. What could not have been anticipated was the overcast, drizzly weather—it was much too dark for the Kinetoscope. There would be no film of the fight and no way for Stuart to recover his losses. Still, the show must go on.

The canvas wall was not high enough for those fans who could climb the canyon walls and a couple of hundred, most of them Mexicans from across the river, did just that. The Rangers, having decided no Texas statutes were in danger of being dishonored, joined them, squatting on the top of the cliffs for a clear view into the ring.[12]

Joe Vendig made himself the doorman and collected admissions of $20 a head, while Bat Masterson stood by, glowering menacingly; no one grumbled. The spectators—among whom was El Paso's Sen. John Dean—continued to place bets with one another right up to the start.

Fitzsimmons stepped from his dressing room in a striped robe around 5:00 P.M. and took the closest corner. Maher took his corner and the two selected gloves—the brown pair went to Maher and Fitz took the light green ones. Timekeepers were announced by Siler—*Chicago Inter-Ocean* reporter Lou Houseman kept the official time, while Bert Sneed of the *New Orleans Times-Democrat* acted for Fitzsimmons and "Parson" Davies for Maher.

Everything was set to go when a snag developed. It came from Martin Julian.

"Siler," Julian called. "Is the money up in cash?"

Tom O'Rourke stepped forward with two checks for $10,000 each, certified by the State National Bank of El Paso.

Julian rejected them. "I told you I did not want checks. I want money. Those checks are no good to us."

O'Rourke was insulted. "This is the first time my honesty has been questioned."

"It is not a question of honesty with us. If Fitzsimmons fights he wants the money, and he'll not fight without it."

This was not exactly an opportune time for such a squabble. A voice from ringside hollered, "How do you know the money will be yours? The other side is not kicking."

Julian shot back at the heckler, "I am not looking out for the other side. I am looking out for our own interests."

A Rangers'-eye view of the Fight of the Century as seen from the Langtry bluffs overlooking the river, canvas walls discouraging all but the heartiest of gate crashers. Courtesy Western History Collections, University of Oklahoma Library.

As Siler and Julian continued to argue, Fitzsimmons stood and said, "We have been given the worst of the deal all the way through; we have consented to everything asked and now I am going to fight to satisfy the public, money or no money. This, however, will be the last time I will ever give under."

He was applauded, and the two fighters were called forward by the referee.

"I told them," wrote Siler that night, "that as the battle was for the championship the spectators, the public at large, and myself in particular, wanted to see the best man win by fair means only. I explained fully as possible what I considered fouls. . . . Either man violating these rules would be declared a loser." Insubstantial blows struck in clinches or on breakaways would be subject to a caution; repeated offenses would result in a victory for the victim.

They went to their corners and waited. Fitz wore dark blue "thigh

And then there were two—after all the preaching, posturing, and politicking, the carnival's star pugilists finally come out punching. From *Chicago Tribune,* February 9, 1896.

trunks" with a belt of red, white, and blue. Maher's black trunks reached halfway to his knees and were held up with a green belt. Siler had them return to the center to shake hands. There was a whistle; five seconds later Lou Houseman called "Time!" and hit the gong.

The heavyweight title fight Dan Stuart began organizing nine months before was at last underway.

"Up sprang Fitzsimmons," reported the *Chicago Tribune,* "advancing with his little eyes flashing like balls of burnished blue." Maher was equally swift to the mark and they met in the center of the ring. There was no hesitant sparring. Fitz swung two quick ones—left, right—and they clinched. Maher landed a right on Fitz's cheekbone during the clinch.

"Ain't that a foul?" cried Fitzsimmons, a call echoed by many of the spectators, especially Julian.

The blow did no damage, and Siler issued a warning: "If you do that again I will decide the fight against you."

Fitz said, "Let it go, I'll lick him anyway."

Hard infighting commenced with two more clinches and two more quick hits by Maher—Siler called the first "a hot right-hander in Bob's body." Still, neither foul blow had material effect. Fitz complained, and said to Maher, "You're a fine fellow to keep your word, ain't you?"

Maher answered with a left to Fitz's lip that drew blood.

Both men went at each other, swinging, hitting, missing, hitting, rushing into Maher's corner, then onto the ropes. A minute into the first round the Irishman appeared to have the upper hand, just the way he had in New Orleans, and Fitz was on the defensive. But Maher wasn't connec-

At long last, Maher and Fitz meet in the ring again—on a sandbar in the middle of the Rio Grande. *El Paso Daily Herald,* February 22, 1896.

ting with the big ones—he "landed several light taps which would have been serious if Fitz's head had not been on a pivot," Stephenson wrote. "Fitz ducked and dodged, but kept his eyes on Maher's chin and several in the crowd began to murmur that 'Maher has got him.'"

But Siler knew it wasn't retreat they were seeing. "Fitzsimmons played the same old game he has so often played before, leading on his opponent until he had him where he wanted him."

Maher closed in and led with his left.

Fitz stepped aside and lashed out with his powerful right arm, his glove traveling but six inches and landing solidly on the point of Maher's chin.

Maher seemed to rise up off the floor, twist halfway around, and then come crashing down. His head struck the boards with a sickening thud.

Siler began counting.

One!

Maher raised his head and attempted to get up but fell back.

Two! Three!

Fitz watched for a few seconds, then walked to his corner and sat.

Four! Five!

Jack Everhart yelled, "Stand up, for heaven's sake, he may come at you." Julian was having a conniption fit.

Six! Seven!

Maher moved, trying to rise. His eyes showed white. From his corner came shouts of encouragement. Despite the cold drizzle, one of his crew tried to throw water on him but was restrained by a spectator.

Eight! Nine!

"Get away from me," Fitz growled at Julian who was trying to get him back on his feet and at the ready. "Get away from me, I tell you, it's all over, he's out."

Ten!

"There, didn't I tell you he was out?"

The long-delayed championship fight lasted, by Siler's account, one minute and forty-three seconds.[13]

Fitz put on his robe while the dazed Maher was assisted back to his corner. It took another fifteen seconds to revive him and he sat slumped over, head down, for several minutes.

Fitz walked over to Maher and stuck out his gloved hand. As the fight's loser reached for it, Fitz jerked it back with a boyish laugh. But after Julian had removed the glove, he held out his hand again and this time they shook.

The jubilant Julian made an announcement. "Gentlemen! Mr. Fitzsimmons has now worked his way up to the top and is now the champion of the world. He is now ready at any time and place to defend his title against any man in the world."

There were no immediate takers.

When Julian caught up with Fitz and the departing crowd, the new champ was poking a stick at a caged wolf Bean had on display. Julian pulled him along to the depot and the waiting westbound train.

Enoch Rector was there, looking almost as glum as Peter Maher. He wanted to know if Fitz and Maher could reproduce the fight in front of his camera on a sunny day—even stretch it to six rounds, but with the same result. Fitz said he'd do it for $5,000 and 50 percent of the net receipts.

When this information was carried to Quinn, he thought the six rounder would be for real, not staged, and wanted a bigger purse. Arguing ensued, and finally Fitz called the whole thing off. "I don't care about fighting before the Kinetoscope," he said. "Every time they want me to do it they want to give the other fellow all the money, and I want some of it."

The train ride back was, understandably, filled with talk of the fight.

"I was sure of him at all stages of the game," said Fitz. "He was afraid the minute he put up his hands, and I knew it." He admitted to a moment of doubt. "He found me three times, and the blow he gave me in the jaw set me dizzy. It was a hot soaker, and for a second I thought I was gone."

Maher was still confused. "He is a clever fighter, and I don't know exactly where I was hit; seems to me it was on the jaw. The back of my head has a big lump on it, and that's where it struck the floor. I thought I had him licked from the start, and so far as my condition is concerned I have nothing to complain of and I would like to get a fight with somebody else—I am not particular which of the heavyweights."

J. J. Quinn: "I was confident Maher would win and he had the best of it until Fitz got in that blow."

Martin Julian: "I told you two months ago that Bob would win. He is the best man in the ring today." He parried talk of a lucky blow. "It was no accident. Fitz started in to do just what he did."

Joe Vendig: "I had money on the winner, but don't claim to be any judge in such matters."

George Ade: "It didn't look like an accident. Fitz wouldn't dare pursue the same tactics with Corbett."

Speaking of whom, the loudest noise came not from the train but from the stage of the Haymarket Theatre in Chicago. At the end of *The Naval Cadet*'s first act, with the expectant crowd getting restless, James J. Corbett stepped in front of the curtain and said he'd make a big announcement at play's end.

He could hardly refuse, given both his personality and what he had said five days before the fight: "I have made up my mind never to allow Fitzsimmons to be champion of the world," he promised. "I hope and pray that Mr. Maher will win that fight, and if he don't I will meet Fitzsimmons anywhere in the world."

Now he was stuck and, as usual, making a theatrical event out of it. He had already sent a challenge to Fitz by telegram. There was a condition, though: "No more Julian for me. Julian does a grandstand play, ending with a song, dance, and a few contortionist specialties. I will take no more chances on this sort of work."

The audience became intrusive during the third act, calling out quips in reply to scripted lines. When Corbett said to his leading lady, "It has been in my heart for a long time—," someone bellowed, "To lick Fitzsimmons!"

After the final curtain, Corbett read his challenge from the footlights and produced $10,000 in cash as a guarantee, handing the sum over to the theater's manager, Will J. Davis. "I never made a bluff in my life," said Corbett, the crowd in his hands. "There are three places I know we can fight. These are England, South Africa, or Australia, and any one of them is agreeable to me." The building shook with applause.

Before the train reached El Paso, Fitz had Corbett's telegram. It must have made him laugh. He also had word that the Mexican authorities would not pursue the matter any farther. The offense that once drew threats of death was now being termed a misdemeanor and not extraditable by the terms of any treaty. Legally, they were home free.

They were not, however, free from the press. No sooner did word of the outcome hit the telegraph wires than the critics were out to get their punches in.

The *New York Sun* chastized Maher as "Pete Quitter, alias 'Alkali Pete.'" The *San Francisco Chronicle* said, "Judged from the standpoint of the pugilist, the encounter between Fitzsimmons and Maher was a great fiasco, because there was no opportunity for the exhibition of much science. . . . A few more encounters of this kind will put an end to pugilism in this country, as the amount of preparation and the expense are out of all proportion to the results."

The *San Antonio Express* saw the whole thing as a civics lesson: "As promoters of peace and good order, Corbett, Maher and Fitzsimmons, together with Dan Stuart and the rest of the gang are unparalleled in the annals of the speedy promotion of legislation. . . . All the leagues, societies, associations, churches, supplemented by the salvation army could not have accomplished this monumental work."

Mexico City's leading paper, *Two Republics,* downplayed the event. "El Paso has gained a large amount of advertising, such as it is. Lovers of the manly-art have probably by this time satisfied themselves that prize-fighting in the United States and Mexico must be reckoned among the lost arts. It will be a long time before another carnival of that sort is billed."

The *Chicago Dispatch* managed to cover the whole thing in two sentences. "As we understand it, Mr. Fitzsimmons walked up to Mr. Maher yesterday, pushed his hands down and struck him violently on the jaw. There isn't anything else to tell."

But even the anti-fight papers couldn't dampen the mood of the winner. Back in El Paso, the new champ left the depot in a carriage; Maher walked. He was greeted by Rose, Nero and Princess at the Grand Central Hotel. Fitz described the whole fight to the lion, who only growled when his ear was boxed.

Rose, on the other hand, needed no such cue. She said she was sure he would win, but now wanted him to quit. "I do wish he'd get out of this fighting business. It's such an awful bother, you know." She wasn't sure what he could substitute for the sport, but was adament about the future. "I wish he'd settle down to something else."

But not right away: "I've made up my mind to allow my husband to engage in just one more ring battle. I want him to whip Corbett," she said emphatically. "I don't think Mr. Corbett has acted like a gentleman towards Bob, and Bob, you know, is always peaceful and well-behaved. If they ever come together Bob will settle all the old scores."

When asked about Corbett and his fusillade of challenges, Fitz smiled and replied, "Tell him to get a reputation."

That Saturday, happy as a schoolboy, Fitz settled in at a blacksmith's shop and pounded out a dozen souvenir horseshoes for his supporters. Saturday was Washington's birthday, and the bank was closed. However, the bank officers were located and Fitzsimmons was soon holding $9,000 in cash and $1,000 in gold.

Dan Stuart looked on and asked, "Gentlemen, have I conducted this affair to please you?"

For a change, Julian was satisfied, and everyone shook hands.

Back in Dan Stuart's hometown, the *Dallas Morning News* was hailing its conquering hero. The paper described the outwitting of "Gov. Ahumada's copper-colored dudes" and reported, "The most artistic thing about the whole affair was the smoothness and ingeuinty [*sic*] exercised by that great pugilistic general, Hold-Fast Stuart in the selection of a battle ground."

The paper even poked some fun at the Rangers: ". . . it was amusing to see the flower of the frontier guard sitting on the crags above with their rifles resting lazily on their laps while that great and unpardonable crime, the big glove contest, was taking place a few hundred yards away."

(This view was shortly countered by a telegram to Mabrey sent by Acting Gov. George Jester that read, in part, "I desire to thank you on behalf of the law-abiding citizens of Texas for the active and successful effort of yourself and command in enforcing our laws and protecting the honor of Texas in preventing the prize fight from taking place on Texas soil.")

Before the local newsmen got back to more mundane stories ("All members of the El Paso Whittling Club are requested to meet at Van Patten's Corral at (1) one o'clock sharp this Sunday"), one ceremony remained—saying good-bye to the hoard of correspondents who put El Paso on the nation's sporting map.

Thirty sportswriters showed up for a "sumptuous supper" at the Palace Restaurant on El Paso Street the night after the fight. New Mexico's Governor Thornton was also present. There were toasts all around, including one from Lou Houseman titled, "Prayer Slipped a Cog." Siler, Ade, and Thornton all made speeches, and Dan Stuart was hailed as a "dead game sport" by one and all. The evening ended with a chorus of "Auld Lang Syne," and then everyone went their separate ways.

After nine months, Dan Stuart's fistic carnival was over.

Corbett was still fuming, of course. "I expect nothing further from Fitzsimmons. He has again showed that he does not want to fight, never did and never will, if he can help it."

But Fitz did an extraordinary thing—he gave up his title, saying, "To show Corbett how little weight his championship presented to Maher carried, I now formally renounce all claims to the belt and refuse to accept it."

The gesture had all the signs of a new fistic carnival in the making. Especially when Corbett responded by saying: "He is a big coward. I will leave it to the public to judge as to whether I am correct or not." His words were intended to provoke Fitz into action. "Mark what I say, that man Fitzsimmons will never meet me," he gamely predicted, "but the public will force him into it eventually. I don't know what Fitzsimmons plans for the future are, but wherever he goes I will go and he will finally have to meet me. There will be no flukes then. You can bet on that. I am not particular about money for a match. I want to beat this imitation whether there is a cent in it or not."

Yup, the two lovebirds were at it again.

Back in Dallas, Dan Stuart finally held a press conference. On his personal losses in the carnival, he said, "I am not kicking. The baby act is new to me. If it was to do over again I would take the same medicine."

Could the fight have been stopped? "They ought to have had President Diaz call a special session of the Mexican congress," said Stuart, aiming a jab at his own state's legislators, "and made provision for policing every foot of the border from the gulf to California. That might have been successful."

Was there ever any doubt in the mind of Hold-Fast Stuart? "I told those people I would provide a place for them to fight free from interference, where no law would be violated. I have done it. The fight is over. All that I had to do with it was to make my word good. I generally do that when it is possible."

Now that it was all over, Dan Stuart was content to step out of the uncomfortable spotlight, but the accolades must have been very satisfying.

The *Houston Post* called him a good leader and businessman, "a genius in certain lines," a square man "strictly on the level," as well as being "modest and unobstrusive." Which made the writer wonder how disgusted Stuart must be "to do business with many of the freaks and macers on the outskirts of the pugilistic camp."

Governor Thornton's *Santa Fe New Mexican:* "The manner in which Dan Stuart outwitted the Mexican authorities shows him to posses rather clever managereal [sic] ability."

The El Paso Daily Herald: "Dan Stuart came in like a meteor and went out the same way . . . he is made of that tenacity of purpose that wins against all obstacles. . . . With the loss of thousands of dollars staring him in the face he never flinched or squealed."

The *New York World* put a picture of Stuart on its front page and captioned it: "DAN A. STUART, WHO OUTWITTED THE MEXICANS. Mr. Stuart is a prize-fight manager who 'pulled off' his fight when the United States Government, the Texas Rangers, the Mexican Rurales, the Arizona militia and half a dozen Governors were united against him. Mr. Stuart is in the pool-room business in Dallas, Tex."

To the victor belongs the laurels.

CARSON CITY AND BEYOND

The sporting public demand a fight between Corbett and Fitzsimmons and neither will be allowed to squirm out of it.

—*El Paso Daily Herald,*
February 26, 1896

IT DIDN'T TAKE LONG for Fitz and Maher to meet again. The two climbed into the ring at Madison Square Garden on February 29, eight days after the Langtry knockout.

Fitz was duly introduced as the Middleweight *and* Heavyweight Champion of the World and received both cheers and huge floral offerings in tribute.

Maher's reception was even noisier. The *New York Times* explained that the reception was because Maher "is the one prizefighter in America, possibly in the world, who fights with his fists, instead of depending on his ability to call names and write letters full of bluff and bluster."

They sparred for three rounds, each landing a few good shots, and never fought each other again.

William Brady was in the crowd and tried to challenge Fitz in the name of Jim Corbett, but he was booed and hooted down by the fans.

Ex-champ Corbett hated being told he had to get a reputation before challenging Fitz, but that was how he had once chided the Australian. While on tour in June, Corbett arranged an exhibition match with Tom Sharkey, the first time he'd been in the ring in eighteen months, and the first hard, meaningful fight he'd had since beating Sullivan nearly four years earlier.

They met in San Francisco for a scheduled four rounds on February 24. Corbett controlled the first two rounds, then Sharkey moved in close and gave him a tough fight and might have pulled off a win, but the police broke it up, and it was ruled a draw.

The next to try "Sailor" Sharkey was Fitzsimmons five months later, and he got a rude surprise. Before the fight even started, Julian charged fraud: "I have it on good authority, we can't win." The referee was ex-Marshal Wyatt Earp, a man whose integrity never quite matched his status as Legendary Western Hero.

Sharkey, by all accounts, was nearly out in the eighth round when he was floored by Fitz, and Earp immediately called the blow foul and awarded the fight to the man writhing on the floor. The partisan crowd was not in agreement and started forward, as if to enter the ring for a spirited discussion. Earp reportedly drew his gun and asked, "Any questions?"[1] He had an engaging way of winning over an audience.

The veteran gunfighter later said, "It was clearly a foul." Fitz saw it differently. "I was simply robbed of $10,000," he charged. "I never struck a foul blow in my life, and no one knows better than Sharkey that I won last night's fight fair and square."

Julian was so enraged he offered to let Fitz meet both Sharkey *and* Corbett in the same ring. The case went to court.

"Australian" Billy Smith, Sharkey's trainer, testified that Earp was hired with the understanding that he was to award Sharkey the fight any time Fitz came close to landing a blow that might be "stretched into a foul," for which Wyatt would be paid $2,500.

The case was thrown out on a technicality—the law made no distinction between a glove contest and a prizefight. Sharkey kept the money and claimed the title, though few outside his own backers recognized it.

Meanwhile, Dan Stuart was feeling unfulfilled. In June of 1895, he had promised a fight between Corbett and Fitzsimmons. He had also promised to build an amphitheater. Neither promise could be carried out, through no fault of his own. Still, for a man with Stuart's sense of personal honor, this was a state of affairs that had to be rectified.

And Corbett was now chasing Fitz the way Fitz once chased him. It just might come off this time. Despite the many laws against prizefighting, there had to be a place in the states where the two men could fight unmolested by politicians or preachers.

Stuart studied the situation, and decided Nevada was the place. Nevada had an anti-fight law, it was true, but laws could be rescinded. With the help of W. K. Wheelock, Stuart set about his task, gaining support from a number of cities before approaching the legislature.

He had picked—not entirely by accident—a most convenient time for his lobbying. George Siler explained it this way: "Stuart quietly and diplomatically turned to the bankrupted Commonwealth of Nevada, with a total population of less than 60,000 and a hopeless insolvency. The Sage Hen State opened wide its arms and embraced Stuart and his enterprise." The bill making prizefights legal passed "with the alacrity of a legislative junketing appropriation."

Corbett met with Fitz and Stuart, the artful stage manager, in December. The place was New York's Bartholdi Hotel, and they signed for a "finish" fight and a $15,000 purse, plus side bets.[2] The big battle was set for St. Patrick's Day, 1897.

Stuart settled on Carson City as the lucky site of the mini-economic boom, and then hired an architect—this time he *would* build an amphitheater.

By March 1, a hundred men were at work, the best carpenters getting $5 a day to nail together the half-million feet of lumber. P. J. Donahue's design was based on Rome's coliseum with one improvement: a canopy could be placed over the ring high enough so as not to block the view from anywhere in the arena. The fighters would be safe from rain, sleet, and snow, even if the paying customers had to suffer.

The same gang of characters trooped to Nevada with the stars of the show—Julian, Brady, "One-Eyed" Connelly, Enoch Rector with his improved Kinetoscope (now called a Veriscope), and John L. Sullivan, who, though fat and out of shape, announced he would challenge the winner. George Siler was again hired as referee and Bat Masterson put in charge of security.

The rhetoric exchanged by both camps in the papers hadn't changed either, though quotes from Fitz and Julian were not as readily available as before. For a fee of $10,000 in cash, William Randolph Hearst had secured exclusive access to Fitzsimmons, sending reporter Robert Hobart Davis to serve as the fighter's "secretary," much to the annoyance of other writers. Competitors were eventually forced to pay Hearst for his syndicated stories.[3]

One new element was the amount of odd fan mail both men received. The quantity of the regular mail was awesome enough. The *Chicago Tribune* noted, "It would take a corps of stenographers big enough to equip the auditing department of the average railroad company" to answer it all. But the contents were often bizarre.

They each received "lucky" rabbits' feet in every delivery, along with "Hoodoo charms of all sorts." A Brooklyn woman sent Corbett the "wishbone of my favorite dove," and directed that it be put in the folds of his belt.

Corbett also received clippings from a bulldog's ear because its owner didn't believe in the powers of amputated bunny appendages. "He never whimpered when he gave them up," wrote the man of the ear clippings. "They are the true symbols of unflinching courage and fighting qualifications. The rabbit foot, with all its fabled virtues, isn't in it with a ring charm of this description."

There was also a new face in the Corbett camp, a hulking youngster named James J. Jeffries. His main task was rubbing down one of the champ's legs. "I never dreamed that any human being could hit so hard," Jeffries commented after sparring with his boss. "I think Jim will tear his head off him."

Julian was now charging a dollar for people to watch Fitzsimmons train and say things (through his "secretary") like, "I am not afraid of anything that breathes," or bits of hyperbole such as, "Altogether I have knocked out 300 men in this and other countries, and I don't propose to stop now."

Then Stuart was brought down with an illness in February that nearly killed him. He was laid up in Carson City for seventeen days; while it lasted, he was saturated with quinine and morphine. He emerged into the daylight ten days before the fight, looking pale and bearded, but recovering.

The *Tribune* paid tribute to his stubbornness. "Dan Stuart figures that it will cost him close to $75,000 to have Corbett and Fitz shake hands on St. Patrick's Day. In this Stuart includes the losses he sustained at Dallas and at Hot Springs. Were he to include the Maher-Fitz affair this sum would be swelled by another $18,000 or $20,000."

When it came time to start easing off the addictive drugs, Stuart told the doctor to stop the treatments entirely. It made him suffer "the tortures of the damned," but, "I'm bound not to become a fiend." Dan Stuart always accomplished what he set his mind to, of that everyone was now certain.

The biggest controversy of the prefight hype came on March 10, when Fitz happened upon Corbett while both were doing roadwork with their trainers and a couple of newsmen. Fitz spied the Pompadour and picked up speed, quickly overtaking him. Their respective dogs instantly got into a fight (like owner, like pet).

Fitz offered his hand as they jogged shoulder to shoulder and Corbett refused, saying, "I'll shake hands with you if you lick me over there on the seventeenth, not before." Unfriendly words were exchanged—the *Tribune* called it "a slanging match"—and as Fitz jogged off Corbett added, "and don't forget to bring the dog with you."

In the next day's paper, Ruby Rob wrote out his version of the encounter and promised, "I will fight a square fight, an honorable fight, but there shall be no mercy, no quarter, no tenderness. I will fight him to the bitter end and conclude this issue and wipe out his insults."

The arena was not as grand as the one attempted at Dallas. The Carson City version would hold only seventeen thousand people, with an estimated gate receipt of $300,000 if it was filled. As always, large sums of money fascinated newswriters and readers alike. It was said that Rector had bid $11,000 for the film rights, with all the money to go to Stuart, weather permitting.[4]

There was snow and slush all that week, and a lot of fingers were crossed. Stuart slept with his window up the night before the fight, and the first thing he said at dawn was, "St. Patrick's Day is with me." Conditions were perfect. The snowcapped Sierras were sharply outlined against a turquoise sky and the breeze was light; more important, the cameras were ready for the first title fight to be captured on film.[5]

Dan Stuart was elated. "This is my one chance to get even, after three years of hard work that I have been through with all these fighters. It marks the beginning of the end with me, and I rather think that when this thing is over that I will be out of the fighting business for good."

At their hotel, Rose Fitzsimmons was overheard praying for her husband's victory. Robert Davis suggested Fitz might care to join her. The Cornishman from New Zealand shook his head and said, quite reasonably, "What's the use? If 'E won't do it for 'er, 'E won't do it for me."[6]

The fight was set for 10:00 A.M. The turnout was far less than expected. Instead of seventeen thousand customers, it looked as if only four thousand made the trip to Nevada. As the fans began arriving, there was spied a sprinkling of women in the crowd. Stuart had not only allowed "properly escorted" ladies to witness the fisticuffs, but had set aside special sections for them away from the rude men. This chivalry did not meet the approval of chauvinist Sullivan.

"I am not in favor of having ladies at fights," reported John L. "It is natural that they should admire fighters. Naturally they think more of a man who can fight than of any other man, because if men did not fight we should all be slaves and the English or somebody else would rule us. George Washington was a fighter, and no man was more admired by the ladies than he was. But ladies ought not to see fights."

Imagine his surprise when Rose Fitzsimmons took a seat near her husband's corner and acted as one of his seconds! By all accounts, this was the first time in the history of boxing that a wife had shared her husband's corner. "She was vigorously cheered when she entered the arena," said the *Tribune*, "and appeared entirely self-contained and unconcerned."

Dan Stuart's prize ring in Carson City on fight day—Siler, Fitz, and Corbett at work left of center. It was a smaller ring than that envisioned for Dallas two years earlier, and the fight was not a sell-out, but Stuart finally did what he set out to do. Courtesy Library of Congress.

In Chicago's City Hall Park, twenty-five thousand people had gathered to hear fight bulletins from the telegraphers. Eight thousand fans were jammed into New York's Herald Square, Broadway and Sixth, each report to be wildly cheered by various factions.

After receiving Siler's instructions, Corbett routinely held out his gloved hand and Fitz, in reflex, nearly took it, but Julian yelled, "No! No! No handshake, remember!" It was a calculated response to the incident on the road and Fitz withdrew his hand. A lot of festering animosities were about to be discharged.[7]

The fight began two hours and eight minutes late. Fitzsimmons started as the aggressor, with Corbett backing and dancing away. There were clinches, hard exchanges, wild misses, and each man got in his share of licks, but no significant damage was done.

In the second, Fitz stayed on the offensive, forcing Corbett into a corner and swinging right and left for the body, but the pompadoured dandy stayed just out of reach. Long-range sparring marked round two, with Corbett's speed dominating. The round closed with a clinch.

Corbett turned on the steam in the third and landed "a left jab hard on the wind." Then he put one into Fitz's stomach and a right to the side of his head. Fitz recovered and there was an exchange of body blows. During a clinch, "Corbett swung right on the jaw." There was hard punching from both and the round was judged a draw.

Rose had sat quietly during those opening rounds, but as the pace quickened so did her excitement. She began rising to her feet to shout encouragement, sometimes standing on her chair and shouting reproaches at her husband's seconds: "You idiots. You don't know how to second a man; you have lost your senses."

The *Chicago Tribune* reported, "As the battle went on she became more and more demonstrative, sometimes breaking out with exclamations which bordered on the profane."

Fitz was "determined but slow" in the fourth, and Corbett picked up the pace. The Australian's punches usually landed short and wide while Corbett's irritating jabs were right on target, including a right under the ear, a left straight in the face, and several more to the stomach. They were in a clinch "and smiling in each other's faces" when the gong sounded.

Corbett felt he was winning. "Left-hand jabs marked his face up pretty well," he wrote later. "He was missing most of the time. . . . a few of his misses were by ten-foot margins, and he looked as foolish as had Sullivan at New Orleans." After five rounds, "I had bothered him by cutting his face to ribbons, jolted him pretty badly, and he was rather tired."[8]

Fitzsimmons hit the deck in the sixth. He opened with two clean misses, appeared to wrestle Corbett against the ropes and drew a caution from Siler. They sparred lightly and again Fitz missed with a roundhouse swing at the jaw.

Corbett landed a left to the mouth and nose that started blood flowing. Now Jim was on the offensive, backing Fitz around the ring. The action was fast and furious when Corbett swung his left and seemed to catch Fitz under the ear; in a blink, the redhead was on his knees.

Corbett's account of the knockdown differed from press reports. "As he crouched there, in a daze, he clutched my legs with his arms. The referee, George Siler, for some reason was not counting, which he should have done, and I told him to make Fitz let go. As I spoke, Fitz released his clutch, and the referee, rather late, did begin to count."

This clutching at Corbett's knees was not mentioned in the blow-by-blow accounts the next day.

"'You're counting slow,' I told him, and he pushed me with his left hand and ordered me to 'step back!'"

Said Corbett, twenty-eight years later, "I don't like to squeal, but Fitzsimmons was on the ground, as you can reckon from the foregoing description, fully fifteen seconds. I have never spoken of this incident before, and feeling I had him at my mercy, I didn't complain then."[9]

By the count of nine, Fitz was again on his feet, keeping away as he let his legendary recuperative powers go to work. He was still slow and took some uppercuts in the clinches, and appeared groggy, but Corbett wasn't able to finish him off.

In his corner Fitz reassured his concerned wife, saying, "Never mind the blood, I've got him licked." It was a game remark with seemingly no factual basis; he looked awful.

Fitz was bleeding heavily now and took more jabs to the face in the seventh—Corbett, said the *New York Times,* "was plentifully besmeared with the Australian's gore."

He wasn't the only one. Corbett noticed a blonde woman screaming in the crowd, "the blood from Fitz spattering her own face." In the midst of the battle he could hear her "yelling at me things that were not at all flattering either to my skill as a fighter or my conduct as a gentleman. The lady was constantly urging Fitz to—'Hit him in the slats, Bob, hit him in the slats!'"[10] At that point, Corbett probably would have backed Sullivan on his bias against female spectators.

More of Bob's blood was drawn in the eighth, from both the nose and mouth. Yet he actually seemed to be getting stronger.

Corbett targeted the gushing nose in the ninth, the way Fitz had once worked on Peter Maher's cut mouth in New Orleans. Fitz was swinging wildly, landing few solid hits beyond one "pile-driver right" to the body.

Rose was screaming at Corbett—"The hound!" "The puppy!"—and urging her husband on: "Punch him, Bob!" she yelled. "Kill him!"

Corbett was slowing down. The bloody Fitzsimmons, earning his "Ruby Rob" nickname, launched a fresh assault in the tenth, connecting with three hard lefts to the head and a right over the ear. Fitz went to his corner looking satisfied; Corbett looked gray and had stopped smiling.

Clinches were frequent in the eleventh with Fitz on the attack, while Corbett appeared to fade, welcoming the bell.

A heavy left to the body came close to doubling Corbett over in the twelfth. Both men went for the face with blows and counter blows. When the bell sounded, Fitz was again bleeding freely.

After two years of talking up a storm, Fitz and Corbett finally clinch in a ring for the heavyweight championship. Courtesy Nevada Historical Society.

In the thirteenth, Corbett paused to spit out a loosened tooth. Fitz later recalled, "I had the satisfaction of knocking out one of his gold teeth, and perhaps two. He looked awful sorry when he got the crack, and flushed to the roots of his hair."

Corbett was not done. After taking a hard right on the short ribs that drove him back a foot, Corbett retaliated, sending Fitz's head snapping back with a "left jolt on the chin," followed by a right uppercut. A left to Bob's nose started a fresh flow of blood but left the recipient looking unconcerned.

In the fourteenth, Corbett thought Fitz's wild swings were "now worse than an amateur, just taking desperate chances. Then I knew I had him," Jim recalled, for he had never before seen Fitzsimmons in such a state. "And to see him flailing away so blindly at me convinced me that he was bewildered and panicky over the fact that he couldn't time me at all and I was outsmarting him. Like all fighters, even the great ones, now that he felt that he was meeting a man who really had it 'on' him, he had forgotten all it had taken so many years and so many and painful battles to learn, and was fighting like a kid." Corbett was smugly confident at that point. "'One good punch,' said I to myself, 'will settle him now.'"[11]

He was right about the end coming with one good punch.

They both went for the jaw, Corbett landing a left and Fitz countering with both a right and left, jarring the Californian. Corbett hooked in another left and Fitzsimmons slammed back a heavy right in response, followed by a clinch.

Then it happened.

Fitz faked a right. Corbett leaned his head and chest back out of the way, just for a second leaving his stomach forward and unprotected.

Said the *New York Times,* "The Australian's small eyes twinkled, and with panther-like speed he drew back his left with the forearm rigid and ripped it up into the pit of Corbett's stomach a little under the heart. Corbett was lifted about a foot off the ground, and as he pitched forward Fitzsimmons swung a right on the jaw and Corbett came heavily down to his knees."

"I was conscious of everything that went on," wrote Corbett, "the silence of the crowd, the agony on the faces of my seconds, the waiting Fitzsimmons, but my body was like that of a man stricken with paralysis."[12]

As Siler began his count, Jim reached for the rope, missed, and fell on his face. The count went on.

There were shouts of "Foul!" because of the punch on the jaw, but such a quick one-two could not have been checked.

The altitude was seven thousand feet, and the air thin. Corbett crawled about on his wobbly knees but could not get up. Siler counted him out, and the fight was over.

Robert Fitzsimmons was the undisputed champion in both the middleweight and heavyweight divisions.

Corbett called the solar plexus shot "a sneaking little punch," and, once he regained his breath, erupted with fury. He fought his way through the crowd now in the ring, swinging wildly, trying to get at the winner. The *New York Times* called him "half-demented" at that point. Corbett landed some jabs while Fitz calmly waited for Brady and others to pull him away.

Enraged, Rose Fitzsimmons climbed into the ring and struggled to get at Corbett, screaming, "I'll kill him! I'll kill the coward!"

Once things had calmed down, Corbett approached the new champ and said, "You licked me fair and square. Now, I want you to give me another chance."

"I will not fight you again," said Fitz, having already proved his point.

"Then I will punch you in the head the first time I meet you on the street."

"If you do," returned Fitz with a smile, "I will kill you."

Corbett remained unconsoled, telling the *Chicago Tribune,* "I believe in the main I fought as well as ever I fought in my life, but luck was against me. The blow which won the fight for Fitz was in a large measure an accidental one."[13]

Fitz dismissed the idea of a lucky punch, sneaky or otherwise. Elaborating on his long road to victory, Fitz commented, "Unmindful of the right I had to challenge him, and totally ignoring the quality of my record, he maliciously maligned me, spat in my face, refused to take my hand, otherwise exhibited conduct unbecoming a gentleman. It took the combined efforts of his manager, Dan Stuart, and the public mind to get him to confront me so either one or the other could prove superiority."

It was estimated Fitz would clear $50,000 on the fight, including side bets.

That night a Montana miner named Dick Bradford, who had backed Fitzsimmons, was shot dead in a Carson City saloon brawl by a Corbett backer named Smith. Smith was jailed, and there was talk of a possible lynching.

"With apologies to Rudyard Kipling," the *Dallas Morning News* published a poem in honor of the new champ on March 19.

Fitzy Witzy

We've met with many pugs from crost the seas,
An' some of them was brave an' some was not;
There's Mace an' Mitchell an' Maher, please;
But Fitzy is the toughest of the lot.

So here's to you, Fitzy Witzy, and the boys will
rush the can;
You are not a howling beauty, but a first-class
fighting man.
We will give you your certifikit an' if you want
it signed
There are others who will romp with you whenever
you're inclined. . . .

So here's to you, Fitzy Witzy, an' the Missus an'
the Kid:

> Your programme was to lick him an' of course you
> went an' did.
> He thumped you right an' left, an' had you in
> the air,
> But for all the odds agin you, you licked him fair
> and square. . . .
> So here's to you, Fitzy Witzy, an' your sunny head
> o' hair—
> You big, red, freckled beggar, you licked him on
> the square.

Ministerial and legislative groups began lobbying against the exhibition of fight films almost immediately.[14]

A big crowd of friends and well-wishers greeted Dan Stuart on his return to Dallas on the evening of March 25—there was a rousing welcome for the weary manager and a party three hours later (attended by Mayor Frank Holland, who won money on Fitz).

Stuart was haggard from his illness in Carson City, now labeled pneumonia, and sported a month's growth of beard. "My tough spell of sickness has made me nervous," Stuart told reporters, "but I shall be myself again after a brief resting spell." No one doubted it, for this was a man who did what he said he'd do.

"I started out to bring Corbett and Fitzsimmons together. It was uphill work for two years and I was continually against the hot end of the poker. I accomplished my purpose, the men met and fought as I pledged my word they would more than two years ago, and now I feel satisfied."

He termed his feat, "The greatest contest in ring history." No one argued with him.

One of the first items of business on return was to place a souvenir of the fight on display in his pool hall: Fitz's right-hand glove (the left glove was in the possession of Tom Williams of the *San Francisco Examiner*).

Of his future plans, Stuart would only say that he would be taking a rest cure at Mineral Springs, then attend to business.

With that, Dan Albert Stuart, the sport from Texas who became a boxing impresario, returned to where he was most comfortable, the background. His work was finished.

Gov. Charles A. Culberson won reelection and went on to become a U.S. Senator, while the law he ramrodded through the legislature lasted more than thirty years; "Knife-to-the-Hilt" Crane became a prominent

Dallas attorney; Thomas Catron became New Mexico's first U.S. Senator; Adjutant General Mabry resigned to fight in the Cuban revolution, where he was killed; Capt. Bill McDonald went on to more Ranger exploits, leading black troops of the 25th Infantry at Brownsville, becoming state revenue agent in 1907 and Woodrow Wilson's bodyguard in 1912; Bat Masterson became a New York sportswriter.

Of the other players in the great fistic carnival, there never again was such a high point in their lives.

Peter Maher's next big fight was with Tom Sharkey on June 9, 1897; the police arrested both of them in the seventh round. Maher never regained his status as a contender and retired.

Around 1920, columnist Westbrook Pegler sought him out. "I found Maher drousing on a barrel on a dock on the Jersey side of the Hudson River. He was a night watchman. I tried to 'interview' him, but he hardly remembered the fight."

John L. Sullivan challenged Fitz, and it was set for July 5, 1898, but was prevented by the police. Not surprisingly, Sullivan opened a bar in New York City. However, he reformed in 1905 and became, of all things, a temperance lecturer. He died in 1918, almost a pauper.

Jim Corbett took on Tom Sharkey again in 1898 and lost on a foul. He tried to regain the title in 1900 from his one-time sparring partner James Jeffries and was knocked out in the twenty-third round. Corbett knocked out contender Charles "Kid" McCoy three months later, sat out the years 1901 and 1902 and tried for Jeffries again in 1903. Jeffries knocked him out in ten rounds.

Jim returned to the stage, made some movies, wrote his autobiography in 1925, and died in 1933. He was elected to the Boxing Hall of Fame in 1954.

"Fitzy Witzy" announced his retirement after the Carson City triumph. "I have given a promise to my wife that I will never again enter the ring, and I will keep my word."

Fighting, however, was in his blood. He had an exhibition in Leadville less than three months later and knocked out a local blacksmith in two rounds. In 1899, Fitzsimmons met Jim Jeffries in Coney Island for the heavyweight title—and the big, strong Jeffries coldcocked him in the eleventh round to win the belt. Jim's manager was William Brady.

As ex-champion, Fitz continued to pummel all comers—his next five fights were all won by knockouts (including one over Sharkey in the second round that helped make up for the Earp fight three years earlier).

In 1902, at the age of thirty-nine, he again challenged the twenty-seven-year-old Jeffries. Jim won with an eighth-round knockout after Fitz had broken both his hands on Jeffries' head.

Fraud was charged in that fight by San Francisco's Mayor Eugene E. Schmitz and others. The mayor said he had heard the fix was in for the eighth round before the fight started. Both fighters denied the charges, and Jeffries picked up a paycheck of $14,346, while Fitz earned $9,564. The *New York Times* said, "even those who charge fraud . . . admit that it was a terrific fight while it lasted."

Rose Julian Fitzsimmons bore two more children, Martin and Rosie, and died of typhoid pneumonia in April of 1903. Three months later Fitz married an eighteen-year-old actress named Julia May Gifford in San Francisco. He was forty-one.

In November of that year, reduced in weight, Fitz took on George Gardner in San Francisco for the World Light-Heavyweight title, winning on points after twenty rounds. He held—and did not defend—the title for two years, losing it to his first opponent, "Philadelphia" Jack O'Brien, by a TKO in the thirteenth.

Despite his earlier disinclination to fight blacks, Fitzsimmons had a go at the up-and-coming Jack Johnson on July 17, 1907. Johnson knocked him out in the second round. (Three years later Johnson would knock out Jeffries and cause race riots and lynchings as the first black heavyweight champ.)

Fitz tried to get the Australian heavyweight title from Bill Lang in Sydney in 1909, and was knocked out in the twelfth.

Fitz still believed in high living and always had financial problems because of it. He once bought a ninety-horsepower race car belonging to racing champ Barney Oldfield, and his chauffeur wrecked it while trying to pass another car at high speed in Batavia, New York. It went into a ditch and Fitz was pinned beneath the rear seat. He was severely bruised and cut. It was 1911; he didn't fight again until 1914.

That year he met K. O. Sweeney on January 29 and Jersey Bellew on February 20. Both went six rounds and ended in no decision. Fitz was then fifty and found himself barred from the ring by the New York State Athletic Commission, which ruled he was "incapacitated by reason of his age and physical condition." An appeals court favored the Commission, and Fitz hung up his gloves, following Sullivan and Corbett to the vaudeville stage.[15]

In May of 1914, just a few days before his fifty-first birthday, Julia sued for divorce, charging he had treated her "with extreme and repeated cruelty" and had once threatened to kill her if she left him. Three years later and remarried, Julia told reporters, "We might have had a wonderful life together if it hadn't been for the whiskey."

Being an aging, ex-champ took its toll.

At the same time, his ex-agent, John Meek, sued him for $2,100. Meek said he prepared Fitz "to undergo the hardships of an actor," and got him a role in *The Girl from Maxim's,* for which he was never paid.

Things became even more complicated three weeks later, when a Middlesex grand jury indicted Fitz and a woman named Temo Ziller for immorality—they were living together without benefit of matrimony. Bob couldn't keep away from preacher-inspired laws.

Fitz went quietly, but Temo put up a fuss and asked the cops to shoot her. They thought it over and declined. The main witness against the sinful couple was Mrs. John Meek.[16]

A subsequent fourth marriage, to Temo, was rocky and in less than a year she sued him for $1,000 just as the sheriff attached his farm, cows and chickens for sale (presumably this also included the stuffed carcass of Nero on display inside). A disgusted Fitz declared he was going to South America to teach boxing, taking along a letter of reference from a big fan, Theodore Roosevelt. There's no evidence he ever went.

Money continued to elude him. On October 28, 1915, he was in his favorite Dunellen, New Jersey, saloon at 64 Market Street when James Hendricks came in and served him with a dispossess order on his farm. The action was brought by Hendricks' brother, a doctor.

Fitz "applied an objectionable epithet" to the doctor's name, and Hendricks slugged him in the mouth. Generally speaking, this is not the wisest thing one can do to an ex-heavyweight champion of the world.

"I started to swing for his jaw," Fitz later told a judge, "and if I had landed he would be asleep yet. I realized that and let the blow go to the solar plexus, and I must admit he was pretty dazed when he went out."

Understandably, as it was the same punch that decked Corbett nine years before. It had lost little in the interim. Fitz was found guilty and given a one-year probation. A sign of his finances is that he was ordered to pay off Hendricks's $10 doctor bill at fifty cents a week.

There was another, almost comic brush with the law in October of 1916. Fitz received a subpoena charging him with assaulting a black man with a pair of brass knuckles. The victim said he still managed to beat up his assailant. Incensed, Fitz declared, "I never saw this man in my life, and I don't think he could thrash me either."

He was right. The man who should have gotten the subpoena was the Reverend Fitzsimmons, a black man.

The lasting worldwide interest in the fistic carnival and the Carson City fight was such that in October of 1916, with war raging in Europe, a member of the French Academy sought to rally his countrymen with an apt analogy.

Maurice Donnay, meaning no disrespect, said in *Liberte* that people should think of Corbett as Germany and Fitzsimmons as France and her allies. "The indefatigable Fitzsimmons gave his opponent no respite. While conserving his own forces, he gradually wore out Corbett by raining incessant blows at a distance." The message being that "Courage, and tenacity had got the better of force." Donnay said the Kaiser's Germany was already "worried, harried, up against the ropes, appears 'groggy,'" and the moment for the famous solar plexus punch of nineteen years before was drawing near.

No Frenchman missed the connection. Such is fame.

Temo took up evangelism and, following a reconciliation, Fitz sobered up and found religion. They were performing together at South Chicago's Calumet vaudeville theater in 1917, when Fitz developed lobar pneumonia. His wife blamed the drafty theater. From his bed at Michael Reese Hospital, Fitz said, "I'm not going to give up until I'm counted out."

There was war news in the paper of the United States poised to head for the Western Front, and snow flurries in the air when, on October 22, after a five-day struggle, Robert Fitzsimmons died.

Eulogizing him as "a modern gladiator," the *New York Times* wrote: "With Robert Fitzsimmons passed away a protagonist of an ancient profession which has always been more or less honored. . . . With bare hands he should have sent some of the heroes of antiquity to sleep."

Texas-born son Robert, called away from a hunting trip, arrived in Chicago and found that all of Fitz's jewelry had been pawned or sold. Temo explained that Bob was "not always provident, but he meant all right." Bob junior argued with the widow over the burial, insisting his father had wanted to be cremated.

When it became clear Fitz would be buried at Chicago's Graceland Cemetery, young Bob snapped, "I'm not welcome here." He returned to New York without waiting for the funeral. "I have a commission as boxing instructor in the U.S.A., a lock of my dad's hair in my pocket, the return end of a round trip railroad ticket in my pocket, and deer waiting for my gun. I'm off." He also inherited his father's temper.

Before several thousand friends and fans, the Reverend Paul Rader of Chicago's Moody Tabernacle, a former college boxer, spoke well of Fitzsimmons and his late baptism, calling it "the symbol of the casting off of the old man for the new." He added, "Bob fought his final fight as he had fought his ring battles—with indomitable courage."

There was a memorial service in New York at the Campbell Funeral Church on 66th and Broadway and many of the all-time great boxers came to pay their respects. For a change, Jim Corbett got up and said nice things about him, about his gallantry and capacity for friendship.

In the Antipodes, on the land known as New Zealand, an old Irishman worked the forge at a Timaru blacksmith shop. Fitz had left the shop almost thirty years before, but the sign over the door still read, "Bob Fitzsimmons, Blacksmith." His fame and success had earned him a memorial before his time.

As Longfellow wrote: "Thus at the flaming forge of life/Our fortunes must be wrought;/Thus on its sounding anvil shaped/Each burning deed and thought."

Fitzsimmons was elected to the Boxing Hall of Fame in 1954.

EPILOGUE

BOXING, of course, survived, despite many more frontal assaults.

In December of 1899, a New York meeting of Methodist preachers condemned the sport as "brutal," "a crime against the peace and dignity of the Nation," "this public shame" that appealed strictly to "every base appetite of depraved human nature," and approved only by "motley" hoards who afterwards "make the night hideous with a saturnalia of vice and crime."

They also condemned newspapers for carrying descriptions of prizefights which "further debauch the public mind" with "page after page of sickening details" that dared to "enter homes of piety and peace. Like Egyptian frogs, these reports penetrated every place with their loathsomeness. The morning trains carried reports written in the most seductive style to every part of the land."

Those who promoted fights were "greedy purveyors of amusement" pandering to "promiscuous audiences."

There was nothing like boxing to bring out the fire and brimstone.

Bowing to such pressure, in 1912 Congress passed a federal law prohibiting the interstate transportation of photos or movies of prizefights, violators to be fined $1,000 for each heinous offense.

Eventually even Texas bowed to the inevitable and legalized boxing, overturning Governor Culberson's legislative pride and joy, though a 1933 statute legalizing it in the Lone Star State did make a notable exception. It prohibited "fistic combat matches, boxing, sparring, or wrestling between any person of the White Race and one of the Negro Race."[1]

And, yes, men continued to die in the ring—nearly five hundred between 1918 and 1988; welterweight champ Benny "Kid" Paret was fatally injured by Emile Griffith on national television in 1962. People continue to debate the nature of the sport to this day, and men at the peak of their physical prowess, scientifically trained to absorb and inflict the maximum of punishment, continue to risk permanent injury and death in the ring. A 1988 *Time* magazine cover of then-champion Mike Tyson asked, "Why the Fascination With Boxing?"[2] Why, indeed?

On June 27, 1988, Tyson whipped Michael Spinks in slightly less time than Fitzsimmons beat Peter Maher that drizzly day on a Rio Grande sandbar. But Tyson and Spinks fought in glitzy comfort in Atlantic City, and both earned millions.

That fight was, in the words of *TV Guide,* the "highest grossing one-day event in sports history," *any* sport, taking in some fifty-eight million dollars from cable and closed-circuit TV rights alone. Ringside seats were $1,500. People who never heard of the Kinetoscope watched live pictures from the Goodyear blimp and endless slow-motion replays.[3]

If nothing else, Tyson and Spinks turned inside-out John L. Sullivan's remark of ninety-two years earlier, on his way to El Paso, that the day of the big $10,000 purses was over.

That fight too received its share of condemnation. *The New Republic* used the same basic arguments of the preachers who tried to stop Fitzsimmons, Corbett, and Maher. Boxing was described as "barbarism," a bad influence on youth ("Boxers get rich without an education"), and predicted that someday "anthropologists will look back at our society and marvel at the persistent popularity of boxing at this late date in human evolution." It was claimed that "homicides increase appreciably after every nationally broadcast heavyweight championship fight."

The *New Republic* called for criminalizing boxing by placing it in the same ranks as "drug use, prostitution, and several other 'victimless' pastimes," and blasted *Time* and others for placing Mike Tyson on their covers.[4]

Foes appeared vindicated when Tyson was convicted of rape in 1992. A hoped-for championship fight with new champ Evander Holyfield that had figured to bring a record $100 million purse was cancelled. In the wake of the conviction, Joyce Carol Oates, while calling the sport "publicly condoned sadism," was moved to write in *Newsweek* (February 24, 1992), "What makes boxing repulsive to many observers is precisely what makes boxing so fascinating to participants."

And the monetary payoff keeps growing. When Evander Holyfield lost his crown to Riddick Bowe, *Newsweek* (November 23, 1992) noted that in two years as champ Holyfield earned an estimated $80 million and commented, "Punishment has its rewards."

Rewarding enough, apparently, to make a fellow masochistic: Holyfield took back his title in a bruising match in Las Vegas on November 6,

1993—a bout estimated to have been worth some $12 million to both fighters. That pays for a lot of dental work.

(Holyfield lost the title to Michael Moorer in a close decision on April 22, 1994, in Las Vegas, Nevada, and Moorer became the first left-handed champ in heavyweight history. Holyfield's true grit was never more apparent when, four days later, it was announced that he had fought the twelve punishing rounds with a previously undetected congenital heart condition that could well have killed him. Knowing when to hang up the gloves, Holyfield retired.)

Fighters haven't changed much over the years, though some are classier than others, and neither have their fans and foes. The continuing popularity of the sport in light of all efforts to stop it and all the body blows it has taken from unscrupulous participants, shows how difficult—if not impossible—it is to legislate any one view of "morality" in an ever-changing society.

As Oates rhetorically asked, "Is there any athlete, however celebrated in his own sport, who would not rather reign as the heavyweight champion of the world?" The mystique lives on.

CHAPTER NOTES

THE FULL STORY of the fistic carnival has never before been told. Consequently, most of the material in this book comes directly from contemporary newspaper accounts. A list of specific papers and dates appears in the bibliography. Book citations and other pertinent (or merely interesting) information in the text follow.

PRELIMS

1. Bernard Grun, *The Timetables of History,* p. 449.

2. Herbert G. Goldman, ed., *The Ring Record Book and Boxing Encyclopedia.* The London Prize Fight Rules did not address fist coverings but did forbid "all attempts to inflict injury by gouging or tearing the flesh with the fingers or nails." Biting, kicking, and head-butting were also considered fouls. Should either contestant prove less than gentlemanly, rule number five provided for a frisk to make sure that the fighters' tights contained no more than what nature provided: "On the men being stripped it shall be the duty of the seconds to examine their drawers, and if any objection arises as to the insertion of improper substances therein, they shall appeal to their umpires. . . ."

3. *New York Times,* September 19, 1886.

4. Donald Barr Chidsey, *John the Great.* Acting did have its shortcomings. The *Houston Post* reported on September 20, 1895, that Sullivan "declares that never again will he tread the boards as an actor. He has an undying hatred for the stage, for it was an actor who seized John's wardrobe in a Southern city, recently, and left John in a condition which would have made it necessary for him to be shipped home in a hogshead did not some kind friends come to the front with some clothes."

5. "Billy Muldoon," said the *El Paso Daily Herald* for January 3, 1896, "is the prince of American trainers. He trained Sullivan for his fight with Jack Kilrain and transformed a bloated and besotted hulking giant into the most perfect specimen of physical manhood that ever stepped into the fistic ring."

6. *Webster's American Biographies.*

7. Elliott Gorn, *The Manly Art.*

8. Ibid, p. 246.

9. James J. Corbett, *The Roar of the Crowd,* pp. 112–14. Sullivan was appalled at the match and asked Corbett if it was true. When the fact was confirmed, Sullivan shook his head and said, "Well, you shouldn't fight a nigger." As for Corbett's

egalitarianism, his was a quest for boxing knowledge: "I have sparred plenty of white men, but here I am soon to crawl in the ropes to fight to the finish with a Herculean black, and I do not know how it seems to stand in front of one of them; there may be something in a dark opponent that is not found in a light one, and, if so, it behooves me to find out. The sooner the better." (*Dallas Morning News,* September 14, 1895.)

10. Corbett, p. 141.

11. In *The Fighting Man,* William A. Brady asserts that "after the thirtieth round both men stopped fighting and did nothing but circle around the ring, striking no blows . . . and the match was declared a farce."

12. Corbett, p. 187.

13. Corbett, p. 201.

14. John L. Sullivan's usual method of fight training was, by today's standards, appalling. The October 17, 1895, edition of the *Dallas Morning News* reported that Sullivan "would do little besides punching the bag and taking short daily 'spins' over the roads, and spent most of his time in carousing after nightfall. . . . He used often to say that the principal part of his training was a shave, a shampoo and a cold water bath just before a fight."

15. Charles Neider, ed., *The Selected Letters of Mark Twain,* p. 224.

16. Richard Rainbolt, *Boxing's Heavyweight Champions,* p. 39.

17. Corbett, p. 326.

18. Alexander Johnson, *Ten . . . and Out!,* p. 125.

19. Because of the lion, purchased at the Wombwell Show during a visit to Coney Island, Fitzsimmons was hardly the best choice as a neighbor. One memorable incident happened while training for the Corbett fight. As he returned home from a bicycle ride to Brooklyn, "one of the knickerbockered, bicycle-mounted policemen who guard the boulevard saw Bob's long legs and red hair tearing along toward Coney Island" at an unlawful speed. The fighter was already home and dismounted before the policeman arrived, puffing, to be met by a lion growling and roaming about the yard. The prudent officer accepted a soda and did not write a ticket. (*New Orleans Picayune,* September 28, 1895.)

20. *New York Times,* October 12, 1894.

21. *New Orleans Picayune,* December 11, 1894.

22. *New Orleans Picayune,* May 10, 1895.

23. *New Orleans Picayune,* May 22, 1895.

ROUND ONE: DALLAS, PART ONE

1. Joan L. Dobson, Dallas County Public Library, personal conversation.

2. *Memorial and Biographical History of Dallas, Texas.*

3. E. H. R. Green, president of the Texas Midland Railway and the son of Hettie Green, the richest and possibly most eccentric woman in the world (known in her day as "The Witch of Wall Street"), was so taken up in the fight atmosphere that he offered to provide Corbett, his favorite, with free training facilities. He also put up a bet of $3,000 on Corbett against $2,000 wagered on Fitzsimmons by John W. Dunne, a Chicago theatrical man.

4. The offer was tendered by a one-time Sullivan backer, Henry Phillips, who guaranteed no police interference. His enthusiasm for prizefighting was not shared by Canadian officialdom. The *Picayune* reported on June 4, 1895, that Attorney General

Casgrain of Quebec flatly refused to have the fisticuffs take place in his province: "I will take all possible means to stop it if any attempt is made to have the contest here."

5. Fair officials were eager for the immense crowds and profits expected in connection with the fight but refrained from publicly being linked with or endorsing the bout.

6. He was paraphrasing a famous line Corbett reportedly used before stepping into the ring to meet Sullivan, "It's all over but the applause."

7. *New Orleans Picayune,* June 8, 1895. In February, Oscar Wilde brought a libel suit against the Marquis of Queensberry, lost, and began a tragic chain of reprisals that ended with Wilde in jail for two years of hard labor, from which he never fully recovered.

8. One such meeting was called by ex-alderman J. H. Webster. "He is laughed at generally," reported the *Picayune,* which called him "the Anthony Comstock of Dallas," referring to the legendary postal prude. The paper chuckled over his ineffectual ravings: "Webster is leading a small and dull meeting at the city hall to-night, whereasing and resoluting against the mill, but worldly Dallas is highly elated over the coming battle" (June 11, 1895.)

9. The bankbook gap was again looming as the deadline for each fighter to hand over a guarantee of $5,000 drew near and then passed. Early in June, the stakeholder, racing tout Phil Dwyer, was dining at Delmonico's when he was asked how much of the fight money he was holding. He replied, "Twenty-five thousand dollars." This did not include the guarantees from either fighter, though Corbett had been fomenting angrily about the absence of money from Fitz. Dan Stuart was firm and got both parties to ante up before he left New York.

10. Dempsey was dying of consumption—he had barely five months to live. The benefit drew some of the biggest names in boxing—Irish champion Peter Maher, Kid Lavigne, Tommy Ryan, Joe Choynski, George Dixon, and John L. Sullivan. Corbett sparred three rounds with John McVey while Fitzsimmons followed them with Frank Bosworth—both Jim and Ruby Rob were given "thunders of applause." The evening ended with Sullivan and Dempsey lightly sparring.

11. Vera soon became Mrs. Corbett for real, and Jim dedicated his 1925 autobiography to her, neglecting to include any of the divorce's messy details.

12. *New Orleans Picayune,* June 22, 1894.

13. *Austin Daily Statesman,* July 4, 1895. (Note: The *Picayune* of the same date referred to the star witness as "Dr. G A. Lyon," while the *El Paso Daily Times* that day christened him "O. A. Lyon.")

14. Fitz and Captain Glori had ended their business relationship acrimoniously back in February. Glori accused his fighter of spending money recklessly at a time when they desperately needed stake money for the Corbett fight. Cited among the unnecessary expenditures were $60 to $90 a week for hotel bills, a $350 diamond ring, and $650 worth of clothes. The two nearly came to blows over the matter in Cleveland and eventually went to court, where Glori was awarded $750 that was due him. Fitz then joined with his brother-in-law to form The Martin Julian Specialty Company.

Glori felt betrayed: "For four months, when he was without a cent, I housed and fed him, out of pure pity for his condition, and after I advanced the money to start out on the road again he takes the earliest opportunity to throw me down." With the dissolution of their partnership, Glori related that "I got the richest cursing I ever heard for my pains."

For his part, Fitz said the money spent on luxuries belonged to his wife, Rose, and that Glori's charges were "absolutely false and malicious."

15. Dallas Historic Preservation League, *Dallas, an Illustrated History,* pp. 113–14.

16. Sam Acheson, *Dallas Yesterday.*

17. Ibid., p. 234.

18. Ibid., p. 235.

19. Corbett, pp. 247–49.

20. Politically, Frank Holland was actually engaged in some adroit fence straddling on the fight issue by drawing clear distinctions between how he felt as mayor, as private citizen, as editor of *Texas Farm and Ranch,* and as a member of the Commercial Club's committee that helped set up the fight in the first place. Each position had its own constituency, and the mayor assured everyone that he was going to help pull off the very fight he morally opposed.

As mayor, Holland claimed neutrality, asserting that the amphitheater lay just outside the city's corporate limits and, therefore, did not officially concern him.

As private citizen, "I am in favor of anything which is legal and which is likely to advertise, draw people to, and benefit the city and state."

As the self-described editor of "the cleanest and most progressive farm and family paper in the south or elsewhere," the mayor tended to write "learned dissertations on the dehorning of cattle and the latest remedy for the potato bug pest," but took time lately to denounce prizefighting for his rural readers. He told them he was not only against prizefighting but had never seen a football game or been inside a gambling house. "On the other hand, I do not believe in persecution, nor am I an admirer of namby-pamby sentimentalism."

As a fight committee member, he not only talked up the fight wherever he traveled but urged "our worthy, diligent and intelligent county officials" to refrain from persecuting the combatants. Mayor Holland was wearing enough hats for a political hydra.

21. *National Cyclopedia of American Biography,* vol. 12. At the time, sixty-eight-year-old William Lewis Cabell was commander of the Trans-Mississippi department of the United Confederate Veterans, with the rank of lieutenant general. A great-grandson of Pocahontas, Cabell senior was once chief of the Creek Indians for the Canadian district, sometimes commanded Indian companies during the Civil War (he resigned his Union commission and joined the Confederacy in 1861), and was commanding a cavalry brigade as a brigadier general when he was captured in Kansas in October of 1864. He remained a prisoner in Boston until September, 1865.

William Cabell took up the law as his post-war profession and practiced in Fort Smith, Arkansas, until he moved to Dallas in December of 1872. After serving four terms as mayor, he spent the years 1885–89 as U.S. Marshal for the northern district of Texas.

22. *Austin Daily Statesman,* Aug. 25, 1895.

23. *Austin Daily Statesman,* Aug. 28, 1895.

ROUND TWO: DALLAS, PART TWO

1. James William Madden, *Charles Allen Culberson, His Life, Character and Public Service.* The chapter epigraph is from this source.

2. Texas State Historical Association, *The Handbook of Texas,* vol. 1.

3. *National Cyclopedia of American Biography,* vol. 12, p. 76.

4. Fred Gantt, Jr., *The Chief Executive in Texas.* A man who liked getting his own

way, by the time he finally left office Culberson racked up a then-record thirty-three vetoes.

5. Bulger the terrier met a dozen feisty rats in the evening's final match; the original bill had called for two dogs battling twenty-five rats each, "but the rats got up a fight of their own and, like the Kilkenny cats, very nearly exterminated each other."

Bulger, noted the *Dallas Morning News,* "was in for record-breaking" within the sixteen-foot pit. "He picked up a rat and in his haste to grab another kept the first one in his mouth and then grabbed still another, having three in his mouth at one time. There was no room for any more, so he dropped them and started in afresh. Bulger finished the twelve rats in about fifteen seconds and was then looking around for more. This ended the entertainment." (And you wondered what people watched prior to television.)

6. The tax collector was protected by a law saying, "if any collector shall give a manuscript or any other species of receipt for taxes, except the regular blank furnished by the comptroller, such collector shall be guilty of a misdemeanor, and on conviction be fined from $100 to $500 and may be dismissed from office." Louis Jacoby was not about to jeopardize his position on the shaky basis of a prizefight.

7. The sheriff of Rio Grande City was one W. W. Shelly, known locally as the "Tall Chaparral of the Rio Grande." He had recently been instrumental in rounding up Catarino Garza revolutionists and deporting them, and was no stranger to violent border clashes. While unsure of his authority on the banco, he was quoted as saying it was time for "another first-class scrap" along the lower border.

8. Culberson's opinion had been sought by the Abilene Athletic Club in June of 1894 before a welterweight fight between a black Texas fighter named Scott Collins but billed as "Bright Eyes," and a Montanan named Billy Bebbs. There was the usual local resistance to the fight, but Culberson's reading of the law prevailed and the fight was held. Bright Eyes lost and the club lost so much money it disbanded. Following the hearing, Culberson insisted he had nothing to do with that earlier decision but had merely referred the matter to the then-comptroller.

9. Fitz was nothing if not creative about his own training routine. The *El Paso Daily Times* reported on September 24 on some unusual roadwork: "A fast trotting horse is hitched to a light wagon, and Bob, in running costume, goes behind the wagon and rests his hands on the back-board. This is in order that he may save his body and get the exercise only in his long legs. The driver whips up the horse and away they go, Bob keeping up with the flying horse and wagon."

During his training in Texas the *Dallas Morning News* (October 12, 1895) related how "Fitz has two maxims in training—never to let your work get monotonous, and never let it get absolutely exhausting. He believes that it is as bad to overtrain as to undertrain."

10. Jackson, it was sadly reported, was in bad shape: "Jackson and old John Barleycorn have pulled off a large number of interesting contests the last eighteen months and the official referee has been compelled to decide that the negro was worsted in every mill that he has fought."

11. The outspoken Gibbs was a former city attorney and state senator from Dallas who was elected lieutenant governor in 1884 and 1886. He served as governor for a few months in 1885 during the absence of Governor Ireland. At the time of the fight he was retired from politics and working as a lawyer in Dallas. The following year he tried for a comeback as a Populist (he had been a Democrat) but was defeated in bids for Congress and the governor's office.

12. Fight fever tended to inspire more than just purple prose from pulpits. Eight days later, the paper printed a folklorish salute to Fitzsimmons by an unnamed writer that would have made Paul Bunyan and Pecos Bill blush:

> I do not wonder that the pompadour front of Mr. Corbett is tremulous with panic. The Red Australian Terror is more terrible every day. He keeps a herd of the most vicious and vivacious lions that ever gambol in a free country, and he can throw down the whole collection with a glance of his left forefinger. . . . They occasionally escape and eat up a large family. But when they see Red Robert they have nervous prostration, and they sink to the size of a common villatic pussy cat. . . . He wears a royal Asiatic tiger around his neck. He keeps thirteen grizzly bears in his house. He boxes every day with a pile-driver. He wears rattlesnakes for safety pins. He catches thunderbolts on the lobe of his right ear and smashes them back and gives the sky the dusky eye. He swats hydraulic rams in the snout and kills electricity with a gesture. He mashes potatoes with a curve of the eyebrow and wrecks the furniture with a wink. He knocks quarries into jelly with the flat of his hand. His right hand weighs 1,000,000 tons and his left 3,000,000. The ground he walks on gets bowlegged and the house he lives in gets curvature of the spine. Corbett will have to poison him. There is no other way of licking him.

13. This was not an age where wives spoke their minds or criticized their husbands, publicly or privately. This particular interview caused a brief scandal (and no doubt some domestic strain) before being retracted by Mrs. Culberson in a few days as being totally fabricated. A sign of the times might be the opinion of Mrs. John V. L. Pruyn of Albany, New York, a leader in the state committee of anti-woman suffragists. She was actively opposed to "the imposition upon women of the unwelcome and unsuitable responsibility of the ballot."

14. The Reverend Alderson was quite a wordsmith when he was on a pulpit. Here are some more excerpts from that peppery sermon:

> . . . the hoard of pickpockets, harlots and thugs who will come—are now coming—in advance of and with the prize fight will make the fair to stink in the nostrils of the people. Moreover, some man visiting the fair will be robbed and murdered, some woman will be outraged. . . . Outlawed by civilization this incarnation of all brutality is dumped on the helpless south. . . . The evil effects of this one exhibition, from the financial standpoint alone, will outlast the present generation. . . . The most brutal elements of our civilization, the refuse of creation, will turn to Texas as the Mussulman to Mecca. . . . Shame upon such venal degradation!
> The brutalizing effect of these fistic encounters is appreciated by but few. The heroes are men brutal to murderousness. . . . The spirit fostered by the contests in the actors and the speculators [sic] is the sheer spirit of murder. . . . No single thing ever devised by infernal ingenuity is so powerful and so far-reaching towards the complete debauching of manhood. Born of the spirit of the gambler and the brute, the prize ring and the purlieus are the putrid hotbed where vegetate and flourish in rank luxuriance every degrading, brutal, murderous passion. There is not a boy in the land who will not absorb of the infernal poison. . . . They come like vampires, to suck the life blood . . . while Dallas and Texas are impoverished, imbruted and disgraced.

15. Maher had lots of fans in New York but not among the authorities. It was common knowledge that New York's anti-knockout law of 1891 was brought about by a Madison Square Garden exhibition where Maher knocked out two men in the space of five minutes.

16. It would have been pointless (and perhaps unhealthy) to remind the fighter that the ear, like the proverbial rabbit's foot, had not done well by its original owner. Most fighters of the period were very superstitious. Often, it was wearing a favorite pair of lucky tights—John L. Sullivan's were green, Jack McAuliffe's were dark blue, Dempsey's were black. Charley Mitchell was terrified of meeting a cross-eyed woman before a fight. Jake Kilrain and Peter Maher believed it was good luck to happen upon a nun or priest before a bout. Jack Ashton was afraid of seeing a funeral lest he end up hearing his final bell. A lot of fighters simply would not fight on a Friday.

17. Fitz also took the occasion of the interview to do some predicting and grandstanding:

> Why of course I am going to win the fight, if it comes off. I'll tell you, I ain't near as scared of the fight as Corbett is. . . . Those two fellows, Corbett and Brady, are a pair of loafers and fakes. . . . If I don't give him the worst licking he ever got in his life—well—I'm no good. He never met a man yet who could give him a fight. Sullivan? Pshaw! He was in such condition the night he was knocked out that Creedon could have knocked him out in two rounds. . . . Corbett only hammered him, and the big fellow gradually sat down. He kept getting lower and lower, and when he got down on his haunches, he keeled over, that's all. . . . [Corbett] tried to back out of this fight with me, but I finally got him cornered, and he can't get out. He don't know what's in store for him.

18. Francis Lubbock won the governorship in 1861 in the election immediately following Sam Houston's ouster for refusing to join the Confederacy. Lubbock won by the narrowest margin in state history, 124 votes. He quickly became friends with Jefferson Davis and was instrumental in Texas committing vast numbers of men and amounts of resources to the South's cause.

19. The statement wasn't quite accurate. Like John L. Sullivan, Fitzsimmons "drew the color line." While staying over in Houston, the challenger qualified his brother-in-law's remark by adding: "I will fight any man in the world, barring color. Since I have been in America I have refused to go in the ring with a negro, and I shall never do so. I am a naturalized American citizen and such events are repulsive to the refined tastes of the American people."

20. The first casualty of the fistic carnival turned out to be Nero, "the fighting lion." As the Fitzsimmons train left San Antonio for Corpus Christi, Nero decided to take in the sights. He slipped his collar and disembarked. Unfortunately for him, the train was going thirty-five miles per hour at the time. When noses were counted and one passenger found to be missing, the train was run back. Nero was found by the tracks in agony due to a severely sprained left hind leg. He was taken on to Corpus, where he could convalesce while his master trained.

21. Culberson found support in many national papers, including the *Nashville American*, the *St. Louis Post-Dispatch* (which said he was backed "by all decent people"), and the *Chicago News*, which wrote: "Gov. Culberson of Texas seems to be of a different mold than anything gentlemen of thumping tendencies have run up against in their generation."

22. Senator Dean was a standout on the floor during this forced debate. According to the *Austin Daily Statesman* (October 3, 1895), "it has often been said that there is not one man in a thousand who can say 'no' and then stick by that assertion. That there is one such a man in the Texas senate was illustrated yesterday. . . . When the first vote was taken on the anti-prize fight bill Senator Dean voted 'no' and he continued to vote 'no' on every roll call until the bill had passed finally, notwithstand-

ing the fact that there were 27 senators voting for the bill. He stands singly and alone in the senate on this great question and will go down to posterity as the one statesman in all Texas who could say 'no' and then stick to it."

23. The bill's particulars take up less than a page in *The General Laws of Texas* passed by the twenty-fourth legislature. Its four sections are as follows:

Section 1. *Be it enacted by the legislature of the State of Texas:* That any person who shall voluntarily engage in a pugilistic encounter between man and man, or a fight between a man and a bull or any other animal, for money or other thing of value, or for any championship, or upon the result of which any money or any thing of value is bet or wagered, or to see which any admission fee is charged, either directly or indirectly, shall be deemed guilty of a felony, and upon conviction shall be punished by imprisonment in the penitentiary not less than two nor more than five years.

Sec. 2. By the term "pugilistic encounter," as used in this act, is meant any voluntary fight or personal encounter by blows by means of the fist or otherwise, whether with or without gloves, between two or more men, for money or for a prize of any character, or for any other thing of value, or for any championship, or upon the result of which any money or any thing of value is bet or wagered.

Sec. 3. That all laws or parts of laws in conflict herewith be and the same are hereby repealed.

Sec. 4. The fact that there is now no adequate penalty against prize fighting and pugilism, or fights between men and beasts, creates an imperative public necessity and emergency requiring the suspension of the constitutional rule requiring bills to be read on three several days, and that this law should take effect and be in force from and after its passage, and it is hereby so enacted.

ROUND THREE: HOT SPRINGS

1. Madden, *Charles Allen Culberson,* pp. 37–38.

2. The full-page circus ads were modesty personified, merely pointing out that the Barnum & Bailey show was "stupendous . . . overwhelming, magnificent and colossal," and had an educational scope "as great as a university." The self-restrained copy writers assured readers that "all hearts are gladdened, all pulses thrilled, all minds amused, all classes instructed, and the people made better" by the coming of the circus. A "Grand New Ethnological Congress" allowed visitors to openly gawk at "Cannibals, Idolaters, Pagans, Buddhists, Hindus, Vishnus, Heathens, Confusians, Fire and Sun Worshipers" and other sights hard to find on the American frontier prior to the invention of airport terminals.

The show was nothing if not mobile, playing twenty-three Texas cities in twenty-nine days. And in case there were doubters, the ad clearly stated, "Truthfully Advertised—Honorably Presented."

3. The 1890 census put the population of Indian Territory at 50,055 Indians, 18,636 Negroes, and 109,393 whites.

4. The name-calling and character assassination got so ferocious at times among the ministers and politicians that some public relations work was often needed.

On October 8, the *Dallas Morning News* printed a press release touting Dan Stuart's community actions: "He has been unsparingly denounced in this campaign, and yet he is a heavy taxpayer, employs a great number of men, has given freely to every public enterprise in this city for the past ten years, and his purse has ever been open to the needy, the distressed and the unfortunate. When a man's vices are hurled broadcast it is not out of place to say a word or two as to his virtues."

5. The two managers were not dissimilar. Brady was thirty-one, Julian twenty-seven; Brady hailed from San Francisco, and Julian was born in Melbourne, Australia. Both had roots in the era's entertainment industry.

Julian's parents were professional acrobats and tumblers and came to America when Martin was still a child. He and his sister Rose toured with them across the country and later did a duo act—Martin as acrobat, Rose as a contortionist—for over a decade. Rose married Robert Fitzsimmons and Martin married the fighter's first wife (which now made her Fitz's sister-in-law).

Since around 1888, Julian had been managing various athletic and vaudeville acts. He was also out of shape.

While handling Jim Corbett, William Brady also had nine theatrical companies crisscrossing the states—three of them doing performances of *Trilby*—with a weekly payroll of some $17,000 to meet.

Both men knew the value of publicity.

6. Fitzsimmons had more than a fight to worry about. Nero went sight-seeing once again on October 8 in Corpus. Until he was found, children were hustled indoors and houses shut tight all along the beach. He eventually returned on his own when he got hungry.

7. The bribery charges were investigated and found to be groundless. A threat of impeachment proceedings over the lobby fight was voted down.

8. Hot Springs was fourth in the nation on the list of hotel accommodations, such was its fame as a health retreat.

9. If worse came to worst, there were still other options, the most imaginative one being offered by Mr. J. McCauly of Dallas. He proposed "to contrive an aerial platform upon which a contest can be had at any time and entirely free from any interference. . . . It is a cigar-shaped balloon of sufficient buoyancy, when highly inflated, to support the principals and their seconds and others necessary to the occasion . . . four aerial machines, one at each corner, electrically arranged with storage batteries, are placed at such angles that when in motion the platform will be held in stable position."

10. General Taylor was a soldier who followed orders. The *Dallas Morning News* of October 16 quoted Taylor as saying, "I know nothing about the law. I am acting under instructions. I do not consult my own feelings in this matter. To indicate my personal preferences I will tell you that I had obtained my ticket to the fight in Dallas and intended to go and see it there myself."

On October 21, the *El Paso Daily Herald* described General Taylor this way: "The brigadier has long hair and a fierce eye and he don't care where he parts his hair."

11. Fitz was having trouble with a badly bruised left hand he had mashed while making a horseshoe on October 14. There was some sparring in the exhibition, where "a large number of ladies were present and seemed to enjoy the sport fully as much as the men."

Meanwhile, Corbett was fussing aloud in the papers again and said he was only in Hot Springs on orders, convinced now the fight would not come off there. On the subject of his opponent, "I'll fight him for fun. Fitzsimmons is doing a lot of blowing and is running a big bluff. . . . If the fight has to be pulled off in private I will be compelled to fight for glory and amusement."

12. The new articles of agreement stipulated a twenty-five-round bout using

"soft," five-ounce gloves, the winner to receive $41,000. To some, the gloves looked as harmless as pillows. Fitz thought so, as did Martin Julian, who called the contract "a big pugilistic fake . . . in order to evade the Arkansas statutes. It will either be a fight to the finish or no fight at all, and you can put that down as official."

13. Fitz was doing more than card playing, of course. He was also hunting—he bagged seventeen ducks and six quail on October 18. And he found time to study a Kinetoscope fight film of Corbett in action. It was only a staged fight, but might still provide an edge.

The challenger's usual loose training regimen was continuing along with his enormous intake of food. In the October 12 edition of the *Dallas Morning News,* it was reported that Fitz, after an ocean swim, a walk, a romp with Pat—his two-hundred pound St. Bernard, and some wood splitting, settled down to a breakfast table usually stocked with "oatmeal, muffins, steak, chops or chicken. He does not believe in diet or special foods." After exercising and a cold sponge bath there was a hearty dinner of "every vegetable the markets far and near can produce. These are flanked by generous roasts of beef, mutton and pork." It certainly sounded better than the fare in an Arkansas jail.

14. The only excuse offered by prosecuting attorney and servant of the people C. V. Teague was this: "The state was handicapped by public sentiment in favor of the fight."

15. Brady, *Fighting Man.*

16. *Austin Daily Statesman,* November 18, 1895.

17. Corbett, *Roar of the Crowd,* p. 247.

ROUND FOUR: THE IRISHMAN

1. Robert Green Ingersoll was the scourge of the pulpits in his day. A champion of agnosticism and rationalism, the self-taught attorney was as great a target for fundamentalists as Huxley or Darwin. When his views on baptism were once demanded, Ingersoll responded, "With soap, it's a good thing." He loved Shakespeare and wrote essays on many diverse subjects. He died in 1899.

2. El Paso was noted for its dry climate, and many tubercular people came to stay for their health. And, thanks to the railroad workcrews settling in El Paso, the city also had a large Chinese community. Hence the pen name of Wun Lung.

3. Shortly after the brief Maher-O'Donnell fight, there came rumors of a setup. Not a fix, just a deliberate mismatching so that Corbett could dump his sparring partner.

Asked about this strategy, Jim Daly commented, "Of late O'Donnell has had the idea that he was a better man that Corbett, and has not hesitated to say so. . . . He went at Jim harder than necessary at times, and finally one day Corbett smashed his nose flat with a left-hand blow that Steve had never seen or heard of before. After that Jim did no more boxing with O'Donnell. . . . That match was made with Maher simply to get rid of Steve O'Donnell."

4. Terry Ramsaye, *A Million and One Nights.* Ramsaye termed Latham's idea to put "the odium of pugilism" on film "a moment of destiny for the motion picture. Amazing consequences and many of the controlling events of all subsequent screen history have their roots in that trifling moment."

5. The new articles of agreement dictated "a fair, stand-up battle with five-ounce gloves," with the winner to take home $10,000 and the *Police Gazette* championship

belt. Dan Stuart was to deposit $3,000 with the *Gazette*'s Richard K. Fox by December 5, and another $7,000 with the final stakeholder by February 9, along with $2,000 "appearance money" guaranteeing the fight, all of which he would forfeit if he could not bring off the contest.

6. Most sources say Maher worked at the Guinness Brewery, but the *New Orleans Picayune* of February 29, 1896, places him in the Phoenix Brewery and his birthplace as Tuam County, Galway. That paper also reported "an amusing incident" during an early fight with a bruiser named Seenan:

"A portion of Maher's costume became disarranged and Seenan, taking advantage of Peter's concern, went for him at once. This roused the big devil in Maher, who, not caring about the state of his dress, fairly plunged into the Belfast man and sent him to sleep with a few terrific thrusts. As may be imagined, Peter was loudly applauded."

7. The match with Sullivan was, of course, off. On March 4, Sullivan issued a list of his preferred opponents beginning with Frank Slavin ("he and his backers have done the greatest amount of blowing"), Charles Mitchell ("the bombastic sprinter") and James Corbett ("who has achieved his share of bombast"). Maher wasn't on the list.

Aside from those named, "in this challenge I include all fighters (first come, first served) who are white. I will not fight a Negro. I never have, I never shall."

8. Texas tended to bewilder the Dubliner. "This is a queer country here, when you think about it," he told the *Dallas Morning News* (October 5, 1895). "Here you have a law that makes boxing exhibitions as serious a crime as manslaughter or an attempt to outrage. At the same time, I understand there are 800 fallen women in your city of 50,000 people. That beats anything I ever heard of. There is not a licensed fallen woman in Ireland, and as fast as they come there they are shipped out of the country, so there are practically none there. There we can have our contests anywhere just the same as any theatrical performances. . . . All we have to do is to keep the gloves on."

9. *El Paso Daily Herald,* December 13, 1895. Fitz told the *Herald* on December 26, "Carroll is not on the level. While acting as my manager he was secretly hoping that Maher would knock me out. I gave him a third of that purse and he was 'knocking' me all the time, while professing to be my best friend. He need not visit my training quarters, as I want none of his kind about me. No Jimmy Carroll in mine."

According to the *Chicago Record* (January 28, 1896), Carroll "would like to see Mr. Fitzsimmons good and thoroughly whipped. With him it is a personal grievance. He worked hard training the red-headed Australian for his big battles and he claims that after Fitz became an undisputed champion he became ungrateful and forgetful of his obligations."

10. Theater manager Sam Jack thought he detected hypocrisy on the part of the police chief and pointed out that Paddy Ryan and John L. Sullivan had obtained a license to fight. The chief replied, ". . . they are a couple of has-beens, fat and out of condition and unable to do each other any kind of injury."

ROUND FIVE: EL PASO, PART ONE

1. *El Paso Daily Herald,* December 16, 1895. "There was some very reckless revolver shooting around on El Paso street last evening when the fire occurred. . . . This thing of firing off revolvers to send in an alarm of fire when there are a half dozen telephones within a few steps, is all foolishness. . . . By last night's shooting a number

of men came near losing their lives, because an excited individual had a revolver and he thought he would shoot out the fire."

2. "Now the 'new man' is coming, and won't he and the 'new woman' have a time fighting for the best pair of pants? Let us hope for the day when all these 'new' things will have become rank chestnuts and disappear into oblivion." (Wun Lung, *El Paso Daily Herald,* December 11, 1895.)

Amelia Jenks Bloomer had died in December of 1894, but the garment ungraciously (and undeservedly) named for her lived on. Bloomers were so much like baggy pants that they were considered male duds and, thus, inappropriate for women. Attitude adjustment to this perceived cross-dressing was not an overnight success:

"An El Paso married man was discussing the woman situation . . . and he remarked that his wife had taken to mannish shirt, collars, cuffs and neckties to such an extent that he was kept on the hustle to secure clean ones for himself, and he simply was compelled to hide his neckties. He also kicked because he had to get up first in the morning for fear his better-half would arise in all her glory and don his trousers, and he wanted to avoid any such catastrophe if possible. Who can blame him?" (*El Paso Daily Herald,* November 21, 1895.)

On February 10, 1896, Wun Lung commented, "The shyness of the bloomer girl in El Paso is a thing to be commended. I have only seen one case of bloomers since I came here, and that was in the restaurant when it glided into a private room from a rear entrance. I haven't heard that the offense was subject to arrest in this locality, but the girl looked as though she were dodging the authorities."

Bloomers were not the only female garments to receive stares in El Paso:

> A young lady bicyclist flashed through the town astride a wheel that looked like a racer. Perhaps she would not have attracted so much attention but for the fact that she was wearing a very nobby bicycle costume of dark goods, the skirt of which came to just about her knees, her le—ah—limbs being very tightly dressed in leggings that fit as snug as silk hosiery. Many a male eye was turned full upon the young woman and her attire, and when she alighted and skipped up the post-office steps, the hearts of all the men who saw her went pit-a-pat at a lively rate. (*El Paso Daily Herald,* October 29, 1895.)

3. Harriet Howze Jones, ed., *El Paso, a Centennial Portrait.*

4. Doc Albers used to tell the story of a customer who was addicted to both morphine and cocaine. He'd come in quiet and unassuming in the morning to get his morphine, then returned at midafternoon in a frenzy, "with his wild eyes starting from their sockets as if he were seeing ghosts. . . . He would demand cocaine and I never bartered words with him. I wanted to get him out as quickly as possible, for he was liable to smash the whole place. This awful and complete change was caused by the effects of the cocaine, the desire for which came upon him at a certain hour every afternoon, and he had to gratify it. But every morning he came back to morphine." Doc gave him *Dr. Jekyll and Mr. Hyde* to read and "he told me that the changes as described in the double character were not greater than took place in him, when he changed from one drug to another."

5. Jones, *El Paso, a Centennial Portrait.*

6. H. Gordon Frost, *The Gentlemen's Club,* pp. 97–98.

7. Hardin was a preacher's son who racked up at least thirty deaths before being jailed for second-degree murder in 1878. On the night he was killed, Hardin had been out of prison for seventeen months. Selman's son had recently arrested Hardin's

mistress for carrying a gun. The ex-gunman became increasingly drunk and abusive towards the younger Selman, and that led to the showdown with John senior. The autopsy showed Hardin was shot in the back of the head; Selman claimed he'd been reaching for a gun. Hardin was forty-two. As a point of reference, Hardin was shot nine days after Corbett and Fitzsimmons had their lobby altercation in Green's Hotel in Philadelphia.

8. Gambling was even more pervasive across the border in Juarez. Wun Lung noted "scores" of games at the fiesta, from "Monte Carlo" to chuck-a-luck, faro, and roulette, with no limit on betting. "By the way, I noticed several ladies wagering 'clackers' at some of the tables, apparently with the keenest enjoyment. They did it, no doubt, just for the novelty of the thing, you know."

9. A "prominent grocery dealer" told the *Times*, "I believe in churches . . . but some preachers are fond of straining at gnats and swallowing flies. Now of course one of those preachers who signed that appeal would not accept from the gambler money he won at faro. But the gambler can give the money to a prostitute and she will give it to me for groceries and then the preacher calls on me for it. By passing through my hands the coin has been cleansed of its wickedness."

10. The *Chicago Record* of January 2 reported that Fitz "enjoyed the sport of throwing Indians heels over head immensely." There were no pads or helmets, of course. The *New York Sun's* report was a bit fanciful: "On New Year's Day the Hon. Robert Fitzsimmons, the crimson topped kangaroo of the bush, played football with eleven little Indian boys, each not more than seven feet high, from Albuquerque. He piled them one on the top of the other, held them in the palm of his left hand, and then threw them over his shoulder to Albuquerque. On Saturday, while trying his lungs, he accidentally blew over a train of sixty three freight cars."

11. The Indians went on to beat Las Cruces and tales of the El Paso game must have gone with them—when Las Cruces then challenged El Paso's motley team, they made certain, non-negotiable stipulations: "The game to be utterly devoid of slugging, unnecessary roughness and all unfair tactics of any nature whatever." The head of the Las Cruces club later disavowed all knowledge of the challenge.

12. Lillian Lewis, a fourteen-year stage veteran, was asked about Fitzsimmons after watching an exhibition. "Why, I think he is just the nicest man—and such lovely blue eyes! . . . And you know he has a magnificent reach—why his great long arms like iron move like lightning when he strikes. I lost $1,800 last time on Corbett because he knocked that Mr. Mitchell out in three rounds. But I am going to bet on Fitz this time and get even."

13. The fiesta was attracting even "decent" folks. One El Paso man complained, "It may be all right for ladies to play the games over at the Juarez fiesta, and some of them appear to enjoy the excitement very much, but . . . I noticed a couple of respectable young ladies sitting at one of the games yesterday and not three feet away were several women of the town, who are notoriously tough. That sight certainly shocked my idea of propriety. . . . A great many of those females who play the games are women of easy virtue, and a respectable woman is liable to rub up against them at any time. . . . I tell you, it doesn't look proper to me."

14. *El Paso Daily Herald,* January 6, 1896. Four days earlier, the *Times* wrote: "Francis Schlatter, the New Mexico 'Christ,' is coming down the Rio Grande through New Mexico and will reach El Paso in a month or two. He is mounted on a milk-white horse and says he has been 'directed' to go to a spot in Central America where he will go into retreat for an indefinite time. He is healing all people who come

to him as he continues his journey." Schlatter, a blond, blue-eyed Alsatian cobber, walked across the Mojave from California to Albuquerque in 1895. In Denver, he was thronged by thousands of people per day seeking his blessing. Then he and his horse Butte vanished. He did not arrive in El Paso, and ten years later there came a report of his skeleton being found in Chihuahua.

15. Weight classes at the time went like this: Heavyweight—158 pounds and up; Middleweight—154 pounds; Welterweight—144 pounds; Lightweight—133 pounds; Featherweight—122 pounds; Bantamweight—112 pounds.

16. "The kodak [*sic*] has been considered an instrument of impertinence, if not of torture. People have resented its prying ways and have denounced the button-pusher as a 'fiend.'" (*Chicago Record,* February 10, 1896.)

George Eastman introduced the Kodak to the world in 1888. By 1895, shutterbugs even had flexible, daylight-loading film to use.

17. The office was at 113 Oregon Street. Before the carnival came to a close, a lot of people would be pointing to that 13 above the door as a bad omen.

18. Nero proved to be good as a hunting dog too. When Fitz and Señor Deguerra took to the Sierra Madres and spotted a javelina—a wild hog—the lion was turned loose and pinned the pig in three bounds. He was well-mannered enough not to kill it, and Fitz brought it back to the city in order to ship it alive to the New York Park Commission.

19. *El Paso Daily Times,* January 15, 1896.

20. The *Herald* had declined to publish the first letter of the ministers because it implied that no legitimate businessmen were contributing to the bonus and that it was all coming from the denizens of the tenderloin.

21. Siler was once the lightweight champ of the East but hung up his gloves in 1893 to become a sports reporter. The *Chicago Inter-Ocean* (reprinted in the *El Paso Times*) wrote: "George Siler is as 'square' a man as lives. He has never been implicated in questionable fights, and his ability and fairness as a referee are everywhere recognized."

22. The *Chicago Record* of January 20 wrote, "Judging by the picture in a southern paper of 'Bright Eyes,' that worthy is almost as horribly ugly as Walcott, whom he is to meet in the ring in El Paso."

23. Frost, *Gentlemen's Club.* Stuart offered to pay all costs for prosecuting the counterfeiters responsible, but no one was apprehended.

ROUND SIX: EL PASO, PART TWO

1. The accident brought to mind an eerie prediction in the *Herald* of January 2: "John L. Sullivan wants to be cremated when he dies. Spontaneous combustion may prevent the gratification of this his last wish."

2. *El Paso Daily Herald,* January 27, 1896. "The whole party are a jolly set and amuse themselves with good natured jibes and jokes on the numerous letters they receive from some sickly sentimental maiden who has just sent them a letter which reads between the lines nothing less than a proposal for marriage. Many of these letters are from girls they don't know and have never heard of, and the whole gang have [*sic*] lots of fun in reading these love epistles to one another and good naturedly quarreling over whose letter is the 'softest.'"

3. Connelly was a character. Known also as "One-Eyed" Connelly, he had a habit of losing his glass eye in a store and offering a $500 reward for its return. He'd leave and a confederate would show up, find the eye, and then be offered $100 for it by

someone expecting to make a nice profit. That entrepreneur would then hurry to Connelly and proffer the eye only to be told it was the wrong one. Connelly would split the hundred with his pal. He kept a stock of glass eyes for just such an occasion. (Corbett, *Roar of the Crowd*.)

Vendig, by the way, much preferred being called "Positive Joe," but editors were not so inclined.

4. Colonel Fountain, once a state senator from El Paso, was most recently an attorney hired by the Southeastern New Mexico Stock Association to prosecute cattle rustlers, a task which made him many nasty enemies. He and his son were returning to Las Cruces when their buckboard was waylaid by three men on horseback. The two were murdered.

Posses were dispatched immediately. The *Herald* of February 4 commented, "Brave determined men compose the parties, and if Colonel Fountain has been murdered, as is undoubtedly the case, and his murderers overtaken, retribution will be speedy. Justice has too long been trifled with in this county. . . . And if the officials whose duty it is to do cannot stamp out crime, then it develops upon the people to take the law into their own hands."

Three men were brought to trial three years later by Pat Garrett. Lacking bodies, the largely political trial ended with a verdict of Not Guilty after seven minutes of deliberation. The possible remains of the victims were found buried high in the Sacramento Mountains in 1900. (A. M. Gibson, *The Life and Death of Colonel Albert Jennings Fountain*.)

5. Robert W. Larson, *New Mexico Populism*.

6. William A. Keleher, *The Fabulous Frontier*.

7. *Congressional Record*, 1896, pp. 1339, 1344–45, 1385.

8. *New York World*, February 7, 1896. The *El Paso Daily Herald* attributed the quote to Governor Ahumada in a wire to Mexico City.

9. Not all the city's ministers were actively involved in the Union. The *Herald* of February 7 printed what it believed to be a complete list: C. J. Oxley, Trinity Methodist Church; A. Hoffmann, First Methodist Church; L. R. Millican, First Baptist Church; E. R. Hallam, Christian Church; Rev. Funk, Congregational Church; A. M. Elliott, Presbyterian Church.

ROUND SEVEN: RANGERS

1. *New York World*, February 10, 1896. The *World* was quick to point out the perceived hypocrisy of bullfighting. After quoting a Mexican journal as saying pugilism was "the most brutal" of all sports, the paper then noted a long and detailed description of a bullfight in that same paper, one in which six bulls were killed and "four poor, blindfolded horses were gored by the bulls until their blood ran in rivulets about the ring, to the infinite delectation of the fashionable and plebeian audience alike."

After reprinting some statistics that revealed 432 homicides and 7,775 stabbings in Mexico City in one year, the *World* saw the root of the bias against prizefighting: no weapons. "There's a good way out of the dilemma. Why can't the men fight with knives?"

(President Diaz, known as a ruthless dictator whose *rurales* were said to be no better than organized marauders, and who "won" his office originally by force of arms when he overthrew the legally elected president Lerdo de Tejada, in 1876, was against bullfighting and had been trying to ease his people away from it with shorter seasons. It didn't work.)

2. Texas State Historical Association, *Handbook of Texas.*

3. Had the Rangers been sent to Dallas, "Jim" shuddered at the possible outcome: "This fight will draw 60,000 people to Dallas. A strong per cent will be of that free and easy brood, the cow punchers. Now a cow puncher doesn't like a Texas ranger, no how, and if he ever meets him in Dallas . . . there's liable to be trouble in a minute. The only chance for a scrap, aside from the fistic performances on the program, will be between rangers and the hostile portion of those who come to see the fight . . . should the rangers come down to Dallas the last of October, with fire in their eyes, they are likely to have quite a time."

4. Boyce House, *Cowtown Columnist.*

5. Albert Bigelow Paine, *Captain Bill McDonald, Texas Ranger.*

6. Texas State Historical Association, *Handbook of Texas.*

7. Paine, *Captain Bill McDonald.*

8. *El Paso Daily Herald,* February 12, 1896.

9. Hughes came to be such a joke that when the *Times* reported a shooting downtown the story began this way: "Last night at about half past eleven o'clock a regular fusillade of pistol shots fired on San Antonio street in front of the Astor House, caused people on the streets to imagine Gov. Hughes of Arizona had arrived with his militia and was storming Dan Stuart's headquarters. . . ."

10. *Dallas Morning News,* February 28, 1896.

11. The five "jurors" were Hugh Fitzgerald of the *Houston Post;* George Siler of the *Chicago Tribune;* Bill Naughton of the *San Francisco Examiner;* Lou Houseman of the *Chicago Inter-Ocean;* and Tom O'Rourke, the stakeholder. Stuart was named chairman.

12. Owen White, *Autobiography of a Durable Sinner.*

13. Fred C. Kelly, *George Ade, Warmhearted Satirist,* pp. 98–99.

14. In 1897, Ahumada was again in Juarez, this time to drive the first spike (golden) in the Mexican Northwestern Railroad (later called the Rio Grande, Sierra Madre & Pacific). During the upheavals of the Mexican Revolution, Ahumada lost his mining and hotel interests and took up exile in El Paso. He was named an Honorary Elk, became a 33d degree Mason, and died at his home on August 27, 1916, of a blood clot on the brain. *El Paso Herald,* August 28, 1916.

ROUND EIGHT: THE MAIN EVENT

1. White, *Autobiography.*

2. The all-male club's name came from a popular song of the era, "Down Went McGinty."

3. C. L. Sonnichsen, *Roy Bean, Law West of the Pecos.*

4. Terence Tobin, ed. *Letters of George Ade,* p. 174.

5. The *Chicago Tribune* estimated the cost of shadowing Maher and Fitz at $50,000, not even counting the special session.

6. Kelly, *George Ade.*

7. Robert K. DeArment, *Bat Masterson, the Man and the Legend.*

8. Texas State Historical Society, *Handbook of Texas.*

9. House, *Cowtown Columnist.*

10. DeArment, *Bat Masterson,* p. 349.

11. Robert J. Casey, *The Texas Border,* p. 213.

12. In his final report to the governor, Mabry wrote, "The statement wired, that I and my rangers crossed the river to see the fight, was palpably made to belittle the force. They knew it was false at the time." What he neglected to mention was that crossing the river was unnecessary—they could see quite well from the Langtry bluffs.

Mabry praised the men under his command, saying that the rangers "conducted themselves in such manner as to reflect additional credit upon the name of a ranger— always a synonym for courage and duty well performed. They were . . . orderly in manner, determined in mien, fearless and vigilant on duty; they thus naturally incur the displeasure of the law-breakers everywhere." (*Dallas Morning News*, February 28, 1896)

13. *Chicago Tribune*, February 22, 1896. The *El Paso Herald* put the time at 1:25. The *New York World* reported it as 1:35.

CARSON CITY AND BEYOND

1. Lester Bromberg, *Boxing's Unforgettable Fights*, pp. 26–27.

2. Ibid, p. 27.

3. Robert Hobart Davis, *Ruby Robert, alias Bob Fitzsimmons*. Davis even blasted one intrepid photographer's camera and tripod with a shotgun to discourage freelancing.

4. *New Orleans Picayune*, March 23, 1897. Financial details always varied. In 1926, Terry Ramsaye wrote that "Tilden, Rector and Stuart financed the fight while the fighters and their managers took twenty-five per cent each of the picture profits and Rector and Tilden divided the remaining fifty per cent with Stuart" (Ramsaye, *A Million and One Nights*).

5. Rector had three cameras and forty-eight thousand feet of film, of which he exposed a then-record eleven thousand feet at twenty-four frames a second.

6. Davis, *Ruby Robert*, p. 134.

7. Bromberg, *Unforgettable*, p. 28.

8. Corbett, *Roar of the Crowd*, p. 262.

9. Ibid., p. 263. Nine years before Corbett wrote those words, Brady wrote: "After the fight was over we claimed he was down longer than ten seconds. . . . But we did that for effect. The truth of the matter is, Fitzsimmons was not badly hurt in this round and simply did what all experienced boxers do: took the benefit of nine full seconds before getting up" (*Brady, Fighting Man*, p. 145).

Robert Davis recalled that Fitz slipped, lost his balance, and slid down the length of Corbett's legs: "Not a blow was struck during that entire performance. It was merely a question of one man off his balance reaching the floor through a little play of tactical dexterity. The moment his right knee touched he let go of Corbett and Siler began to count" (Davis, *Ruby Robert*).

10. Corbett, *Roar of the Crowd*, p. 264.

11. Ibid.

12. Ibid., p. 265.

13. *Chicago Tribune*, March 18, 1897. In his autobiography, William Brady wrote: "Corbett was taken to his room, broken-hearted, and I believe that he contemplated suicide."

14. According to Brady, the Veriscope film "made between six hundred thousand and seven hundred thousand dollars. They were exhibited everywhere, the world over." But Brady was still bitter: "Mr. Stewart [*sic*] took the films to New York,

formed a corporation with himself as president and his brother as treasurer, took the entire management of the thing out of our hands, and left us helpless—thankful for what we could get. I think each man received about eighty thousand dollars."

For his part, Brady obtained a copy of the film and made a most ingenious, if fraudulent, use of it. "I laid before Corbett a little scheme that I had conceived and worked out" to convince the public that his man had been robbed of the title in round six.

"The people at that time," Brady confessed, "knew very little about this new form of entertainment [or] that one could run the picture fast or slow." At a New York showing Brady bribed the projectionist to "run his machine very slowly" as soon as Fitz went down, then invited viewers to take out their stopwatches. Naturally, Fitz seemed to stay down for thirteen seconds! (Brady, *Fighting Man,* pp. 148–50.)

15. Jeffrey T. Sammons, *Beyond the Ring—The Role of Boxing in American Society,* p. 65.

16. *New York Times,* June 7, 1914. Temo's surname is a matter of conjecture. Robert Davis says "Ziller," while newspapers at the time give both "Sloan" and "Slonim." Likewise, her nationality was variously reported as German, French, and Italian.

Epilogue

1. *General Laws of the State of Texas, 43rd Legislature, Regular Session,* 1933.
2. *Time,* June 27, 1988.
3. *TV Guide,* June 25, 1988.
4. *New Republic,* August 8 and 15, 1988.

BIBLIOGRAPHY

NEWSPAPERS

Austin Daily Statesman. July–November, 1895.

Chicago Record. January–February, 1896.

Chicago Tribune. June, 1894; June–December, 1895; February, 1896; March, 1897; October, 1917.

Dallas Morning News. September–October, 1895; February, 1896; March, 1897.

El Paso Daily Herald. October–December, 1895; January, 1896; February, 1896; March, 1897.

El Paso Daily Times. July–December, 1895; January–February, 1896.

El Paso Herald-Post. October, 1917; May, 1962.

Houston Daily Post. August–September, 1895.

New Orleans Picayune. December, 1891; January–March, 1892; March, 1893; June 21–22, November–December, 1894; March–November, 1895; March, 1897.

New York Times. December, 1886; August, 1889; October, 1894; October–November, 1895; March, December, 1896; March, June, 1897; July 1898; December 1899; August 1900; July, 1902; July, 1903; June, 1911; June, 1912; April, 1913; May, June, 1914; August, 1915; November, 1915; October, 1916; October, December, 1917.

New York World. February, 1896.

BOOKS AND OTHER SOURCES

Acheson, Sam. *Dallas Yesterday.* Dallas: Southern Methodist University Press, 1977.

Ade, George. *Letters of George Ade.* Edited by Terence Tobin. West Lafayette, Ind.: Purdue University Studies, 1973.

Brady, William A. *The Fighting Man.* Indianapolis: Bobbs-Merrill Company, 1916.

Bromberg, Lester. *Boxing's Unforgettable Fights.* New York: Ronald Press Co., 1962.

Casey, Robert J. *The Texas Border.* New York: Bobbs-Merrill Co., 1950.

Chidsey, Donald Barr. *John the Great.* Garden City, N.Y.: Doubleday, Doran and Co., 1942.

Congressional Record. February 5 and 11, 1896. Washington, D.C.

Corbett, James J. *The Roar of the Crowd.* New York: G. P. Putnam's Sons, 1925.

Dallas Historic Preservation League. *Dallas, an Illustrated History.* Dallas: Privately printed, 1982.

Davis, Robert Hobart. *Ruby Robert, alias Bob Fitzsimmons.* New York: Doran, 1926.

DeArment, Robert K. *Bat Masterson, the Man and the Legend.* Norman: University of Oklahoma Press, 1979.

Encyclopedia Americana. Danbury: Americana Corporation, 1979.

Fell, John L., ed. *Film before Griffith.* Berkeley: University of California Press, 1983.

Frost, H. Gordon. *The Gentlemen's Club.* El Paso: Mangan Books, 1983.

Gantt, Fred, Jr. *The Chief Executive in Texas.* Austin: University of Texas Press, 1964.

Gibson, A. M. *The Life and Death of Colonel Albert Jennings Fountain.* Norman: University of Oklahoma Press, 1965.

Goldman, Herbert G., ed. *The Ring Record Book and Boxing Encyclopedia.* New York: Ring Publishing Corp., 1987.

Gorn, Elliott. *The Manly Art.* Ithaca, N.Y.: Cornell University Press, 1986.

Grun, Bernard. *The Timetables of History.* New York: Simon and Schuster, 1982.

Hardin, John Wesley. *The Life of John Wesley Hardin.* Norman: University of Oklahoma Press, 1961.

House, Boyce. *Cowtown Columnist.* San Antonio: Naylor Co., 1946.

Johnson, Alexander. *Ten . . . and Out!* New York: Ives Washburn, 1927.

Johnson, Frank W. *A History of Texas and Texans.* Chicago: American Historical Society, 1914.

Jones, Harriet Howze, ed. *El Paso: A Centennial Portrait.* El Paso County Historical Society, 1972.

Keleher, William A. *The Fabulous Frontier.* Santa Fe: Rydal Press, 1945.

Kelly, Fred C. *George Ade, Warmhearted Satirist.* New York: Bobbs-Merrill Co., 1947.

Larson, Robert W. *New Mexico Populism.* Boulder: Colorado Associated University Press, 1974.

————. *New Mexico's Quest for Statehood, 1846–1912.* Albuquerque: University of New Mexico Press, 1968.

Madden, James William. *Charles Allen Culberson, His Life, Character and Public Service.* Austin: Gammel's Book Store, 1928.

Memorial and Biographical History of Dallas County, Texas. Chicago: Lewis Publishing Co., 1892.

National Cyclopedia of American Biography. Clifton, N.J.: James T. White and Co., 1975.

Paine, Albert Bigelow. *Captain Bill McDonald, Texas Ranger.* New York: J. J. Little and Ives Co., 1909.

Rainbolt, Richard. *Boxing's Heavyweight Champions.* Lerner Publications Co., 1975.

Ramsaye, Terry. *A Million and One Nights.* New York: Simon and Schuster, 1926.

Rogers, John William. *The Lusty Texans of Dallas.* New York: E. P. Dutton and Co., 1951.

Sammons, Jeffrey T. *Beyond the Ring—The Role of Boxing in American Society.* Urbana: University of Illinois Press, 1988.

Sonnichsen, C. L. *Pass of the North.* El Paso: Texas Western Press, 1968.

———. *Roy Bean, Law West of the Pecos.* New York: Devin-Adair Co., 1958.

Twain, Mark. *Selected Letters of Mark Twain.* Edited by Charles Neider. New York: Harper & Row, 1982.

Texas State Historical Association. *The Handbook of Texas,* 1952.

Webster's American Biographies. Springfield, Mass.: G. & C. Merriam Co., 1975.

White, Owen P. *Autobiography of a Durable Sinner.* New York: G. P. Putnam's Sons, 1942.

INDEX

Abilene Athletic Club, 217n.8
Ade, George, 190; on bullfighting, 135–
36; on interviewing Fitzsimmons, 174;
on odds against carnival, 151–52, 155;
on Stuart's determination, 142; and Sullivan, 166–67
advertising tie-ins, 38, 125. *See also* publicity
Ahumada, Miquel, 136, 167, 227n.8;
arrives in El Paso, 152; background and
character of, 153; at bullfight, 165; and
fight exhibition, 155; interviewed, 154–
55; and ministers, 154; post-carnival
career of, 228n.14; and Sullivan, 164
Albers, A. K. ("Doc"), 90, 96, 112; on
drugs, 224n.4; on surveillance, 161–62
Albuquerque Indian Industrial School,
113–15
Alderson, Rev., 54, 218n.14
Allen, R. B., 56
amphitheater, 19, 22, 29, 46, 70; at Carson City, 194, 196, (photo) 197; at
Dallas, 49, 57–58; at El Paso, 116–17,
124; at Hot Springs, 70, 73; at Langtry,
180, 182, (photo) 183
Anderson, Charles E., 49
anti-fight bill. *See* Catron, Thomas B.;
Congress, U.S.
Ardmore, Okla., 64, 65
Arizona Citizen, 164
Arkansas: anti-prizefighting statutes of,
66; militia of, 71–72, 77; and search for
Fitzsimmons, 76–77
Armour, P. D., 86
Armstrong, Albert, 50
Arriola, Tito, 153
articles of agreement: for El Paso, 222–
23n.5; for Hot Springs, 221–22n.12

astrology. *See* superstitions
Aten, Ed, 171, 173
Augusta Chronicle, 62
Austin Daily Statesman, 32; on Austin
ministers, 27; on bancos, 44; on crowd
in Little Rock, 79; on decoys, 31; on
letters of Culberson and Cabell, 33–
34; on Senator Dean, 219–20n.22; on
Hot Springs, 66, 73; and river fight
scheme, 31
Austin Ministerial Association, 29, 54

balloon, as fight site, 221n.9
bancos, 44, 154, 155
Baptist Young People's Union of Amer-
ica, 28
Barnum and Bailey Circus, 63–64,
220n.2
Barry, Jimmy, 117
Bates, Jim, 40, 41, 45, 173, 182
Bauche, Manuel, 170–71
Bean, Roy, 173; background and charac-
ter of, 178–80; photo, 179
Bebbs, Billy, 217n.8
Bellew, Jersey, 205
bloomers, 88, 224n.2
border jurisdiction, 154, 155
Borglum, Gutzon, 13
Bowe, Riddick, 210, 211
Bowser, Oliver P., 52
boxers. *See* prizefighters
boxing. *See* prizefighting
Brady, William, 16, 20, 60, 65, 75, 79,
204; background of, 221n.5; castigates
critics, 66; challenges Fitzsimmons, 192;
on Corbett-Jackson bout, 214n.11; on
El Paso site, 80; and film fraud,

230n14; and Hot Springs ministers, 71
Brisbane, Arthur, 75
Brooks, J. A., 148
Browning (Indian Commissioner), 65
Bryan, William Jennings, 37, 83, 85, 126
bucket shops, 140
Bulger (the terrier), 40, 217n.5
bullfights, 102, 106, 122–23; Ade on, 135–36; Fitzsimmons attends, 110, 165; hypocrisy of, 227n.1; Maher attends, 119
Burge (El Paso photographer), 124, 173
Burges, Will, 109
Burleson, Albert, 65
Burns, Jim 108–109
Burns, Peter, 122, 176

Cabell, Ben 33–34, 42, 43, 44
Cabell, William L., 34, 44, 216n.21
Campbell, Robert, 109, 163
Canada, 20, 214–15n.4
Carr, Frank, 135
Carroll, Jimmy, 112, 161; and Fitzsimmons, 102, 223n.9; on Maher, 100, 122
Carroll, Rev. W. Irving, 42–43
Carson City, Nev., 194
Catron, Thomas B., 127, 204; anti-fight bill, 139–40, 141; background and character of, 139
Cavanaugh, Tommy, 40, 41, 45
Chicago Dispatch, 188
Chicago Inter-Ocean, 182
Chicago News, 219n.21
Chicago Record: on betting, 145; on border fight, 141, 147–48; on commercialism, 124; on Fitzsimmons, 128; on Maher, 138, on Nero, 128; satire in, 80–83; on Stuart, 141–42; on Sullivan, 160; on uncertainty of fight, 155; on verbal sparring, 67
Chicago Tribune, 20, 122; on Arkansas phase, 83; on Culberson, 22, 39–40; on 1892 Fitzsimmons-Maher bout, 99; on fan mail, 194; on film rights, 94–95; on Langtry fight, 184; on New York city violence, 87; on odds against the carnival, 145; on Rose Fitzsimmons, 198; sandstorm cartoon in, 162; on Stuart's investment, 195; on Texas Rangers, 150; on Vendig, 77; on verbal sparring, 72
Chinese, in El Paso, 107, 156–57
Choynski, Joe, 24
Christian Courier, 53

Cincinnati Enquirer, 132
Citizens Reform League, 108, 109
Civil War veterans, 29–30, 37
Clark, Etta, 125
Clark, George, 26
Clark, George (Judge), 52–53
Clark, Hatti, 23
Clarke, James P., 41, 45, 60, 90; and bribery charge, 68, 221n.7; combativeness of, 68–69; declares prizefighting illegal, 69; in Hot Springs, 72; and Texas anti-fight law, 66; threatens fighters, 80; threatens military force, 71. See also Arkansas
Clemens, Samuel [pseud. Mark Twain], 10
Cleveland, Grover, 85, 142, 170
Clint, Judge, 42
Cockrell, J. V., 138
Cole, Billy, 23
Collins, Scott, 117, 119, 122, 138, 165, 217n.8, 226n.22; and fire, 136
Colorado River, 31
Columbia Baptist Association, 71
Commercial Club (Dallas), 28, 36–37
conditioning, 9. See also training
Coney Island, 46–47
Coney Island Fiasco, 5–6
Coney Island Jockey Saloon and Restaurant, 18
Congress, U.S., 43, 140
Connelly, Michael, 135, 143, 165, 194, 226–27n.3
Conroy, James, 161
Corbett, James J., 60, 71, 194; as actor, 10, 15–16, 102, 187; arrested in Hot Springs, 72, 75; career of, 7–11; divorce of, 23; ego (inability to accept defeat), 7, 9, 10, 21, 201, 202, 229n.13; eulogy for Fitzsimmons by, 208; and fight with Jackson, 7–8, 214n.11; and fights with Sharkey, 192, 204; and fight with Sullivan, 9–10, 215n.6; film contract of, 94, 95; and film fraud, 230n.14; and Fitzsimmons, 11, 13, 15, 187–88, 197–202; and fracas with fireman, 131; gold tooth of, 200; in hotel fight, 32–33, 67, 68; and knockdown in Carson City, 198–99, 230n.14; on Maher-Fitzsimmons match, 102; and O'Donnell, 222n.3; parodied, 80–83; photos of, 8, 95, 197, 200; physique of, 22; post-carnival career of, 204; retirement of,

75, 84, 96, 130; ring strategy of, 48; on Riordan, 24–25; training style of, 47–48; and verbal sparring, 15, 20, 21, 32, 67–68, 72, 74, 83, 92, 93, 130, 166, 190, 195, 202, 221n.11
Corbett, Joe (brother), 32–33, 65
Corbett, Ollie, 23
Corbett, Vera, 23, 215n.11
Corpus Christi, Tex., 33, 67, 72, 76, 219n.20
Cortazar, Joaquin, 134
Courtney, Peter, 10, 94, 95
Crane, Martin M., 26–27, 203–204; on militia, 34–35; parodied in poem, 50–51; test case, 45, 55
Cravens, Rev. George W., 27
Crawford, Bill, 26
Creedon, Dan, 13
Creelan, Danny, 166
Crotty, John, 49
Culberson, Charles A., 22, 36, 46, 203; and anti-fight law, 58, 62–63, 220n.23; background and character of, 39; and championship belts, 59; criticized, 163; on legality of fighting, 30, 217n.8; letters to sheriff from, 34; national newspaper support of, 219n.21; parodied, 50–51; Rangers sent by, 109, 110; calls special session, 55–56; on test case, 52; veto record of, 216–17n.4
Culberson, Dave (father), 39, 53, 150
Culberson, Sally (wife), 39, 53, 218n.13
cultural diversions, 87–88
Cushing, Jack, 94

Daguerra (fiesta manager), 110, 136
Dallas: business leaders of, 31, 33; economic problems in, 19; history of, 36; photo of 30; Rangers and, 228n.3
Dallas Athletic Club, 41, 173
Dallas Coliseum. See amphitheater
Dallas Morning News, 31, 42, 56, 58, 75; on amphitheater tourists, 49; on Corbett's demeanor, 67; on Fitzsimmons' training, 217n.9, 222n.13; on Hot Springs, 71, 76; on Indians and sport, 65; on Maher, 60; poems in, 50–51, 202–203; on Stuart, 189, 220–21n.4
Dallas Pastor's Association, 21–22, 42–43, 54
Daly, Jim, 222n.3
Dalzell, John, 140
Darbyshire, B. F., 89

Darrow, Mrs. George, 130
Daughters of the Confederacy, 37
Davenport, Gypsy, 125
Davies, Charles ("Parson"), 11, 48, 76, 167, 182
Davis, Robert Hobart, 194, 229nn. 3, 9
Dean, John M., 58, 124, 182, 219–20n.22
decoy rings, 163–64
Dempsey, Jack "Nonpareil," 4, 14, 23, 215n.10
Dempsey, William Harrison ("Jack"), 4
Denver, Colo., 11, 16
Detroit Journal, 43
Diaz, Lamedax L., 136
Diaz, Porfirio, 44, 90, 136, 141, 147, 227–28n.1
Dixon, George, 117, 138, 155, 165
Dixon, Rev. Thomas, 87
Donahue, P. J., 194
Donnay, Maurice, 207
Donovan, Joseph, 47–48, 102–103
Donovan, Mike, 47
Drescler, Cosias, 88
Dr. Jekyll and Mr. Hyde, 224n.4
drug use, 107, 163, 195, 224n.4
Duffie, A. M., 69
Dunn, Jere, 48
Durango Democrat, 139
Dwyer, Phil, 21, 215n.9

Earp, Wyatt, 193
Eastman, George, 226n.16
Ebert, W. P., 86
Edison, Thomas, 87, 94
Eidoloscope Company, 94
Elkins, Stephen, 139
Elliott, Rev. A. M., 121
El Paso, 80, 163, 223–24n.1; city council of, 163; and fight, 89–90; history of, 105–107; and Paderewski, 87; photo of, 103; Rangers in, 110, 148; special session vote and, 58; vice in, 108–109
El Paso Daily Herald, 89, 112, 177; arrival of Rangers, 148; on carnival, 90, 116, 117, 152; Clarke's resolve, 71; on crowds, 126; on editor's pro-fight stand, 132; on Fitzsimmons-Corbett match, 192; on fire alarm system, 223–24n.1; on Mabry, 149; on Maher, 101, 131; ministers quoted in, 121–22; on Nero, 120; poems in, 85, 91, 104; on Stuart, 105, 191; on Sullivan, 129; on verbal sparring, 67; on women smokers, 106

El Paso Daily Times, 27, 31, 65, 89, 90;
    and bullfight, 106; on Fitzsimmons, 76,
    110–11, 217n.9; on Fitzsimmons-Maher
    match, 96–97; on Maher, 119; and min-
    isters, 120–21, 138–39; and New Year's
    festivities, 113, poems in, 124–125, 142–
    43; on Stuart, 92, 95, 160, 169; on Sul-
    livan, 79, 166; on Texas Rangers, 157
El Paso Evening Telegram, 110
El Paso Ministers' Union, 120, 132, 134,
    138; appeal to citizens by, 120–21, 167–
    68; at Juarez meeting, 154; members of,
    227n.9; photo of, 133; and public back-
    lash, 138–39, 141, 142–43, 225n.9
El Paso Telegram, 143
El Paso Tribune, 130
El Paso Womens' Christian Temperance
    Union, 115
Empire Athletic Club, 92
Evangelical Pastors Association, 29
Everhart, Jack, 117, 119, 167

Fallon, Jack, 97, 98, 101
fiesta, 102, 104, 115, 134, 137, 158,
    225nn.8, 13. *See also* gambling
Fink, E. M., 113–14
Finley, Nat, 25–26, 55
fistic carnival, 19, 20–21, 92; alternative
    schemes for, 31, 44, 64, 147, 154,
    221n.9; breaks up, 163, 169; bullfights
    and, 122–23; court test of, 44–45; eco-
    nomic impact of, 31, 53, 57–58;
    fighters signed for, 117; postponed, 163;
    public opinions on, 49–50; rattlesnakes
    and, 123, 144; rodeo and, 123; test
    fights for, 40, 43. *See also* Stuart, Dan
Fitch, J. B., 130
Fitzsimmons, Bob, Jr. (son), 102, 129, 207
Fitzsimmons, Charles (son), 46
Fitzsimmons, Robert: as actor, 94, 205,
    206, 222n.13; arrested, 78, 206; arrives
    in El Paso, 110; arrives in Houston, 57;
    and bear, 176; at bullfight, 165; career
    of, 13–15; on Carroll, 223n.9 and car
    wreck, 205; challenges Corbett, 11, 13,
    15; on championship belt, 102; on con-
    dition before fight, 170; on Corbett-
    Sullivan bout, 13, 219n.17; citizenship
    of, 137; death of, 207; debts of, 67, 75,
    83, 116, 206–207; dreams of, 55, 128;
    and Earp, 193; fan letter to, 218n.12;
    and fight with Corbett, 194, 197–202,
    229n.9, 230n.14; and fight with

Dempsey, 14; and fight with Hall, 137;
    and fights with Jeffries, 204, 205; and
    fight with Johnson, 205; and fight with
    Maher (1896), 183–86, 192, and fights
    with Sharkey, 193, 205; and football
    game, 113–15; and funds, 215n.9; and
    Glori, 215–16n.14; in hotel lobby fight,
    32–33, 67; in illustration, 185; on Irish
    roots, 112; and light-heavyweight title,
    205; and Mabry, 157–58; on Maher, 100,
    174; and manslaughter trial, 24–25; and
    Nero, 128, 129, 226n.18; parodied, 80–
    83; personality of, 14, 111, 165; photos
    of, 12, 200; physique of, 22, 47; post-
    carnival opponents of, 204–205; post-
    fight comments of, 187; quits carnival,
    83; renounces title, 190; and retirement,
    102, 205; on ring strategy, 48; supersti-
    tion of, 55; surveillance of, 157, 161;
    throws a fight, 137; training of, 46–47,
    217n.9, 222n.13; traveling to Texas, 55;
    and Vendig, 77; verbal sparring by, 16,
    20, 21, 32, 68, 75, 112, 189, 195–96, 202
Fitzsimmons, Rose (wife), 55, 102, 196,
    204, 205; background of, 221n.5; on
    Corbett, 189; in husband's corner, 196,
    198, 199, 201
Florida: and prizefighting, 10–11, 15
Florida Athletic Club, 15, 21, 56, 63, 65,
    74
football, 89; Fitzsimmons and, 113–15,
    225n.10; photo of, 114
Ford, Henry, 87
Fort Bliss, 106, 158
Fort Sill, 57
Fountain, A. J., 138, 227n.4
Fox, Richard K., 131, 223n.5
French Impressionists, 87
Friend, Emanuel, 20, 67, 102

Gallagher, Fred, 100
Gallagher, Reddy, 16
Galveston, 28, 102, 168
gambling, 18, 29, 100, 102, 108, 135,
    167–68, 214n.3; at fiesta, 115, 134, 136,
    158; on national level, 145
Gardner, George, 205
Garrett, Pat, 227n.4
Garza, Catarino, 148, 217n.7
Gem Saloon and Dance Hall, 92, 118,
    119, 122, 141, 166; photo of, 123
Gentleman Jack, 16
Geronimo, 155

Gibbs, Barnett, 49–50, 52, 217n.11
Gifford, Julia May, 205, 206
Gillespie, John P., 41
Girl from Maxim's, The, 206
Glori, Captain, 11, 112, 128, 143, 215–16n.14
Goodwin, Ethel, 124
Gough, J. R., 56
governors. *See* Ahumada, Miquel; Clarke, James P.; Culberson, Charles A.; Hughes, Louis; Lowry, Robert; Thornton, William
Greeley, Clarence, 10–11
Green, E. H. R., 214n.3
Green's Hotel, 32–33, 67, 225n.7
Gross, Joe, 5

Hall, Jim, 24, 128, 176; and Fitzsimmons, 136–37
Hallam, Rev. E. R., 138, 169–170
Hardin, John Wesley, 109, 224–25n.7
Harris, Will, 89
Haymarket Theatre, 187
Hearst, William Randolph, 194
Henderson, David B., 140
Herald, Frank, 6
Hoffman, Rev. Adolph, 121
Hogg, James Stephen, 26, 52, 148, 150; and Bean, 178–79
Holland, Frank P., 31, 33, 216n.20
Holyfield, Evander, 210, 211
Homan, Rev. W. K., 53–54
Honest Hearts and Willing Hands, 6
Hot Springs, 66, 221n.8; economic conditions in, 69–70; ministers in, 71; photo of, 70
Houpt, Robert, 69, 70–71, 73, 77; photo of, 78
Houseman, Lou, 48, 182, 184, 190
Houston Post, 33, 191
Hubbell, F. T., 41–42
Hughes, Gov. Louis, 155–56, 159, 164, 167, 168, 228n.9
Hughes, John, 148, 157, 170, 173
Hurd, Jesse, 76, 80
Hurt, James M., 44–45, 55

Ike, Greasewood, 144
Indians, 64, 65, 139; on football team, 113–15, 225nn.10, 11
Indian Territory, 57, 64–65, 220n.3
Ingersoll, Robert G., 89, 222n.1
International Law and Order League, 10

Jackson, Peter, 11, 23, 49, 217n.10; and Corbett, 7–8, 214n.11
Jacksonville, Fla., 10, 11, 15
Jacksonville, Tex., 59
Jacoby, Louis, 41–42, 217n.6
Jeffries, James J., 195; and Corbett, 204; and Fitzsimmons, 204, 205; and Johnson, 205
Jersey Lilly, The, 173, 178, 179, 180
Jester, George, 189
Johnson, Jack, 205
Johnson, Rutabaga, 57
Jones (Arkansas representative), 68–69
journalism: hazards of, 130, 132, 135
Juarez, 35, 64, 89, 102, 104; and fiesta, 115; and gambling, 225nn.8, 13; and ministers' meeting, 154; photo of, 153; and troops, 160–61, 170–71
Julian, Martin, 25, 55, 65, 79, 91, 96, 221n.5; claims forfeit, 165; and El Paso, 104, 105; and film rights, 94–95; and Fitzsimmons, 111–12; on hotel lobby fight, 33; and Hot Springs, 67, 74, 77; in Langtry, 182, 186, 187; on London offer, 143; on prize money, 101–102; on referees, 49; on stake money, 83; taunting Corbett, 57, 165, 166; and training, 129, 195

Kearby, Jerome, 50
Kelly, Spider, 40
Kilgore, Rev., 110, 127
Kilrain, Jake, 6, 48, 213n.5, 219n.16
Kinetoscope, 94, 182. *See also* motion pictures
King, Marie, 23
Kinsworthy, E. B., 76
Kirk, W. A., 72
knockdown, in Corbett-Fitzsimmons fight: 198–99, 229n.9, 230n.14
Knox, William, 140
Kodak, 226n.16

Lang, Bill, 205
Langtry, Lillie, 178
Langtry, Tex., 173, 175, 178
Las Cruces, 119, 131, 138, 173
Las Vegas, Nev., 210, 211
Las Vegas, N. Mex., 134
Las Vegas Optic, 152
Latham, Grey, 94
Latham, Otway, 94
Lawlor, James, 57, 122, 155

Leatherman, Judge, 73
Leeds, Horace, 117, 128, 134
Leonard, Michael, 94
Lewis, Lillian, 115, 225n.12
Liberte, 207
Life and Battles of Bob Fitzsimmons, The, 122
Little Rock, 72, 79
London Prize Fight Rules, 5, 213n.2
London Sporting Life, 100
Longfellow, Henry Wadsworth, 14, 208
Louisiana, 15
Lowery, Rev. John R., 73–74
Lowry, Robert, 6
Lubbock, Frank, 57, 219n.18
Lung, Wun, 222n.2. *See also* Whitmyer, Colonel
lynching, 86, 202

Mabry, Woodford Haywood, 132, 148, 170, 173; background and character of, 148–49; and Bean, 180; death of, 204; and Fitzsimmons, 157; and Hughes, 156; on Langtry fight, 229n.12; and ministers, 160; photo of, 149; and Stuart, 158, 160; and Thornton, 151
McCoy, Charles, 204
McDonald, Bill, 170, 173; background and character of, 150–51; and Masterson, 177; post-carnival career of, 204
Mace, Jem, 14
McGinty Club, The, 170
McGown, W. C., 109
McKinney, Tex., 59
McVey, Jim, 10
Madden, Billy, 97
Madison Square Garden, 29, 58, 192, 218n.15
Maher, Peter, 49, 55, 74; on acting, 159; arrives in Arkansas, 71; arrives in El Paso, 118–19; background of, 97, 223n.6; and benefit in New York, 112, 116; and blindness, 161, 163; citizenship, 158; exhibition, 122; and Corbett, 84, 131; and fans, 177; and Fitzsimmons, 183–86, 187, 192; on Fitzsimmons, 97–100, 158, 170, 176, health problems of, 144; illustrations of, 6, 162, 172, 184, 185; and ministers, 60; and O'Donnell, 92; post-carnival career of, 204; and sandstorm, 151, 162; suicide attempt by, 100, superstition of, 219n.16; training of, 131; and women, 223n.8, 226n.2

Marquis of Queensberry rules, 9, 10
Marshall, Jake (Jerry), 117, 118, 119, 165
Martin, H. H., 66
Martin Julian Specialty Company, The, 215n.14
Mason, Cactus, 144
Masterson, William Barclay "Bat," 136, 141, 145; arrives in El Paso, 138; in Carson City, 194; fight prediction of, 148; on Fitzsimmons, 120; in Langtry, 182; and McDonald, 177; on Maher, 119–20; as sportswriter, 152; on Stuart, 152; and train security, 175
May, Jane, 88
Meek, John, 206
Mexico, 28, 31, 64, 134, 136, 147, 158, 176; violence in, 227n.1
Millican, Rev. Leander R., 121, 138
Mills (Texas representative), 26
Mississippi City, 5
Mitchell, Charley, 10, 100, 219n.16
Mitchell, Gene, 40
Moorer, Michael, 211
Moreno, Jose de, 122
motion pictures, 87, 93–95, 117–18, 144, 157, 222n.4, 229nn. 4, 5; Corbett and, 222n.13; and fight films, 203; film fraud and, 229–30n.14. *See also* Kinetoscope; Veriscope
Muldoon, Billy, 7, 213n.5
Muncie, Ind., 11
Murphy, A. M., 131
Murphy, Johnny, 117, 161
Murray (New York Superintendent of Police), 4
Myar Opera House, 104, 107, 159, 161; Fitzsimmons at, 111–112; Maher at, 122; photo of, 108; Sullivan at, 159, 166

National American Woman Suffrage Association, 88
National Sporting Club of London, 143
Naval Cadet, The, 102, 187
Neeley, George, 72
Nero, 15, 55, 57, 110, 120, 188, 206; at Coney Island, 214n.19; at Corpus Christi, 221n.6; and goat, 129; and hunting, 226n.18; at Juarez training camp, 128–29; and train mishap, 219n.20
Nevada, 193–94
Newman, S. H., 108
New Mexico, 139

New Orleans, 9, 11, 14; Fitzsimmons-Hall fight in, 137
New Orleans Picayune, 4, 22, 56; on carnival crowd, 29; on Corbett-Fitzsimmons meeting, 20; on Fitzsimmons-Hall bout, 137; on legality of carnival, 40; poem in, 3; on Rangers, 150; on special session, 52; on Stuart, 18, 21; on test case, 45; on troops, 57
New Orleans Times-Democrat, 182
New Republic, The, 210
newspapers: on Langtry fight, 188; on Stuart, 191
Newsweek, 210
New Woman, The, 88, 106, 224n.2; and anti–woman suffragists, 218n.13
New York Athletic Club, 47
New York Herald, 15
New York Sun, 62, 188, 225n.10
New York Times: on bullfighting and boxing, 227–28n.1; on Clarke, 79; on Corbett as actor, 11; on fights, 14, 199, 201, 205; Fitzsimmons eulogy in, 207; on Hot Springs, 80; on Maher, 192; on Sullivan, 6, 7
New York World, 93, 96; amphitheater (Langtry), 180–82; cartoon in, 154, 172; on bullfights, 135; on carnival, 135; on decoy rings, 163–64; on fashion, 88; on fiesta, 115; on fight reactions in Mexico City, 147; on Fitzsimmons, 25, 46–47, 75, 170; and Maher telegram, 170; on prizefighting's popularity, 4–5; on Rangers, 149–50; on Stuart, 140, 191; on Texas hypocrisy, 62; train boarding, 174
New Zealand, xiii, 14, 208

Oates, Joyce Carol, 210, 211
O'Brien, Jack, 205
O'Donnell, Steve, 13, 49, 71; in bout with Maher, 92, 93, 222n.3
Oldfield, Barney, 205
Olympic Club, 11, 13, 14, 15, 16
O'Rourke, Tom, 155, 167, 172, 182
Oxley, Rev. Charles J., 121, 138, 151

Paderewski, Ignace, 87
Pegler, Westbrook, 204
Philadelphia, 32–33, 131, 155
Philadelphia Times, 62
photography, 49, 226n.16
pickpockets, 174–75

poems, 85, 91, 104, 144; *After the Prize Fight*, 124–25; *The Arena*, 91; *The Carnival*, 156; *Crane and Guv Bird*, 50–51; *Fitzy Witzy*, 202–203; *The Prize Fight*, 142–43; *Texas Talks*, 62–63; *The Village Smithy*, 14, 208
Police Gazette, 131, 222n.5
preachers: *See individuals*
prizefighters: celebrity of, 4, 124; lifestyles of, 5; superstitions of, 55, 219n.16; and weight classes, 226n.15. *See also individual fighters*
prizefighting: Arkansas opposition to, 66, 69, 71, 72, 73–74, 75; Arkansas popularity of, 70, 79; Austin opposition to, 27–28, 29; Dallas opposition to, 21–22, 42–43, 215n.8; El Paso opposition to, 110, 112, 120–21, 122, 126, 132–33, 136, 138, 151, 163; El Paso popularity of, 121, 124; euphemisms for, 4; films of, 203, 209; and ministers' opposition, 4, 6, 10–11, 15, 138–39; New York opposition to, 4, 24–25, 218n.15; official opposition to, 66, 69, 72, 73, 75; popularity of, 4–5, 11, 19, 29, 31, 40–41, 43, 176, 218n.12, 222n.14; post-carnival history of, 209–11; Texas opposition to, 26–27, 34–35, 55–57, 58, 62
prostitution, 54, 107–109, 125, 167–68, 223n.8, 225n.9
Pruyn, Mrs. John V. L., 218n.13
publicity: for carnival, 125; Fitzsimmons book and, 122; photos of, 124; Stuart's efforts for, 117. *See also* advertising
Pullman, George M., 86
Pullman, Rev. Joseph, 88

Quinn, John J., 79, 101, 119, 135, 172, 176, 186, 187; challenges Fitzsimmons for Maher, 93; on Corbett's title, 131; on ministers, 161

race: Corbett and, 213–14n.9; Fitzsimmons and, 205, 219n.19; Johnson and, 205; Maher and, 131; Sullivan and, 7, 213n.9, 223n.7; in Texas, 107, 209. *See also* lynching
Rader, Rev. Paul, 207–208
Ramsaye, Terry, 222n.4
Rector, Enoch J., 94, 117–18, 157, 171, 229nn. 4, 5; in Carson City, 194; in El

Paso, 141; in Langtry, 186. *See also* motion pictures
referees, 21, 48–49
Reiger, John F., 56
religion. *See* prizefighting: and ministers' opposition
Richburg, Miss., 6
ring deaths, 5, 24, 155, 209–10
Rio Grande, 105, 173, 180–82
Rio Grande City, 44, 217n.7
Riordan, Cornelius, 23, 24, 25
Roeber, Emile, 55, 113, 127
Rogers, J. H., 148
Roosevelt, Theodore, 206
Rose, Rev. A. J., 28
Ross, Lawrence Sullivan, 26
rules, 5, 9, 10, 213n.2
Rurales, 161, 171
Ryan, Paddy, 5, 76, 223n.10
Ryan, Si, 119, 122, 159
Ryan, Tommy, 49

St. Louis Post-Dispatch, 219n.21
San Antonio Express, 122, 188
San Antonio Jockey Club, 55, 60
Sanderson, Tex., 177
San Francisco, 7, 9, 23, 205
San Francisco Chronicle, 188
San Francisco Examiner, 203
Santa Fe New Mexican, 191
satire, Gorbett-Fitzgibbons bout: 80–83
Schlatter, Francis, 116, 225–26n.14
Schmitz, Eugene E., 205
Scholl, William A., 11
Seasholes, Rev. C. L., 42
Selman, John, 109, 224–25n.7
Sharkey, Tom, 10; and Corbett, 192, 204; and Fitzsimmons, 193, 205
Shea, Jack, 143
Shelby, W.W., 217n.7
Sherman (U.S. representative), 140
Siler, George, 172, 190; and Ahumada, 154–55; background of, 226n.21; as carnival referee, 122; in Langtry, 182, 183, 184, 185, 186; on Nevada, 193–94; on Stuart, 145; on Vendig, 77–78
Silven (architect), 49
Simmons, F. B., 109
Slavin, Frank, 100
Smith, Billy "Australian," 102, 113, 143; on Fitzsimmons-Sharkey fight, 193; in photo, 114
Smith, Billy "Mysterious," 49

Smith, Denver Ed, 132
Sneed, Bert, 182
solar-plexus punch, 201, 206, 207
Sousa, John Phillip, 37
Southern Pacific Railroad, 107, 175
special session, of Texas legislature, 55–58
Spinks, Michael, 210
Spraggins, Rev. E. L., 21
Spring Lake, Arkansas, 71
statutes, anti-prizefighting, 10–11, 15, 26, 209
Stelzner, Jack, 116, 127
Sterrett, William Greene, 43–44
Stuart, Dan, 16, 21, 35, 40, 96, 203; background and character of, 18–19, 102–103, 189, 190, 191; and bullfights, 122–23; and carnival plans (Dallas), 19, 20–21; community standing of, 220–21n.4; on Corbett retiring, 92, 93, 95–96; and El Paso, 92; Grand Jury summons of, 65; and Hot Springs, 74–75; and Hughes, 159; illness of, 195; illustration of, 19; investments by, 63, 93, 123, 134–35, 190, 195; and Mabry, 151, 158; and Maher, 96–97; and Masterson, 141; on Mexican threats, 155; and motion picture, 94–95, 117–18, 229n.4; and Nero, 129; in Nevada, 193–94; optimism of, 116, 123, 126, 127, 134, 135, 145–46, 168, 170; promotional efforts by, 117; on Rangers, 171; on special session, 56, 58; on test case, 45–46
Sullivan, John L., 204; as actor, 6, 166, 213n.4, 223n.10; and Ahumada, 164; and black fighters, 7, 213n.9, 223n.7; and booze, 166–67; at bullfight, 165; career, 5–7; in Carson City, 194; on Corbett's retirement, 104; and Corbett-Sullivan fight, 9–10; and El Paso, 159; fight prediction, 148; on Fitzsimmons, 13; on future of boxing, 73, 152; and goat, 118; and Hot Springs, 78–79; and Maher, 97, 98; on opponents, 223n.7; as poet, 3; rejected as referee, 48; in train accident, 129–30; and training, 214n.14; on "windy war" of words, 76; on women at fights, 196
Sullivan, Yank, 24
superstitions: astrology and, 164; fighters', 219n.16; Fitzsimmons's, 55; and lucky charms, 194–95
surveillance: on Albers, 161; cost of,

228n.5; on Fitzsimmons, 161, 171; on Maher, 163, 167
Sweeney, K. O., 205
Syracuse, N.Y., 23, 25

Taylor, George P., 71–72, 221n.10
Taylor, J. J., 90, 92
Templeton, Rev. W. G., 42
Texas Christian Advocate, 53
Texas legislature: and anti-fight law, 26, 58, 209, 220n.23; and Congress, 140; special session of, 52–53, 55–57, 58
Texas Rangers, 109, 110, 171, 173, 174, 175, 228n.3; described, 149–50; in El Paso, 110, 148; in Langtry, 180, 189, 229n.12; photo of, 149. *See also* Mabry, Woodford Haywood; McDonald, Bill
Texas State Fair, 21, 37, 215n.5. *See also* amphitheater
Thomas, Cullen T., 56
Thornton, William, 139, 140, 144; and Catron, 139, 141; and Mabry, 151; and ministers, 132–34, 138; and prizefighting, 138; and Stuart, 151, 191
Tilden, Samuel, Jr., 94, 229n.4
Timaru (New Zealand), 14, 208
Time, 210
training: Corbett, 47–48; Fitzsimmons, 46–47, 97, 98, 117, 144–45, 217n.9, 222n.13; Maher, 97, 98, 131, 137–38; Sullivan, 213n.5, 214n.14. *See also* conditioning
TV Guide, 210
Twain, Mark. *See* Clemens, Samuel
Two Republics, 90, 188
Tyson, Mike, 210

Vendig, Joe, 15, 20, 40, 65, 74, 77–78, 91, 128, 182, 227n.3; arrested, 76; arrives in El Paso, 135; on Hot Springs, 75; and motion picture, 94–95
Veriscope, 194, 229–30n.14. *See also* motion pictures; Rector, Enoch

Village Smithy, The, 14, 208
violence, in everyday life, 86–87, 115, 138, 227nn. 1, 4

Waco Telephone, 41
Walcott, Joe, 117, 119, 138, 143–44, 155, 165
War Department, 57
Washington Post, 43
Waters, W. W., 66, 74, 90
Webster, J. H., 215n.8
weight classes, 226n.15
Wheelock, W. K., 64, 76, 119, 120, 121, 193
White, Alward, 161, 165
White, Charlie, 55
White, Owen P., 166, 169
Whitlock, W. T., 56
Whitmyer, Colonel [pseud. Wun Lung], 91; on fiesta games, 225n.8; on fight site, 168; on football game, 113–14; and ministers, 110, 112; on Nero, 128–29; on New Woman, 224n.2; pen name of, 222n.2; poem by, 144; on prayers, 126; on Sullivan, 159
Whittington Park, 70, 73
Wicklow Postman, The, 166
Wilde, Oscar, 87, 115, 215n.7
women: against fights, 136; and anti-woman suffragists, 218n.13; and gambling, 225nn. 8, 13; at fights, 121, 196, 199, 221n.11; and smoking, 106
Women's Christian Temperance Union, 87
Wortham, Louis, 49

Yandell, William, 164–65
Young, Rev. W. C., 50

Ziller, Temo, 206, 207, 230n.16

Bw